Non-White Immigration
and the "White Australia"
Policy

Non-White Immigration and the "White Australia" Policy

H. I. London

071677

New York · New York University Press
1970

Copyright © 1970 by New York University
Library of Congress Catalog Card Number: 71–95763
SBN: 8147–0264–3
Manufactured in the United States of America

Acknowledgments

Excerpts from Justice Sugarman's judgment in the Prasad case, © 1965 by *The Advertiser,* and from a statement by Charles Perkins, © 1965 by *The Advertiser.* Reprinted here by permission of *The Advertiser* (Adelaide).

Excerpts from the reproduction of a speech by Sir Robert Menzies, © 1961 by *The Age.* Reprinted here by permission of *The Age* (Melbourne).

Excerpts from letters to the editor, © 1964, 1965, 1966, 1966, 1966, 1967 by *The Australian,* without reference, in text or footnote, to the authors of the letters, and from editorial comment, © 1964 by *The Australian,* and three cartoons * by Collette, September 21, 1966, February 6, 1967, May 24, 1967, © 1966, 1967, 1967 by *The Australian.* Reprinted here by permission of *The Australian.*

Excerpts from A.N.A. *Advocate,* January–February, 1962, © 1962 by the Australian Natives' Association. Reprinted here by permission of the Australian Natives' Association.

Excerpts from articles and editorials in *The Bulletin,* © 1961, 1963 by the Australian Consolidated Press Limited, and a Rushton cartoon * from *The Bulletin,* September 17, 1966, © 1966 by the Australian Consolidated Press Limited. Reprinted here by permission of the Australian Consolidated Press Limited (*The Bulletin*).

---

* The cartoons referred to above appear on the jacket of the New York University Press edition distributed in the United States and Canada.

vi *Non-White Immigration and "White Australia" Policy*

Excerpts from letters to the editor, © 1964, 1965, 1966, 1966, 1966 by *The Canberra Times,* without reference, in text or footnote, to the authors of the letters. Reprinted here by permission of *The Canberra Times.*

Excerpts from Sir Alexander Downer's address "The Influence of Migration on Australian Foreign Policy," the Roy Milne Memorial Lecture for 1960, © 1960 by The Australian Institute of International Affairs. Reprinted here by permission of The Australian Institute of International Affairs.

Excerpts from a statement by General Cariappa in *The Courier-Mail,* © 1954 by *The Courier-Mail.* Reprinted here by permission of *The Courier-Mail* (Brisbane).

Excerpts from *The Daily Telegraph* relating to court action in the Prasad case, © 1965 by *The Daily Telegraph.* Reprinted here by permission of *The Daily Telegraph* (Sydney).

Excerpts from commentary on the Prasad case in a *Sun-Herald* television program, August 15, 1965, printed in the *Sun-Herald,* © 1965 by Associated Newspapers Limited, and a Molnar cartoon * from the March 11, 1966 *Sydney Morning Herald,* © 1966 by Associated Newspapers Limited. Reprinted here by permission of John Fairfax Feature Services, acting for Associated Newspapers Limited.

Excerpts from letters to the editor, © 1965, 1965 by the *Fiji Times & Herald Limited,* without reference, in text or footnote, to the authors of the letters, and from a statement by Sir Alexander Downer, © 1965 by the *Fiji Times & Herald Limited,* and from a statement by Reg Powditch, © 1965 by the *Fiji Times & Herald Limited.* Reprinted here by permission of the *Fiji Times & Herald Limited.*

Excerpts from *Hansard* and other government publications, including those from the Department of Immigration, © by the Acting Government Printer, Canberra. Reprinted here by permission of the Acting Government Printer, Canberra.

Excerpts from a letter to Roy Prasad from Peter Heydon, 1964. Reprinted here by permission of Peter Heydon.

Excerpts from F. M. Daly's "Recommendations for the Immigration Committee," unpublished, 1965. Reprinted here by permission of F. M. Daly.

Excerpts from J. Cairns's *Living With Asia,* © 1965 by Lansdowne Press. Reprinted here by permission of Lansdowne Press.

---

* The cartoon referred to above appears on the jacket of the New York University Press edition distributed in the United States and Canada.

Acknowledgments

Tables from Arthur Huck's *Australian Attitudes to the Chinese,* © 1964 by Arthur Huck. Reprinted here by permission of Arthur Huck.

Excerpts from statements regarding the Prasad case, © 1965, 1965 by *Mirror Newspapers Limited.* Reprinted here by permission of *Mirror Newspapers Limited* (Sydney).

Statistics and tables relating to the public attitude toward non-European immigration, from The Gallup Poll (Australia's Public Opinion Poll), for the years 1943 to 1967, © by The Roy Morgan Research Centre Pty. Ltd. Reprinted here by permission of The Roy Morgan Research Centre Pty. Ltd.

Excerpts from letters to the editor, © 1960 by *The News,* without reference, in text or footnote, to the authors of the letters. Reprinted here by permission of *The News* (Adelaide).

Excerpts from my "Foreign Affairs and the White Australia Policy," © 1969 by *Orbis* (The Trustees of the University of Pennsylvania). Reprinted here by permission of *Orbis.*

Two tables from O. A. Oeser's and S. B. Hammond's *Social Structure and Personality in a City,* © 1954 by Routledge & Kegan Paul. Reprinted here by permission of Routledge & Kegan Paul.

Excerpts from B. A. Santamaria's "Social Justice Statement, 1951, on the Future of Australia," quoted in *Rural Life,* 1959, © 1951 by B. A. Santamaria, and from an address by Rev. G. J. Dullard, O.S.A., M.A., to the Annual Convention of the National Catholic Rural Movement, 1960, quoted in *Rural Life,* 1964, © 1964 by B. A. Santamaria, and from statements in *The Sunday Magazine,* © 1962 by B. A. Santamaria. Reprinted here by permission of B. A. Santamaria.

Excerpts from *The Straits Times,* © 1966 by *The Straits Times.* Reprinted here by permission of *The Straits Times* (Malaysia).

Excerpts from Olabisi Ajala's views of the Prasad case in *The Sunday Mirror,* © 1964 by *The Sunday Mirror.* Reprinted here by permission of *The Sunday Mirror* (Sydney).

Excerpts from letters to the editor, © 1949, 1959, 1963, 1965, 1965 by *The Sydney Morning Herald,* without reference, in text or footnote, to the authors of the letters. Reprinted here by permission of *The Sydney Morning Herald.*

Excerpts from statements by Professor Robin Winks, 1963, and private letters to Robin Winks, 1963. Reprinted here by permission of Robin Winks.

Excerpts from editorials, © 1966 by *The West Australian*. Reprinted here by permission of *The West Australian* (Perth).

Excerpts from Kenneth Rivett's "Statement of Aims" of the New South Wales Association for Immigration Reform, © 1962 by the N.S.W. Association for Immigration Reform. Reprinted here by permission of Kenneth Rivett on behalf of the N.S.W. Association for Immigration Reform. Excerpts from a private letter from Kenneth Rivett, 1967. Reprinted here by permission of Kenneth Rivett.

Contents

	Preface	*xi*
Part One		
1	The Development of the "White Australia" Policy	*3*
2	Recent Liberalization of Immigration Policy	*25*
3	Non-Europeans in Australia	*53*
4	Political Parties and the "White Australia" Policy	*77*
5	Pressure Groups: Immigration Reform Versus the Status Quo	*107*
Part Two		
6	Public Opinion	*145*
7	World Opinion of the "White Australia" Policy	*179*
8	Foreign Affairs and Immigration Policy	*205*
9	The Prasad Deportation: A Test Case	*229*
10	Conclusions	*259*
	Appendix: Australian Newspapers	*267*
	Notes	*271*
	Bibliography	*297*
	Index	*307*

Preface

Since World War II anti-colonialist feeling has increased and racism, whether overtly or tacitly expressed, has been condemned by a growing number of the world's people. But the fact is that, even in those states vocally denouncing it, racism still exists. Australia with its non-European immigration policy is in a particularly awkward position due to its proximity to and involvement with the newly emerging national forces in Asia. In attempting to establish more friendly Asian ties Australia has been forced to examine one primary aspect of national practice —the concept of "White Australia." It is the examination of "White Australia" and the decisions to revise it that will be analyzed in this book.

In March, 1966, Mr. Hubert Opperman, Minister for Immigration, announced modifications in Australia's policy regarding the admission of non-European immigrants. The lack of public response to these changes led one clergyman to remark, "the innovations are neither dramatic nor sudden." Mr. Opperman described them as changes "not departing from the fundamental principles of our immigration policy." Nonetheless, the change in policy did continue postwar pressure, both internal and external, exerted on the Government to liberalize the seemingly rigid White Australia practice. It also marked an unparalleled effort to treat non-Europeans on the same basis as Europeans and to obviate charges that modification was enacted without public discussion. Aside from the steps taken in 1956 and 1957 permitting non-European naturalization, Mr. Opperman's proposals were among the most significant in the truncated history of liberalization. The residence requirement for non-Europeans was reduced from fifteen to five years, the categories for their eligibility were relaxed, and an indication was given that the intake "will be somewhat greater than previously." That pressures played a role in these changes is beyond question. But what were these pressures and how and why did they operate?

Kenneth Rivett, an immigration reformer, has attributed changes to the Immigration Department's attitude itself, partly to other Commonwealth departments embarrassed by the White Australia concept, and partly to unofficial critics within Australia. The Australian Council of Churches, and Associations for Immigration Reform are two of the groups of unofficial critics actively campaigning for change. Australian public opinion itself has been tacitly changing in the direction of liberalization for the past two decades, but it has only recently developed into an effort to clarify and reform the ambiguities in the policy.

Historical realities of the postwar world have helped, too, by shifting Australia's devotion from atavistic isolation to regional collaboration. Economic and military considerations have led government departments to question the feasibility of maintaining a primarily exclusionist policy at the same time as trade and defense pacts are negotiated with Asian states. All of these factors, as well as a considerable portion of international public opinion which sees a non-European immigration policy as being specifically racist (the White Australia policy is almost never defended this way, but is usually denounced as such), account in large part for the increasing trend toward liberalization.

Australia's non-European immigration policy was described

by Mr. A. Downer, Minister for Immigration in 1960, as one which did not permit persons of non-European descent entry into Australia for permanent residence. However, six years later Mr. Opperman announced his modification proposal with the suggestion that these steps were taken in order to "enable more non-Europeans capable of becoming Australians and of joining in our national progress to come here to live." In six years' time the thrust of non-European immigration policies had undergone major revision. The revision itself, while a topic frequently mentioned and described by academics, has not been adequately explained. A. C. Palfreeman, in *The Administration of the White Australia Policy,* suggests that liberalization is based on motives such as humanitarianism and the Australian ethos for "giving a mate a fair go." But these factors were part of the national heritage before Federation; why should they suddenly account for modifications? Even foreign policy pressures do not in themselves account satisfactorily for the recent changes. Immigration was and still is a domestic policy determined ostensibly by the national interest and is not within the purview of foreign states or international bodies. The rationale for modification of the policy is a complex phenomenon depending on a combination of internal and external pressures not yet clearly identified.

It is the intent of this book to shed some light on these factors in the effort to explain the nature of liberalization. Why, for example, did the Australian Labor Party, historically devoted to the traditional policy, abandon the term "White Australia" in its party platform? Why has the Government made a concerted effort to modify its *de jure* policy? Why has continued revision occurred in the sixties? What is the future of the White Australia policy? To what extent has the public kept abreast of changes and exerted pressure for or against them?

In order to determine how the nation is responding to modifications I have relied considerably on newspaper reportage. My reason for doing so is that newspapers, despite the recent emergence of radio and television as influential media, are widely

recognized as Australia's "chief medium of communication." *
In addition, since the immigration policy has not been discussed as frankly and openly in official records and documents as its importance warrants, any research in this area will depend to an exceptional degree on newspaper opinion. Although *Hansard* (*Commonwealth Parliamentary Debates*) has a record of some discussion of immigration policy, particularly the recent attempt at liberalization, there are conspicuous gaps in the reports, e.g., during the controversial and widely discussed Nancy Prasad case (see Chapter 9).

Wherever possible newspaper reports are corroborated or rejected by interviews, letters, and other primary sources. None of the outstanding secondary sources in the field bears directly on this book. Such histories as Myra Willard, *History of the White Australia Policy,* and A. Yarwood, *Asian Migration to Australia: The Background To Exclusion, 1896–1924,* have carefully examined the *raison d'être* for Australia's immigration policy and A. C. Palfreeman, *The Administration of the White Australia Policy,* has analyzed ministerial administration of the policy, but there has been surprisingly little written about recent attempts to liberalize immigration.

Because I wanted to present as wide a range of public opinion as possible, there is no restriction on the choice of newspapers represented in the text. However, in order to apprise the reader of the differences in stature, objectivity, circulation, and influence of the newspapers cited, a brief note appears as an appendix.

It is difficult to give credit to all the people who have assisted in the compilation of information and in the final draft of this document, but special thanks are due some. First, my deepest appreciation is accorded my wife for her understanding, editorial work, and devotion. Without her assistance this book

---

* W. Sprague Holden, "Metropolitan Daily Newspapers in Australia Today," *Journalism Quarterly,* XLV, No. 4 (Winter, 1968), 713.

would not have been possible. Special mention must also be made of several members of the Australian National University faculty—Professor Robert Parker, Dr. Charles Price, and Dr. Donald Rawson—whose advice and recommendations were most helpful; Dr. Kenneth Rivett of the University of New South Wales, whose assistance was invaluable; and Professor Robin Winks of Yale University, whose suggestions for revision were most perceptive.

Mention must also be made of the Australian-American Educational Foundation, which made a year in Australia possible, the departmental secretaries who labored over my unintelligible script, and the staff at the Australian National University libraries, who were always cooperative and resourceful.

At the governmental level acknowledgment should be made of Mr. Opperman, former Minister for Immigration, his successor Mr. Snedden, Secretary of Immigration Peter Heydon, as well as the staff in the Department of Immigration. In addition help was given by several members of Parliament, Mr. Fred Daly, Dr. J. F. Cairns, Mr. Arthur Calwell, and Mr. Richard Cleaver.

If this work makes any contribution to an understanding of the liberalization of Australia's immigration policy, and if it will put the forces responsible for change into sharper focus, it will have accomplished its purpose.

H.I.L.

Part One

1

The Development of the "White Australia" Policy

While "White Australia" has been vehemently denied as a policy it has continued to receive vigorous endorsement as a principle. This paradox is at least partially responsible for the confusion surrounding the immigration of non-Europeans to Australia and the Department's vacillations in administering the policy equitably.

"White Australia is journalese," commented Mr. Arthur Calwell, former Minister for Immigration.[1] "There is no white Australia policy and there never has been one," said another.[2] But in contradistinction to this view is another argument emanating from the same ministry: "Our primary aim in immigration is a . . . predominantly homogeneous population";[3] or as Mr. A. Downer argued, ". . . in general persons not of European descent are not eligible to enter Australia for permanent residence."[4] These four statements, albeit simplified reactions to a complex issue, represent the views of three ministers of immigration, each representing the Department of Immigration and their respective political parties in the postwar period.[5] For the casual observer the contradictions seem glaringly apparent. But are these views contradictory? They might represent a subtle consistency, or perhaps a rhetorical exercise in Orwellian double-think.

"White Australia" was the manifestation of a movement not solely confined to Australia but uniquely appropriate to her geographic position and fortuitous historical experiences. The philosophy of nineteenth-century social Darwinism, which gave a political rationalization as well as moral justification for the subjugation of non-whites around the globe, permeated, somewhat surreptitiously, the isolated continent of Australia. Herbert Spencer was probably not read by most Australians of the day but the essence of his ideas, embraced by most British migrants, bridged the gulf of Australian isolationism as a "feeling" if not an academic axiom. With all the goodwill in the world Australians as well as most whites, assured of their superiority, believed it was the White Man's Burden to "Christianize" or "uplift," or "teach," or "civilize" the natives. Many nineteenth-century anthropologists believed that a primitive society was by no means synonymous with a "simple" or "inferior" culture but to most Europeans this was an absurd contradiction. Outwardly, in fact, Africans and Asians were inferior to Europeans: stone axes were not more functional than finely honed steel blades; ancestral remedies were not as effective in curing disease as modern drugs. If Europeans were not already convinced of their "inbred" superiority, comparisons with Asian and African life were likely to convince them. Subjugation was the natural concomitant of contact between the races.

The very fact that the white man went on with his successful colonization seemed to justify the quasi-scientific views of the social Darwinists. "Does not Anglo-Saxon dominance demonstrate superiority?" is a question that the Stoddards, Gobineaus, Strongs, Chamberlains and Sumners asked. And reason for this superiority was construed as being inherent in the Darwinian notion of "natural selection." White men had emerged through nature's struggles as the "fittest" species, they argued, and it is not at all surprising that effective restrictions on the immigration of Chinese laborers were promulgated by the mid-eighties in Canada, the United States, New Zealand, and Australia. Not only was the white man requested to civilize "the half-naked, half-wild child," he was obliged to maintain the homogeneity of his own race and avoid, at all cost, "racial contamination." Sophisticated theory was not the concern of the man in the street, but prejudice implicit in social Darwinism was well enough known to provide an outlet for those predisposed to crude racial antipathy.

Fears and antagonism engendered by differences, and exacerbated by direct competition, made it possible for the bastions of white supremacy to pass legislation against the non-white intruder. California passed discriminatory taxes against Chinese miners in 1850 and in 1879 prohibited any "corporation from employing a Chinese or Mongolian."[6] In 1875 British Columbia deprived Chinese of the franchise, even if Canadian-born.[7] The New Zealand Parliament passed a Chinese Immigration Act in 1881 that virtually excluded all Chinese immigrants.[8] And by the 1880's Australian colonies had already imposed a capitation tax on every Chinese arrival.[9] Non-white exclusion and white supremacy were widely practiced by all of these non-European countries in the late nineteenth century.

It is impossible to say with any accuracy whether social Darwinism fomented racial exclusiveness or whether racial exclusiveness was a corollary of historical circumstances. In Australia both factors were present and they combined to produce an exclusive immigration policy. The British migrant who came to the land Down-Under already had a set of widely accepted assumptions that proved one general axiom: non-whites were inferior. Being closer to Asia did not diminish the migrant's psychic distance from the Asian continent. He was imbued with notions of British superiority, and asserted his exclusive Caucasian heritage by maintaining the homogeneity of his race and developing a fierce national loyalty in Australia. It was his way of preserving British culture against possible intrusions by races that would be unable to "fit into" Anglo-Australian life.

Myra Willard argues that the immigration policy was primarily a manifestation of national forces resolved "to maintain the British character and institutions. . . ." "If non-Europeans had come to Australia in large numbers," her argument continues, "its effect would have been to alter, perhaps destroy the British character of the community." [10] Furthermore, the development of Australia's democracy would have been impeded by allowing races "unfit to exercise their political rights" into a milieu that required the fulfillment of political duties.[11] It was reasoned that if the Government allowed these migrants into Australia, racial divisions would have been inevitable and the fabric of the representative system torn asunder.[12] As Sir Henry Parkes advised, any race "whom we are not prepared to advance to all our franchise, to all our privileges as citizens, and to all our social rights including the right of marriage, should not be admitted." [13]

Closely related to the desire for retaining British culture was the belief that "a small leak could become a swift stream where a pent-up torrent of Chinese is concerned." [14] There were nineteenth-century illustrations of migrant population explosions in Queensland and New South Wales that gave this argument considerable justification. At the same time, rumors spread by the off-hand remarks of recently arrived migrants substantiated fears that were already extant. The "thin edge of the wedge" represented a gross simplification for Australians who thought that millions of Asians would press for entry once a few were admitted. Since Australia was underpopulated and potentially wealthy it was believed that Asians would use the country as a safety valve for its relatively poor and overcrowded population.[15]

The inextricable interweaving of tradition, fears, and historical inertia produced the notion that preservation of the nation

The Development of the "White Australia" Policy

was dependent on a white Australia. Moreover, steadfast adherence to British colonial restrictive policies assured the resolute continuation of this exclusion as part of the national purpose. Hostility to privilege, dislike of social gradations, hatred of economic exploitation, and an abiding scepticism about the claims of those exalted over their fellows were values in the national character and correspondingly values in the immigration policy deserving of the utmost loyalty.[16]

Economic mobility of Australians increased in the second half of the nineteenth century and helped to create the illusion that economic independence and social equality were virtues immutably tied to the national consciousness. Nationalism came to include an expression of a brash, self-assertive, optimistic way of life which rejected European conventions and politics categorically. Defense of this attitude was based on an emotional commitment to the equality of Australian life. This, no doubt, helps to explain why many Australians were so embittered by the supposed threat of a potential migrant population challenging their "inherited social and economic levelling."

Before the first gold discovery in 1851, indentured Chinese labor was brought into the country to replace convicts employed on the sheep-runs. After the importation of this labor, inchoate nationalist fervor became a working-class fear of lower wage standards.[17] Undesired social effects of Asiatic migration had previously been the basis for objections raised by Australians. These objections grew more bitter when Chinese miners came to Australian gold mines in increasing numbers.[18] The miners were not at first in direct competition with Australian diggers, but as the yields and consequently the incomes of diggers declined, irrational attributions were made. Distinct in appearance, separated in clans, and devoted to foreign religious and social customs, the Chinese and their "absurd superstitions" became the focus of digger distemper.[19] Europeans were even more incensed by the uncanny ability of Chinese to eke out a commendable living by "tailing" abandoned and reputedly effete claims.[20] Under these circumstances minimum conditions for conflict were established, i.e., contact, visible differences, and competition.[21]

The Victorian Government was alarmed by the rapid growth of Chinese immigration. From 1853 to 1857 the Chinese population increased from two thousand to more than forty thousand.[22] When one Chinese remarked that "all were coming" some Australians pictured a vast yellow invasion.[23] The thirty-two thousand Chinese arriving in Victoria between 1855 and 1859 were believed to be a portent of future tidings for that colony.[24]

Even before the enormous influx of Chinese, riots were threatened at Bendigo fields in 1854 and demands were reportedly made to check the growth of this "pagan and inferior race" of Chinese immigrants.[25] An *ad hoc* Gold Fields Commission set up to investigate the disturbance recommended the restriction of Chinese immigration and the establishment of an entrance tax imposed exclusively on Orientals.[26]

The Bill of 1855 passed by the Victoria legislature followed the advice of the Commission and established restrictive legislation, but the law did little more than transfer the port of arrival from Victoria to South Australia or New South Wales. It was not until these colonies passed similar restrictive legislation that Chinese migrant traffic abated.[27] In New South Wales declining gold yields, characteristic of conditions throughout Australia in the late 1850's, sparked a series of miners' riots at Lambing Flat in 1861. Chinese were often attacked and their pigtails were reportedly cut off and kept as souvenirs. Shortly after these riots the New South Wales Government passed an act limiting the landing of migrants which was almost identical to that passed by Victoria.

Restrictive laws in Victoria and New South Wales became unnecessary and were repealed in the 1860's. By the following decade the direction of migration shifted to the Colony of Queensland where the proportion of Chinese to Europeans was one to ten, and at Palmer Diggings in 1877 Chinese actually outnumbered Europeans.[28] To curb the flow a discriminatory license tax was imposed on Chinese migrants in 1876 and "a later Act excluded the Chinese from any goldfield for three years." [29]

The Chinese had almost entirely withdrawn from the goldfields by the late 1870's when a new problem moved the focus of attention from miners to trade unions. The decision of the Australasian Steam Navigation Company to employ Chinese in their ships led to a company-wide strike (1878) which won the support of workmen throughout eastern Australia as well as the Government of Queensland. The public also pressured the Government to withdraw its mail subsidy to the company. Faced with these bitter threats, the company finally acquiesced and dismissed all of its Chinese employees.[30]

This strike helped to bring the Australian colonies closer together on the issue of Oriental immigration. At an intercolonial conference in 1881 the delegates agreed to introduce uniform restrictive acts that in part reflected colonial action taken earlier. As a practical consequence of this agreement it was decided that ships could bring only a limited number of Chinese, all of whom were subject to a capitation tax.[31]

Anti-Chinese Leagues organized as a result of the increasing number of Chinese laborers in the furniture trade added to the developing colonial governments' solidarity. Allegations were legion that cheap labor forced white carpenters out of the industry. In fact, as David Johanson illustrates, "the low price of Chinese manufactured furniture was the result of greater efficiency and calculated specialization rather than of cheap labor." [32] Obviously this view did not receive widespread circulation.

When the commercial possibilities of sugar became apparent in the 1860's, "blackbirders" recruited Pacific Islanders against their will for the purpose of developing the Queensland sugar plantations. It was paradoxical, indeed, that at the moment Chinese labor was being excluded Kanaka labor was forcibly being brought into the country. Traders in human cargo exploited the situation since it was widely believed that only Polynesian labor was suited to work in Queensland's tropical north. Growing out of this employment scheme were some of the worst evils of the old indenture system: indenture provisions were usually abrogated by the plantation foremen; the Kanaka death rate on the canefields was scandalously high; and a quasi-slave institution was developed not unlike the plantation system in the southern United States.[33] Procurement practices and treatment of the Kanakas on the plantations were severely criticized by missionaries and government officials, but "growers protested that the industry could not survive without such labor." [34] In spite of growers' protests, the Queensland Government passed a Polynesian Labourers Act (1868) to control the recruitment and regulate the treatment of Kanaka laborers. The ineffectiveness of this law was made glaringly apparent by the atrocious crimes committed in ships outside the bounds of Australian jurisdiction. In 1872 a law was finally passed to close existing legal loopholes. A joint Colonial-Imperial naval squadron was sent to the Pacific to serve as a police force, and in 1875 a West Pacific High Commission with sovereignty over all British subjects was empowered with magisterial authority to investigate kidnapping cases.

The severe maltreatment of Kanakas aroused public sentiment against the importation of any non-white labor. In the Queensland election of 1883, contested largely on the non-white labor question, Sir Samuel Griffith, a rigid restrictionist, won an overwhelming majority of the votes. After repealing an Immigration Act permitting Indians to come into the country and tightening up the Chinese Restriction Act, he made Kanaka recruitment regulations stricter and working conditions more humane.[35] After this modification in policy total suppression was a foregone conclusion.

At the Intercolonial Conference of March, 1896, delegates from five colonies resolved that the parliaments they represented should amend their anti-Chinese laws and apply them to all colored races.[36] Joseph Chamberlain, then British Secretary of State for the Colonies, influenced by Queen Victoria's pledge not to distinguish among British subjects on the basis of race, origin, language, or creed, asked the colonies to find an inoffensive way of administering restrictive policies.[37] Australia followed the example of Natal's Immigration Restriction Act of 1897, which required literacy in any European language. Under this system a man's color did not appear to be the criterion of acceptability, albeit immigrants of any non-European nationality were at a disadvantage and any "undesirable" could be excluded by giving the dictation test in any language he did not understand. Due to pressure from the Japanese Government, already involved with England in the Anglo-Japanese Treaty of Commerce and Navigation 1894, the dictation test was amended so that it could be given in "any prescribed language."[38] This was intended to mollify Japanese objections to the racial intent without, at the same time, forfeiting the right to exclude non-Europeans. Japan's ability to exert its influence on the policy was a function of its military strength in the South Pacific, highlighted by the embarrassing defeat of Caucasians in the Russo-Japanese War. While the Australian Government feared Japanese power, and was accordingly sensitive to her diplomatic demands, it had no intention of granting Japan a stronger influence on domestic policy by allowing her citizens to migrate.[39]

By 1901 Commonwealth legislation directed at Kanakas and Chinese reflected a united desire for non-European exclusion. These acts were given rhetorical support by eugenic theories that filtered into Australia at the turn of the century. "Racial unity is essential for national unity" was a well-known slogan of the day.[40] Notwithstanding Myra Willard's claim that "the leaders of the people were not actuated by any idea of the inferiority of the mentality or physique of the excluded people," e.g., Deakin, there is considerable evidence to the contrary. Prime Minister Edmund Barton told the House, "I do not think that the doctrine of the equality of man was really ever intended to include racial equality." J. Wilkinson, a notable parliamentarian, said, "Preserve Australia for all future time to the best races of the world and not to the servile race of Asia." And in perhaps the most racial slur of all, J. C. Watson, Labor leader, remarked, "the objection I have to mixing of coloured people with the white people of Australia . . . lies in the main in the possibility and probability of racial contamination." [41]

As these statements indicate, crystallization of White Australia sentiment was clearly apparent by 1900. In a Queensland election of 1899 it was argued that one votes either for "White Australia and Democracy or Toryism and Reaction." [42] The voter did not appear to have much choice. Loyalty to White Australia very quickly became "an expression and, at the same time, a condition of national self-determination and survival." [43]

When the Commonwealth of Australia was inaugurated on January 1, 1901, the Immigration Restriction Bill, based on the dictation test, was accepted as the law. One member of the new Federal Parliament asked that the new nation retain "the noble ideal of a White Australia—a snow-white Australia if you will. Let it be pure and spotless." [44] The implementation of the Act, directed at excluding all non-white people, became the White Australia policy.

Edmund Barton, the first Prime Minister, endorsed the policy on palpably racial grounds; his great fear was miscegenation and eventual assimilation.[45] He joined most of his contemporaries in approving a dictation test—a way of controlling the leakage of colored immigration which at the same time cautiously avoided any offense to Japanese or Indian nationals.[46] But not all parliamentary leaders explained the policy in this way. Charles McDonald, first Labor Speaker of Parliament, opposed colored migration "because it was unwilling migration recklessly organized by irresponsible Europeans." He objected to what was reputed to be virtual "slave labor" in Queensland.[47] Alfred Deakin, one of Australia's most important early leaders, supported restriction with yet another argument: "We here find ourselves touching the profoundest instinct of individual or nation—the instinct of self-preservation—for it is nothing less than the national manhood, the national character, and the national future that are at stake." [48]

Whether motivated by fear, nationalism, humanitarianism, or racial superiority, the early leaders were almost unanimously behind the objectives of the policy. A. T. Yarwood indicates another reason for this unanimity that is still embraced as an argument for maintenance of the status quo: "From the viewpoint of international amity, the Australian Act of 1901, though regarded with hostility at the time for its severity, had the merit of preventing the growth of minorities whose presence might have led to recurring diplomatic crises." [49]

It was apparent that men of different political persuasions rallied behind the policy. Some partisan historians attributed the policy solely to the Labor Party which represented trade union fear of the infiltration of substandard Asian labor. But considerable evidence affirms the notion of a non-partisan approach to this issue.[50] The development of restrictive efforts in pre-federation days and the impetus for joint action on immigration once the colonies were unified is evidence of national, rather than narrow party, endorsement of White Australia.

To a very great extent Australian defense policy was nothing but a disguise for the protection of White Australia against "the yellow peril." Sir George Pearce, an early leader of Federation, said, "Our white Australia legislation is so much waste paper unless we have the rifles to back it up by force." [51] Former Prime Minister William Hughes paraphrased this remark and identified with its spirit when he commented: "If the White Australia Policy is to be a permanence in this country, there must be behind it a sufficient force of white Australians ready, if necessary, to make good their claim. There is no other way." [52] A defense policy based on White Australia was perhaps myopic but it should be recalled that the immigration policy had been elevated to a national faith on which it was believed self-preservation depended. In addition, policy administration, guided as it was by national welfare, was not monolithic. Japanese migrants received far more lenient treatment than Chinese migrants. Likewise, Australian reliance on the panoply of British naval superiority to maintain White Australia often meant granting some very slight imperial concessions to non-white Commonwealth members, particularly Indian migrants.[53]

In the years after 1902 the Restriction Act underwent few changes. The changes that did occur were largely due to Japanese diplomatic pressure and the fear of aggressive intrusion in Australian affairs. Deakin's attempted negotiations with Japan for a reciprocal treaty were considered to be an unmitigated attempt to palliate Japan's dissatisfaction with the policy. According to his proposals, "each party bound itself to restrict emigration to the other" which he believed placed Japan and Australia "on an equal footing" and "removed any suggestion of race superiority. . . ." Furthermore, he took steps to exempt from the dictation test "citizens of any country with which the Commonwealth had made an agreement regulating their admission."[54] Japan refused these concessions, but they nonetheless indicated a government effort to conciliate in order to maintain the basic principles in the White Australia policy.

At the Versailles Peace Conference of 1919 Japanese representatives put pressure on the Australian Government by suggesting that a clause guaranteeing equal treatment to all races be inserted into the Covenant. Prime Minister Hughes, the Australian delegate to the conference, indicated that such a proposal was unacceptable to Australia and was an encroachment upon the right of countries to determine their own domestic policies.[55]

After Versailles, when Japan demonstrated parity with Western industrial standards, some eugenic theorists euphemistically substituted "difference" for "inferior or superior." Correspondingly the Australian immigration policy was decreasingly

The Development of the "White Australia" Policy

defended on racial grounds and increasingly denied to be an expression of bigotry. One senator, obviously disregarding Japanese industrial advancement, described "White Australia" as "economic, not racial." [56] When Hitler's abstract racist notions developed, it was rather awkward for the Australian Government to argue its policy with racial overtones. Nonetheless, Japanese aggression to the south gave fresh, but ephemeral, impetus to racial outpourings. Racialism directed at Japan was neutralized to some extent, however, by the respect accorded Japanese military power and technical skills.

Before World War II there were relatively minor modifications in the White Australia policy and few internal remonstrances for change. Since the war, however, the forces for change have gathered considerable momentum and have induced an often reluctant Government to liberalize immigration policy. Undoubtedly the war itself forced Australia, with traumatic suddenness, to reject its isolation and consider prospects of increased collaboration. This increasing collaboration together with several *causes célèbres* has resulted in the claim that the White Australia policy could no longer serve the needs of contemporary Australia. While this was recognized by a majority in several public opinion polls (see Chapter 6), government proposals have often been slow in meeting the demands of public opinion and the changing Australian-Asia community. But forces set in motion during the war made some liberalization of immigration policy impossible for the Government to refuse.

During World War II the colored population of Australia swelled with the forced migration of Asians fleeing the Japanese invasion. These migrants were given a sanctuary in Australia with the understanding that they would return when the war ended. But many of the migrants married or just found life in Australia congenial, and refused to accept their obligation. In 1947 the Labor Government tried to deport fourteen Malay seamen, all of whom married Australians and most of whom had families. The Government insisted its position was predicated on assurances that the stays were temporary pending the termination of the war.[57] As soon as the repatriation decision was announced vocal opposition erupted in the press, attacking the policy on moral grounds and later as an expression of "administrative callousness." Mr. Arthur Calwell, Minister for Immigration at the time, refused, after considerable delay, to reconsider his decision. Malayan Seamen's Defence Committees were organized in Sydney, Melbourne, and Brisbane. To satisfy some of the opposition's demands the Government offered to pay for the transportation of the families to Malaya.[58] But the bitterness of the struggle remained and organizational weapons for reform were created. All that was necessary to evoke a more vigorous resentment was another *cause célèbre*. The reformers did not have to wait long.

In the same year Mrs. Annie O'Keefe, an Indonesian, provided opponents of the White Australia policy with a new *cause célèbre*. Mrs. O'Keefe, whose first husband was killed in an airplane crash during the war, was rescued from the Indonesian jungle with her family of eight children and brought to Australia. It was stipulated at the time of her entry, according to statutory safeguards, that she would leave the country when required to do so. She became one of many war refugees accepted as temporary entrants, subject to the Minister for Immigration's authority. After several years in Australia she received an offer of marriage and applied for permanent residence credentials from the Department of Immigration. She soon learned that marriage to an Australian conferred no privilege of permanent residence for a war refugee accepted as a "prohibited migrant."[59] Mrs. O'Keefe appealed the decision to the High Court (1947), which ruled in a majority decision that Mrs. O'Keefe did not qualify as a prohibited migrant since she had not taken the dictation test (which was used to determine that status), and therefore the Minister for Immigration no longer had authority to deport her.[60]

The ruling applied not only to Mrs. O'Keefe but to hundreds of other war refugees in the country. In order to deal with this "recalcitrant minority" Calwell introduced several bills designed to restore ministerial control over aliens allowed entry during the war—a control, argued Calwell, that the High Court had preempted in its decision.[61] If implemented, the proposals could have been used against Mrs. O'Keefe and approximately 800 other Asian war refugees. The bills were passed, but before any repatriation action could be taken, a general election was held. A change in government occurred, and a more liberal attitude to these non-European war refugees was adopted.[62] Mrs. O'Keefe was accepted as an Australian citizen.

"White Australia," despite the O'Keefe case, continued to be prominently displayed in the headlines of most Australian newspapers. No sooner had O'Keefe left the front page than another, more volatile case appeared. Sergeant Gamboa, a United States citizen of Filipino parentage, was refused the right to reenter Australia even though his Australian wife and children lived there.[63] The Immigration Department, under Calwell's leadership, argued that marriage could not be used as a means of entering the country, whatever the personal hardships involved. He offered to pay the fares of Mrs. Gamboa and the children to either the Philippines or the United States, but Gamboa would not accept the offer. Instead he challenged the Department's decision by pointing out directly to Eleanor Roosevelt and several United Nations' delegates that Australia's immigration policy was a violation of the United Nations' Charter, which specifically prohibited racial discrimination.[64] Due in part to the publicity the case received, Calwell's judgment was rescinded by the new Menzies Government in its attempt to reverse what Senator E. B. Maher described as "the fanatical . . . and . . . unchristian policy that was applied by the member for Melbourne [Mr. Calwell]. . . ."[65]

The 1949 swing to the Liberal-Country Party and the appointment of a new Minister for Immigration, Mr. Harold Holt, changed the climate in which the immigration policy was administered. With the exception of a few minor cases, the

1950's were almost entirely free of incidents related to the White Australia policy. Most Australians, due very largely to Holt's more flexible attitude to the subject and new immigration legislation enacted in 1956 and 1957, believed that the general tenor of the policy was changing.

Since many returned soldiers had had contacts with Asians for the first time during the war, they developed a "new respect and an ease of personal relationship which opened the way for the closer relations . . ."[66] between Australia and Asia in the 1950's. Many of these former soldiers favored easing the immigration regulations, but few accepted the idea of abandoning the White Australia policy completely.

Postwar participation in the Colombo Plan and other exchange programs made it possible for large numbers of Asian students to attend Australian colleges and universities for the first time. Contact with these students led to renewed inquiries about the rationale for a White Australia policy. In the late 1950's at the University of Melbourne "successive S.R.C.s [Student Representative Councils] battled with National Union of Students to have condemnations recorded"[67] or at least to have student views aired. Student Action and Associations for Immigration Reform actively engaged in publicizing the White Australia policy and they were joined by such interested allies as church organizations, Apex, and the National Civic Council in a new effort to modify or abandon White Australia. Protest groups such as these may not have been directly responsible for change but they did influence the climate in which change occurred.

Minister for Immigration Downer faced far more harassment than his predecessor. Every *cause célèbre,* and there was no dearth of them in the early 1960's, was exploited by protest groups excoriating the abuses in the policy. Deported Darwin pearl divers were sympathetically called "Downer's exports" by Student Action leaders vigorously protesting department actions. No sooner had this banner become dated than it was replaced by "Downer's Wong Move," a reference to Willie Wong who was deported to Hong Kong in 1962 and allegedly shipped off to Red China. Force for change, latent in the fifties, manifested itself in the mass media and reached the Commonwealth Government in the sixties. In one of the few times (1966) in its sixty-five-year history, the House of Representatives conducted a full-scale debate on the White Australia policy.

Change in attitude within Australia was bolstered by diplomatic pressure outside the continent such as the chastizement of Australian policies by non-white members of the United Nations. In spite of the United Nations' legal assurances that domestic policies were not within its purview, White Australia was very often opposed by the full thrust of anti-racial vindictiveness. Whether or not the immigration policy represented racialism was often overlooked in opinions that dismissed Australian foreign policy arguments with an exposure of her omnipresent "Achilles heel."

A deterioration of military security was another inextricable link in the pressure for reevaluation of the White Australia policy. After World War II the British reduced the size of their forces in Asia and the South Pacific. The British navy no longer served as a military shield to protect Australian separation from Asia and concomitantly her White Australia policy. In addition, the states of Asia who were "held in check" by the yoke of colonialism before the war began to gain independence. Dependent peoples by their very status cannot denounce the practices of an independent country, and low living standards and high illiteracy rates characteristic of Asia in the pre-war period contributed to the relative insularity and muted protest of the colonial subjects.[68] But the spirit of the postwar era partially erased passive resistance. Anti-colonial states of Asia and Africa, having won their sovereignty from white nations and taken their place in an international body, became extremely critical of any policy based on racism. An intellectual elite, educated in the Occident, spoke out in most Asian states denouncing what they often referred to as "Western hypocrisy"—a combination of solicitousness for non-whites and compunctions about eliminating the vestiges of racial and colonial institutions. Lastly, the White Australia policy was protected by geographic and psychological isolation before the war. But Australians found, rather uneasily, that any separation in the postwar world could be maintained only because (not in spite) of a *modus vivendi* with Asians.

"Coexistence through separation had to be replaced or supplemented by co-existence through cooperation" [69] in the face of Asian consciousness and the vulnerability of Asian states to Communist ideology. Keeping a balance between collective security based on American strength and directed at Asia, and the simultaneous cultivation of friendly relations with Asian states, became the essence of the new Australian foreign policy. For some the two ideas were mutually exclusive. Would the rapprochement with the United States increase Australia's "distance" from Asia? was the question that went directly to the heart of the matter. Nonetheless, Australia made a commitment to a "good neighbor policy" with Asia and a reduction of the psychological distance associated with her earlier policies. One fundamental aspect of this change in attitude was the modification of the White Australia policy. Those facets of the policy morally exceptionable to Asians were to be revised. On this point, albeit there were differences of opinion on the degree of modification, most Australians agreed. The history of the White Australia policy after the war was marked by an increasing realization of Asian sensitivities and a decreasing emphasis on the "established policy" formulated at Federation.

That the White Australia policy has changed only moderately while the conditions responsible for its enactment have themselves changed drastically probably means that the policy has been propagated by and serves the needs of a multiplicity of forces not easily identified in Australia's historical antecedents. Its racial overtones have over the years been vehemently denied. The policy's proponents have groped for rhetorical responses to explain immigration laws without giving offense. And very often they

The Development of the "White Australia" Policy

have led themselves not into explanations but into a mass of confusion.

Particularly irritating to many Asians is the policy's categorical grouping of diverse individuals on the basis of skin pigmentation. Whereas this method of exclusion could be justified as an economic precaution earlier, the continued exclusion of industrially and technically advanced Asians now seems to point to an underlying racialism. Should the Japanese, with living standards nearing a par with Australia's and proficiency in applying Western technology, be considered as part of the "lumpen-Asiatics"?

Even at the turn of the century, the economic argument for exclusion was not entirely valid. The proposition that Asian labor would work for lower wages and cause Australian unemployment could have been opposed with some justification by the concept that an increase in the labor force would have led to increased production and effective demand, culminating in a higher standard of living for both Australians and Asian migrants. But the argument in favor of a restrictive policy was not only used by laborers; it was part of the rhetoric of professional men and skilled artisans as well. Many of them argued that Asians who secured skilled positions might cause friction in the community and prejudice on the part of any men displaced. This logic ignored the conflict that arose when any two men competed for a position only one could obtain; it likewise ignored the Australian dedication to fluid mobility and "giving each bloke a fair go." What appeared through this argument was that, for some, having an Asian in a higher rank than an Australian was plainly objectionable.

Some Australians assumed that because Asians were ignorant of the representative system they would impede the growth of democracy. W. K. (later Sir Keith) Hancock reasoned, "No country can, without danger, give a share of power to aliens unable or unwilling to accept and defend what it most values." [70] If Asians were given the franchise, the corollary ran, they would not know how to use it; on the other hand to withhold it would endanger the Australian democratic tradition. Sponsors of this reasoning used sweeping generalizations that consciously ignored the growth of political independence in Asia during the twentieth century. This became glaringly apparent when the Government initiated a postwar immigration program to augment population growth. When European immigrants became indiscriminately more acceptable than Asian immigrants, it grew legitimate to ask if postwar Russians and Italians were more democratic than Indians. Similarly, exclusionist theories depending on a maintenance of the British character became paradoxical with widespread acceptance of Europeans. After all, is India less British than Poland? From this perspective the political rationale for exclusion seems very questionable.

The desire to retain a homogeneous population, unanimously accepted by every Minister for Immigration,[71] depends for its logic on the meaning of the word homogeneous. Homogeneity as a manifestation of racism was flatly denied by most of the former Ministers for Immigration. But if homogeneity is not equated with whiteness what does it mean? If it means religion should the Government discriminate against Christian Filipinos? If it refers to wealth should not wealthy Hong Kong merchants be encouraged to migrate? If it connotes culture, should the Government restrict entry for thoroughly Anglicized Indians?[72] And if it means "men of goodwill," why encourage European migration and control Asian migration? Are Asians, notwithstanding the morality of Buddha and Confucius, more decadent than pop culture enthusiasts of the Occident? Perhaps, as O. A. Oeser and S. B. Hammond point out, "the major subjective component underlying the policy appears to be a perception of difference in 'way of life' between people of the various countries and Australia. . . . Immigrants are expected to 'fit in' and to become Australians and opposition is strongest to those groups which are believed to be unlikely to do so."[73]

Whether or not it has been denied, color plays an important

The Development of the "White Australia" Policy

role in determining eligibility for migration. Before Syrians were considered "European" enough for Australia, Secretary of Immigration Hunt wrote in their defense:

> swarthy appearance, with dark hair, and of sallow complexions, but approximate far more closely to the European types than to those of India or parts of Asia further East. So far as general appearance goes they cannot be distinguished from the people of Southern Italy, Spain or Greece and in fact are considerably lighter in complexion than Turks.[74]

The same criterion excluded an Englishman of mixed descent who was refused entrance in 1961 on the ground, according to the acting Minister, "that he was predominantly non-European in appearance. . . . this is in line with immigration policy since Federation." [75]

If the criteria for assimilation were regarded without concern for color and "out-group" association it would be noted that Chinese already resident in large urban centers such as Melbourne and Sydney are generally peaceful and adjusted to Australian living.[76] Racial incidents, as a concomitant of these multi-racial communities, have been almost entirely absent in this century.[77] It is interesting to note that Australians often refer to the United States, England, or South Africa in order to illustrate the incompatibility of different races, but ignore the experiences in their own multi-racial communities. It is true that a white population accepts a few non-white people more readily than substantially larger numbers, but this does not detract from the harmonious relations between Asians and Australians and the relatively smooth assimilation of Chinese into the society. Perhaps the fears aroused by the American and British experiences in the past two decades have obscured Australia's successful absorption of non-Europeans. Whether it be fear of foreign experiences or a reliance on nineteenth century historical antecedents, the criterion of color as a guide to assimilability remains as an essential, but seemingly unjustifiable, ingredient in ministerial administration of the White Australia policy.

2

Recent Liberalization of Immigration Policy

With a sound hardly more audible than a whimper the Minister for Immigration in 1956 announced important modifications in the White Australia policy. The announcement received almost no fanfare or newspaper coverage. A trial involving a university academic and a twenty-year-old student as well as the Hungarian revolt and the Suez crisis shunted the Immigration Department's news to the fifth page of most major dailies. Yet the modification itself was the most far-reaching example of liberalization of immigration policy in the century. The Government decided to modify the conditions for the entry and stay of non-Europeans so that:

- a) persons already permitted to remain here without getting periodical extensions of their stay should be eligible to qualify for naturalization;
- b) certain non-Europeans already in Australia who normally would have been expected to leave, should be allowed to remain for humanitarian reasons;

c) distinguished and highly qualified non-Europeans should be admitted for indefinite stay; and
d) the conditions for the admission of persons of mixed descent should be clarified and eased.[1]

Naturalization for a significantly large group of non-Europeans was permitted for the first time. Furthermore, the new requirements established a precedent for easing the regulations still further. In September, 1956, non-European spouses of Australian citizens were eligible to qualify for naturalization on the same basis as European spouses. And in 1957 other non-Europeans admitted for temporary residence were given the right to apply for naturalization after fifteen years' residence.[2]

These changes in the established policy were due in no small part to the *ad hoc* reaction of immigration officials to the war refugees, political refugees, Japanese brides, displaced persons, and other non-Europeans who came to Australia for asylum after the war. Government sympathy for those fleeing the Japanese invasion led ultimately to a review of the White Australia policy.

While the Government accepted political refugees during the war, it did so with one stipulation—a guarantee of return when hostilities ceased. But when the time for return came the political, as well as ideological, map of the East had changed. What was once Nationalist China and an ally had become Communist China and an enemy. The Government was faced with the dilemma of either deporting refugees to Communist China or modifying the White Australia policy so that the refugees could remain in Australia.[3] If the Government had deported them, it would have been labeled hypocritical in its anti-Communism and insensitive to the plight of migrants; if, on the other hand, it had modified the White Australia policy radically, some people would have considered the act tantamount to violation of the "national faith." One other possibility, deporting the migrants to Hong Kong or Singapore, was rejected by authorities in these places who insisted that migrants, even political refugees, required a visa for entry. Their fear of being a "dumping ground" for unwanted refugees and their proximity to Communist China undoubtedly influenced this decision. Conscious of the limited alternatives, authorities gradually modified the policy. In this way, it was thought, the problem of non-European war refugees could be remedied and the staunchest defenders of the policy, unaware of the revisions, mollified. Political motivation prompted the decision. But the choice, once made, induced some rather awkward political rhetoric as a defense of the concessions. It was not unusual to hear politicians say in sentences juxtaposed, "the very basis of our immigration policy shall not be disturbed" and "we support the proposals [revisions] announced by the Minister." [4]

When the decision to naturalize non-Europeans was made it was only a matter of time before other regulations, even the numbers of entrants, would be revised. If you permitted non-Europeans entry and naturalization could you exclude their spouses, children, and immediate relatives? And if you decided to ease these categories for entry could you maintain a rigid exclusionist policy? The decisions of 1956 and 1957 unwittingly paved the way for further liberalization. In 1959 Australian citizens already domiciled in Australia were permitted "to introduce for residence their non-European spouses and unmarried minor children, who would then be eligible to apply for naturalization." In 1960 this provision was extended to those "with residence status in Australia" or those "about to attain it" and in 1964 liberalized regulations applying to persons of mixed descent made their entry into Australia easier.[5]

In early March, 1966, Mr. Opperman announced his proposed changes to a disingenuous House of Representatives. He suggested at the outset that the measures should be recognized as important "but as not departing from the fundamental principles of our immigration policy." [6] First, he declared that non-Europeans already in Australia under temporary permits, but likely to be there indefinitely, could apply for resident status after five years instead of the previous fifteen-year waiting period. This removed the most objectionable and blatantly discriminatory aspect of the policy, although the provision did not imply the ruling applied to everyone admitted to Australia for limited temporary residence. Students in particular were not given the right to settle after five years' study. Mr. Opperman argued, with considerable justification, that Chinese—allowed to stay on as a result of the July, 1956, decision but unable to bring their wives and children to Australia since they lacked citizenship or settler status—would benefit from the new provision almost immediately. Second, applications by "well qualified people" were to be "considered on the basis of their suitability as settlers, their ability to integrate readily and their possession of qualifications which are in fact positively useful to Australia." [7] The changes also specified that migrants could bring their immediate families with them on first arrival. "The number of people entering the country," said the Minister, "will be somewhat greater than previously, but will be controlled by the careful assessment of the individual's qualifications, and the basic aim of preserving a homogeneous population will be maintained." [8]

The most significant debate since Federation on non-European immigration policy emerged in the House of Representatives at this time. Much of the debate and most of the decisions, on both sides of the House, had been consummated behind closed doors, but the debate, in spite of its non-partisan character, was a noteworthy departure from the historic silence on this issue. Mr. Fred Daly (Labor M.P. for Grayndler), who initiated the debate on the proposals, set the non-partisan atmosphere by referring to the "united support" the non-European immigration policy "has enjoyed" and the "correct" decision made by the Minister to preserve "the principles underlying our immigration policy." [9] The only warnings inserted into his speech were assurances that "non-Europeans will not be brought in to meet general labour shortages, and that there will be no large-scale admission of workers from Asia." [10] In general, this speech as well as the others were rationalizations for and endorsements of the established policy and the government position. "The policy is not, and never has been directed to the total exclusion of non-Europeans, nor is it based on any assumption of racial superiority," [11] declared Mr. Daly, omitting some of the historical reasons for the policy and its administration. Sir Keith Wilson (M.P. for Sturt), a stalwart supporter of the policy, argued "that following upon the proposed reform Australia now has the most liberal immigration policy of any country." [12] His logic relied on the elimination of color or race as grounds for acceptability and the judicious exercise of ministerial discretion. In addition, Sir Keith referred to the restrictive immigration policies of Malaysia, Burma, Ceylon, India, the Philippines, Cambodia, Japan, Vietnam, and most African states. However, he neglected to mention Australia's ardent migrant recruitment and Asia's overpopulation. But as arguments for restriction they were most effective. Perhaps the *sine qua non* of the policy was alluded to in Wilson's plea for assimilation:

> We do not want Australia to be a little Italy, a little Germany, a little Greece or a little any other country. We want our migrants to become Australians and our migration system is based on admitting people who, having come here, want to become Australians. We do not want people to come here just to make what money they can and then return to their own countries. We want them to be part of the Australian community.[13]

This emphasis on "Australianizing" migrants to "fit in" or assimilate is not only an essential ingredient in the White Australia policy; it is an expression of the national ethos and a devotion to the white Anglo-Saxon tradition in which the nation evolved. "Opening the door," or relaxation of the regulations was deemed a threat to Australia's homogeneity and an invitation to racial strife. On this point there was almost no disagreement. "The history of the world today demonstrates clearly that there is a degree of incompatibility between certain races," claimed Mr. E. W. Peters (M.P. for Scullin).[14] His view, shared by many of his political colleagues, relied on the belief that assimilation of non-whites in a predominantly white society was virtually impossible. One Labor stalwart (C. K. Jones, M.P., Newcastle) fearing the consequences of Opperman's moderate proposals, noted, "I am greatly afraid that if we indulge in a policy of bringing in large numbers of these people we are going to import into this country troubles and problems that we do not want."[15] This Labor notion, extant since Federation, seemed to inject a degree of partisanship into the debate. But the representatives of both labor and industry in the House based their opposition to an influx of Asian immigrants on economic grounds. Likewise, both parties viewed the maintenance of the policy, with only the minor revisions suggested by Mr. Opperman, as a reflection of the national interest.

In order to mollify antagonists of the policy who bemoaned its "static" administration, many of the spokesmen in this debate made references to the almost 39,000 non-Europeans in Australia, the 12,400 Colombo Plan and other non-European students at Australian schools, and the modifications made in the policy since 1956. Another argument employed to illustrate the concern of the Department of Immigration for South East Asia involved the fact that students would not be permitted permanent residence after five years in order "to encourage" them to "return to their homelands and assist in their development." Australia, this spokesman insisted, "must not bleed other countries of their skilled workers."[16] However, this statement and the Minister's desire to consider application requests by "well qualified people" do appear contradictory.

One Member of Parliament categorically denied the rigidity associated with the policy and claimed that vindictiveness directed at it was due largely to the phrase, "White Australia," rather than the intent of the policy.[17] He endorsed Sir Alan Watt's suggestion "for a public burial ceremony for the phrase . . ." and a strong rebuttal to publicists that insist on using it. Moreover, he implied that, with the exception of the Country Party, the phrase "White Australia policy" and the racial intent in its original usage had been discarded by the major parties.[18]

While the debate was characterized by a general approval of Mr. Opperman's proposals there were two moderate yet notable exceptions. Mr. L. R. Johnson (M.P. for Hughes) forthrightly suggested:

> there is a case for a real change in our policy, not merely in its words but also in the implementation of its words. Australia needs non-European migrants to enrich its own culture. This will not mean opening the flood gates any more than we have opened them to people from European countries. There is a need for us to permit the intake of non-European migrants so as to increase our understanding of our neighbours and to equip ourselves for participation in the international councils of the world. Of course, there is also the need to increase the intake in order to remedy what has been the fairly disastrous impact of our policy throughout Asia.[19]

With the historian's dispassion, Mr. K. E. Beazley (M.P. for Fremantle), a notable Labor spokesman, also challenged one of the primary assumptions on which the policy was predicated. Asians, he observed, do not cast "hungry eyes on Australia" even though the White Australia policy implies they do.

> If Asians had had the aggression and the determination to migrate that Europeans had in the nineteenth century, this country would have been settled by Asians long before Europeans ever saw it. After all, we do subscribe to the myth that a country is discovered when it is seen by Europeans—preferably Englishmen—but in point of fact Australia had been seen by Asians for generations before any Englishman came here. The Malays traded with Australia. They were perfectly familiar with it, and they did not wish to migrate to it.[20]

Despite the implications in this argument, Mr. Beazley accepted the Opperman proposals as a moderate step toward liberalization consistent with the "realities of migrant absorption."

With almost monotonous persistence cliches were employed by most of the spokesmen in the debate. "It's a sensible approach" was substituted by "it is better than a quota system" for effect and perhaps style, but the arguments were consistently the same. Equally redundant were the references to "not opening the floodgates," "maintenance of our homogeneity," and "the ability to integrate." Not once during this extended discussion did a Member ask for an explanation of phraseology or a definition of terms such as "homogeneity" or "integration." The lack of severely critical remarks and bipartisan acceptance of the proposals was testimony to limited views and political conservatism. A coalescence of opinion was inevitable when leaders and spokesmen in both parties were reluctant to jeopardize their political positions for a more idealistic posture. It was noteworthy that party "whips" did not delegate any of the more extreme spokesmen on this issue to present their views. To discuss the issue at all was progress of a kind. But few politicians were willing to expose their "warts" to the acidic treatment of adversaries. In accordance with a bipartisan agreement moderation was unstintingly practiced and praise of the policy was a natural result of this mutual understanding. The policy proposals were described as "humane, sensible and progressive" or "reasonable and desirable" by both government supporters and government detractors.

One reason for the lack of lively debate between the parties was that Mr. Opperman, before making the proposals, assured the Labor Party that liberalization did not constitute an unrestricted flow of migrants or a major deviation from the established policy.[21] Labor would probably not have supported the modification without these assurances. As a gesture of good faith and an endorsement of a restricted policy Mr. Opperman agreed to review the admission categories in order to curtail "category jumping"—switching admission status in order to obtain permanent residence—and to control, within limits mutually acceptable, the total number of migrants permitted entry. This *quid pro quo* gave the Government bipartisan endorsement on a potentially volatile subject and the Labor Party an opportunity to reject its historically rigid position on this issue without discarding its allegiance to the principles of the White Australia policy. Several months before Mr. Opperman made his proposals, the Immigration Committee in the Labor Party recommended:

> That the proposals be not opposed and the assurance given by the Minister be accepted, that is, that there is to be no departure from the accepted and established principle of our Immigration policy, and that it will be administered with understanding and tolerance.[22]

The Labor Party's concern with the phrase "White Australia" in its platform prompted a 1965 hearing and intra-party discussion of the basic principles of its immigration policy. Some of the more liberal members of the Immigration Committee, i.e., Mr. Donald Dunstan (later Premier of South Australia) and Mr. F. E. Chamberlain, West Australian party leader, suggested the elimination of distinctions between European and non-European migrants—a suggestion considerably more liberal than any Liberal proposal. In order to appease this faction in the Committee and at the same time satisfy the large majority of conservatives on the Committee and in the Party, Mr. Fred Daly, a conservative and the party's "Shadow" Minister for Immigration, with some support from his colleagues, Messrs. Collard, Steward, and Fitzgerald, prepared a brief list of recommendations the party could adopt without alienating either faction. The first recommendation dealt with replacing the phrase "White Australia" in their platform with "predominantly homogeneous population." (The phrase "homogeneous character of our population" was excluded from the policy proposal because of its ambiguous nature. But the principle of homogeneity was the essence of the new statement.) The second set of recommendations, and by far the most important, related to administrative practices. In fact these recommendations constituted Labor demands in the February–March negotiations with Mr. Opperman. The satisfaction of these demands was the quintessential feature of the bipartisan debate on the Opperman proposals. The Labor Committee desired: rejection of an Asian quota system; a review of the categories established for the entry of non-Europeans with "the object of improving or increasing the categories where considered necessary"; "making the period of residence for non-Europeans eligible for citizenship the same as that applying to Europeans, namely five years . . ."; preventing transfer of student visa to migrant visa status (a student's visa, it was argued, should be issued for only a twelve-month period subject to a review before renewal); control of tourist visas so that the holder "cannot transfer to a migrant visa" (this was considered necessary in order to leave no doubt about the limitation of the visa and to overcome deportation problems and the consequential publicity).[23]

These reforms demanded by the Committee and unanimously approved by the party were not incompatible with any of the Opperman proposals. However, the Labor concern with "category jumping" indicated a disenchantment with the flexible administration of the policy which had permitted several thousand migrants in the past ten years to transfer categories and remain in Australia, and the adverse publicity directed at the Department as a result of several deportation cases, e.g., Nancy Prasad (see Chapter 9). The Labor Party tried to tighten categories of acceptability (i.e., "improving or increasing the categories") and simultaneously present an image of fairness and humanitarianism. This condition was accepted by Mr. Opperman mainly because the Government never intended his proposed modifications to abandon the principles on which the policy had been based. One prominent member of the Liberal Immigration Committee remarked: "We cannot allow large numbers of Asians into this country and import trouble. We can accept only 'good quality' Asians." These comments preceded the statement that liberalization was due to "a recognition of inequality in the policy, our involvement in Asia and our humanitarian spirit." [24]

This view was to a great extent a reflection of government and Labor opinion. But not all the Members of the House of Representatives shared this sentiment. Tightening the categories of entry and easing naturalization requirements for non-Europeans, the mutually acceptable criteria for reform, were cynically dismissed by one Member of the House of Representatives. He argued these recent changes would cause "more tightening and less reform"; this revision "is consistent with post-1963 Immigration Policy which because of a sluggish economy, security reasons and a large number of Asian students has had to be limited." [25] Another Member, very well informed about non-European immigration, labeled the Opperman proposals "a distinction without a difference" and "a slight change of method not principle." He continued: "There is absolutely no change in the policy. There is nothing Opperman can do now that he could not do ten years ago. The apparent change is nothing but a 'confidence trick.'" [26]

Notwithstanding the few dissenters, a non-partisan view of immigration has been part of Australia's heritage since Federation. It came as no surprise that this tradition was continued in 1966. Most Members of the House still regard the non-European immigration policy with a respect bordering on reverence. Fundamentalists argued that if changes must occur "let us at least maintain the traditional principles." Or as one of the elder statesmen put it: "The established policy is and always will be the best one." [27] The politically-minded, eager to avoid "jugular issues" that might jeopardize local support, tried to avoid the topic of non-European immigration or opted to maintain the status quo. With these attitudes prevalent it was surprising, indeed, that any modification was approved.

Under the leadership of Mr. Peter Heydon, Secretary of Immigration, the Department had been discussing modification proposals for several years. As Sir Robert Menzies was opposed to any major change in the traditional policy, he usually rejected the proposals. Late in 1964 the Department of Immigration submitted reforms to the Cabinet and the Prime Minister, including a five-year residence requirement for non-Europeans and further flexibility in the categories of acceptance. While most of the Cabinet members, particularly the Ministers for External Affairs and Trade, approved the proposals, Menzies summarily rejected them.[28] A Department of Immigration official remarked: "The 'old man' did not want liberalization of 'White Australia' on his record." [29]

When the late Mr. Harold Holt succeeded Menzies and Mr. Opperman retained the Immigration portfolio, a policy shift was possible. Mr. Opperman, a conservative party man, was willing to accept, without reservations, the Prime Minister's direction on this issue. After only a few months in office Holt asked the Department to disinter the 1964–1965 modification proposals and resubmit them for Cabinet approval. Before there was any hint of a shift in policy the Secretary of Immigration broached the subject with the Immigration Advisory Council. This body, composed of representatives from trade unions, employers' organizations, the Returned Servicemen's League, voluntary welfare bodies, the Chamber of Commerce, professional associations, and a Member of Parliament, was a reflection of different sectors of public opinion, albeit mostly conservative. The Department's consultation with this council and a subsequent visit by the Minister refined the carefully worded modification proposals. Mr. Opperman's appearance at the council meeting was unprecedented for a Minister for Immigration, but it gave him an opportunity to rehearse his presentation to the Cabinet and later the House of Representatives. One factor for a possible shift in policy, discussed at the meeting, was the estrangement of Asians separated from their immediate families for fifteen years. It was suggested that this undue hardship could be eliminated for "well qualified migrants" without "radically altering the policy." Mr. Opperman also indicated, as he reasserted later, that a more flexible approach to the administration of the policy did not constitute a major shift in traditional principles.[30] With only minor opposition the proposals were accepted by the Advisory Council.

Government acceptance of these proposals was influenced by several factors in addition to Mr. Holt's personal predilections. Early in the year Mr. Gough Whitlam, Deputy Leader of the Opposition, made a stern rebuttal of racial discrimination in Australia's immigration policy at the Citizenship Convention in Canberra. He urged that Australia "remove as far as possible any racial aspects of discrimination" and specifically noted that the fifteen-year residence requirement for Asians was glaringly racialist.[31] Despite government disclaimers to the contrary, the timing of the Opperman proposals made them seem like a government rebuttal to Mr. Whitlam's attack of the policy. In much the same way the Nancy Prasad and Aurelio Locsin cases—*causes célèbres* of the 1965–1966 period—seemed to influence the timing, if not the content, of the proposals. One political analyst wrote: ". . . it seems likely that the timing of the changes had a lot to do with the unfavorable publicity Australia was receiving overseas as a result of the Nancy Prasad and Aurelio Locsin cases." [32] As a result of the Aurelio Locsin case the Manila press, particularly Maximo Soliven, a columnist for the *Manila Times,* vigorously attacked Australia's non-European immigration policy. It was pointed out that Locsin had two university degrees and accountancy experience, yet his application to migrate to Australia was rejected. The Immigration Department supported its decision by claiming "that Mr. Locsin could not be regarded as coming within any of these five categories" of acceptability. His academic qualifications did not enable him to be classified as a "person possessing outstanding cultural or other attainments" and his experience as a bank officer could not grant him acceptance under the category for "professional or higher technical appointments for which local residents are not available." [33] This explanation for the decision did not satisfy either the Philippine Government or the press. Some Philippine newspapers "urged breaking diplomatic relations and Australia's expulsion from SEATO." [34] The Philippine Ambassador to the United Nations pushed a resolution through the United Nations Commission on Human Rights condemning racial discrimination "in all its forms, wherever it exists . . ." and appealed for the enactment of "urgent and effective measures for its complete elimination." It was reported that the Philippine delegate moved the resolution "because of growing resentment in his country to the White Australia policy." [35] But by the time the United Nations considered these resolutions the Holt Government had modified its conditions for naturalization and entry of non-Europeans. The Secretary of Immigration denied, in fact, that there was any relationship at all between recent liberalization of the policy and the Locsin and Prasad cases,[36] but one political analyst claimed that the liberalization, while it might not placate Afro-Asian resentment of the policy, "could prevent abrasive incidents" such as the Locsin case.[37]

Within the Government the Departments of External Affairs and Trade were reportedly indignant about the Locsin decision and the immigration policy. A representative from External Affairs said, "the immigration policy is sometimes an albatross around our necks in foreign policy matters." He also remarked candidly, "Australia as a white, rich, developed nation, with a restricted immigration policy makes presentation of any foreign policy issue difficult." It was impossible to determine the extent to which External Affairs influenced Department of Immigration recommendations. But there were overtures by officials in the Department of External Affairs for the modification of the policy. An official in External Affairs often questioned about immigration in his African and Asian posts remarked: "The policy [non-European immigration policy] is always at the back of our minds. You are forced to bend over 'blackwards.' " It was gratuitously admitted that the policy, largely misunderstood, "has been a deterrent to political relations with non-European states."

Because the policy is regarded with such scorn by Asians, noted this official, "one is obliged to be more polite, scrupulous and sensitive. This is done instinctively. You never know when the policy could be offensive to a non-European." [38]

Moderate pressure for change was exerted outside of government circles. Student Action and the Immigration Reform Groups were, by 1965, relatively inactive in exerting pressure for a modification of the policy, but representatives from the Associations for Immigration Reform, the most active of the reform groups in this period, met with Mr. Opperman before his March announcement. Both Mr. Opperman and the representatives denied that pressure by these groups affected the decision. "We listened politely while he gave his talk and he listened while we asked that a non-political commission be appointed to examine the problem." [39] Another group seeking reform, the Australian Council of Churches, passed a resolution in late January calling for several reforms in the policy:

1) To remove as soon as possible the racial discrimination involved in the rule that non-Europeans may not normally be naturalized in less than fifteen years.
2) To raise the number of non-Europeans granted permanent residence to some 1500 a year.
3) To reconsider Australia's policy concerning the entry of skilled and professional people of non-European race.[40]

This Church Council did not have a direct line to government circles through the Immigration Advisory Committee or the Cabinet. It is therefore highly unlikely that its proposals affected the Opperman announcement directly. But it may have been significant that the Council's resolution was quite similar to the Immigration Department's proposals.

Newspaper opinion early in 1966 also contributed to the pressure for reform. The Aurelio Locsin case gave many Australian editors an opportunity to evaluate and criticize the immigration policy. Could Australia realistically increase its Asian awareness at the same time it pursued the "hated White Australia policy"? was the question many prominent newsmen asked. One editor answered the question with the following statement: "to restrict immigration on the grounds of race and color, as Australia does, is not only immoral; it invites furious reactions of the sort we have seen in the past few days from the Philippines." [41]

Another newspaper editorial claimed that Mr. Locsin was prohibited entry for an "absurd reason." His rejection, it was alleged, reversed efforts of the Departments of Trade and External Affairs to increase trade and friendship in the Philippines. The Department of External Affairs warned, before Immigration officials made their decision, that Australia's image would be tarnished by the refusal of Locsin's application, but the Immigration Department apparently felt it could not make a "special allowance." The editorial argued "it would have been far better to risk bending the immigration policy" than refusing Mr. Locsin's admission.

> Obviously, the Immigration Department is unable to take account of such matters as Australia's prestige in Asia. Until our policies can be reviewed in full to remove the stigma of racial prejudice—and this should be swiftly—a new system should be introduced that allows greater flexibility in administration. Moral considerations apart, trade and our foreign relations are far too important to be left open to being undermined by outmoded immigration rules.[42]

The *Sydney Morning Herald,* in the same vein, asked rhetorically: "Can we do business with the Japanese, sell them wool and iron and buy their cars and radios, yet refuse to take their citizens?" [43] Looked at in this way the policy did give a prejudicial impression. Even though the Department of Immigration labored at destroying the notion of racial grounds for entry, editorials insisted that the policy belied these efforts. "While this impression remains," claimed one editorial, "we can never hope to persuade our neighbours of our good intentions or of our friendship for them because our immigration policy reminds them at all times that we consider ourselves superior to them." [44]

The appeal for reform of the Immigration laws in these editorials was shared by most of Australia's newspapers, but there was at least one exception. The *West Australian* pointed out:

> The purpose of the immigration laws is to build up a homogeneous community and avoid the creation of mixed racial problems. It is also to avoid any development of sub-standard economic conditions.
>
> Australia has to live with Asia by reason of geography. We want to be friends with Asians but Australians are essentially of European stock. We cannot become Asians and do not wish to.
>
> As the population increases it will be reasonable to admit more Asians by administrative action, as is being done now, and allow more to settle if they have something useful to contribute to the economy or culture of the country.
>
> The Immigration Act itself does not require amendment.[45]

Approval of the reforms appeared in *The Courier-Mail*—"a step in the right direction, though a somewhat timid step." [46]—and the *Canberra Times,* whose editorial bemoaned "the conservative way" the changes were presented, but described them generally as an "important step in a liberal direction." [47] These modifications, announced the *Mercury,* "should go some way towards satisfying critics of the so-called 'White Australia policy.' . . ." [48] "Liberalization of the old rules deserves hearty applause as a step in the right direction . . ." pointed out another editorial.[49] The *Sunday Telegraph* described the changes as "a sensible move forward." [50] The *Sydney Morning Herald* characterized the new steps as "a reasonably bold step in the right direction in the present still evolving climate of political opinion on the subject." [51] *Advertiser* editors responded to the announced changes by writing, "Mr. Holt and the Minister for Immigration [Mr. Opperman] may not have finally buried the White Australia policy with their announced changes, but they have at least given it a decent covering."⁵²

In 1965 and 1966 there was no evidence of foreign political pressure exerted on the Government to modify the policy, with the one exception of Philippine recommendations to the United Nations' Commission on Human Rights. If other foreign pressure did exist, it was subtly manifested through the Departments of Trade and External Affairs. A brochure entitled *Australia's Immigration Policy* announcing the changes was distributed to all non-European embassies and drew mainly polite, muted responses. But there were several exceptions. The Malaysian Prime Minister, Tunku Abdul Rahman, who had previously alternated between calling for changes and supporting the policy, stated that relaxation of the laws were "a step in the right direction" and indicated an Australian "desire to be more friendly with Asian countries."⁵³ An English-language newspaper in Malaysia claimed, "there would be general applause for the Australian move."⁵⁴ Perhaps the most enthusiastic response came from another English-speaking, British-controlled newspaper, the *Kuala Lumpur Daily:* "Canberra's problem has been to reconcile a perfectly honorable desire to maintain a homogeneous population with a felt need to correct the damage done by immigration policy in the past. In this light the new rules represent a masterly compromise."⁵⁵ A street poll conducted by an Australian-managed newspaper in Hong Kong, *The Star,* elicited a generally favorable comment from most of the residents questioned. One respondent said: "I've always found the White Australia policy disgusting, but I am certainly glad to hear Australia plans to be more flexible in its policy."⁵⁶ The *South-China Morning Post* featured the reform modifications on its front page and the Philippine Foreign Secretary, Narciso Ramos, called the action "welcome news."⁵⁷ Officials in the Singapore Government announced privately that "Australia's new immigration rules would be welcomed in Asian countries."⁵⁸ In India, *The Hindu* of Madras maintained, "the White Australia policy had been a 'major stumbling block' in

establishing goodwill between Australia and Asian countries.
. . . Liberalization that is now planned would help Australia
forge firmer friendships with Asian countries." [59] *The Times of
India* noted: "Relaxation of rules no matter how slightly is
reassuring indication of Australia's growing awareness that its
policies, internal and external, must be determined by its geographical contiguity to Asia rather than Europe." [60]

The *Straits Times*, although it responded approvingly to the changes, argued that the "White Australia" issue was given exaggerated importance by Australians.

> Australians, to their credit, worry much more about their country's immigration policies than do the Asians, who are supposed to feel so mortally offended because they cannot go to live there.
>
> So Mr. Holt's indication that small changes are under review is bound to set off more discussion inside Australia than outside.
>
> Any country's immigration policy is its own affair and while Asians will feel gratified if Australia should moderate its discrimination against them, not many will want to join the debate.
>
> It will be enough if the racial barriers which now prevent them even considering settling in Australia are slowly whittled away, and if in the meantime the absurd rejections and expulsions which so damage Australia's reputation do not recur.[61]

In much the same vein the former President of the Philippines, Mr. Diosdado Macapagal, said most Asians do not think the White Australia policy exists: "the majority of democratic Asian nations believe there is no color bar in Australia. It seems to me, personally, that the isolated cases of colored people being refused admission to Australia come from other reasons than color." [62] Many of Mr. Macapagal's countrymen, however, did not share his view. After the changes Mr. Aurelio Locsin was asked if he would reapply for admission. He replied: "As for my applying again—never. They [Australians] should have come to their senses earlier than this. I wonder whether the new rules would really use the same yardstick for whites as well as for half-breeds with Caucasian features as well as for plain Filipinos and Asians?" [63] Mr. Maximo Soliven, columnist of the *Manila Times* and bitter opponent of the White Australia policy, welcomed modification, but he said, "I doubt whether there was really anything new in the rules." [64] According to his informants, "Australian Embassies in Asia had always had instructions to permit non-European applicants 'from prominent families' and with 'the best qualifications' to immigrate to Australia." It was the "same old buggy except that it had been given a new coat of paint," he remarked.[65]

Was there anything "new" in these proposals? Did they represent a departure from the established policy? Could the modifications be accurately labeled "liberalization?"

It is difficult, indeed, to evaluate a policy that primarily depends on ministerial discretion. The announcement that liberalization would occur brought with it assurances of more flexible administration. But flexible administration was very often a function of the criteria used for admissibility. The "old" admission categories were:

1) non-Europeans, who are the spouses, unmarried minor children and aged parents of Australian citizens, or of British subjects permanently resident here, may be admitted for permanent residence;
2) a European British subject proceeding to Australia from overseas for permanent residence may be accompanied by his non-European spouse and unmarried minor children;
3) non-Europeans who have been admitted for temporary residence may qualify, on residential and other grounds, for permanent resident status and subsequently for naturalization;
4) in addition to those non-Europeans admitted for temporary residence for commerce and trade, provision has been made for the admission on a selective basis for indefinite stay of highly qualified and distinguished people who seek to reside here;

Recent Liberalization of Immigration Policy   45

5) included in this latter category would be those non-Europeans who have taken educational courses at the tertiary level in Australia, who have spent at least five years in their own countries after having completed their courses, and who have qualifications from which the Australian community would benefit;
6) those non-Europeans, whose continued residence in Australia was induced by political events in their own countries, have been permitted to remain here indefinitely.[66]

The "new" categories which replaced them were:

1) Persons with specialized technical skills for appointments for which local residents are not available.
2) Persons of high attainment in the arts and sciences, or of prominent achievement in other ways.
3) Persons nominated by responsible authorities or institutions for specific important professional appointments, which otherwise would remain unfilled.
4) Executives, technicians, and other specialists who have spent substantial periods in Australia—for example, with the branches here of large Asian companies—and who have qualifications or experience in positive demand here.
5) Businessmen who in their own countries have been engaged in substantial international trading and who if admitted would be able to carry on trade with other countries which would be of significant value to Australia.
6) Persons who have been of particular and lasting help to Australia's interest abroad in trade, or in other ways.
7) Persons who by former residence in Australia or by association with us have demonstrated an interest in or identification with Australia that should make their future residence here feasible.[67]

Categories of the "new" set were seemingly more liberal. Expressions such as "highly qualified" and "distinguished" were eliminated. Furthermore, the new statement included a paragraph which claimed: "Applications for entry by well qualified people wishing to settle in Australia with their wives and children may be considered on the basis of their suitability as settlers, their ability to integrate readily, and their possession of qualifications which are in fact positively useful to Australia." These criteria represent a departure from an earlier policy statement which maintained: "It is fundamental to the policy that these people coming to Australia for permanent residence should be capable, both economically and socially, of ready integration into the community. Consequently preference is given to persons of European origin."

Two of the seven categories listed by Mr. Opperman could be described as "new"—categories six and seven. While the number admitted under these categories was and will probably continue to be small, the reforms involved were overdue and commendable. In the same way the abolition of the fifteen-year residence requirement was a welcome change. It eliminated the most obvious racial slur in the written policy and made less credible abusive attacks directed against the policy. The other five "new" categories, however, were only less ambiguous and extended definitions of provisions which existed since 1956.

Mr. Opperman's reaffirmation of the old tenet, preservation of a homogeneous population, made it clear that although the modifications had broadened the categories of acceptability, they had not appreciably improved the chances of admission. After these changes were enacted, the Government's refusal to consider Nancy Prasad's readmission, even though she had clearly "demonstrated an interest or identification with Australia" (category seven), indicated that the "new policy," like the old, was to be administered by "individual decisions on individual circumstances."

Denis Warner, a columnist for *The Courier-Mail* favorably disposed to the changes, said they must not be exaggerated. "The categories under which they will be admitted here for permanent residence are still limited enough to preclude significant migration." [68] Julie Rigg, columnist for *The Australian,* called the modification "a shrewd politician's assessment of the extent of immigration reform currently acceptable to a majority of Australian voters." [69] An official in the Malaysian Embassy said: "Most of those who qualify under 'new' regulations are professional men who are relatively well off in Malaysia. This new legislative decision does not affect us. We have few emigrants that qualify for admission anyway." [70] It should be recalled that Mr. Opperman himself said the changes "would not depart from the fundamental principles of immigration policy." He assured the Opposition that any reform would be combined with a concomitant effort to prevent category transfers, illegal extensions of temporary permits, and a close scrutiny of applications for entry. But what the reforms did to mollify antagonists was pointed out by Mr. Richard Gan, Secretary of the Malaysian-Singapore Students' Association: "Australia's liberalized immigration policy was a step forward in removing the stigma that Australia had a white supremacist attitude." [71]

Whether the Department actually changed the policy can only be determined by a comparative examination of non-European entrees and naturalization in the period before and after the announced changes. Even this method is flawed since the March decision could not yet have had very significant results and as such might only reflect partial aspects of liberalization. Naturalization figures five years from 1966 will better reveal any possible increase in the number of non-European temporary residents who qualify for citizenship. The number of permanent residents admitted should also be higher in five years' time when the dependents of naturalized non-Europeans are invited to Australia. Since the exact figures cannot, therefore, be determined, 1966 figures will be considered in comparison with preceding years and rather tentatively with the succeeding period. Some differences between 1965 and 1966 were apparent in the semi-annual report of non-Europeans admitted and in residence during the half-yearly periods shown.[72]

Class of Person	6/30/65	12/31/65	6/30/66	12/31/66
Permanent residents	149	145	120	171
Long-term temporary residents	227	209	286	271
Total		730		848

In addition, in 1965, 407 non-Europeans, excluding registered British subjects and non-Europeans in New Guinea, were naturalized as opposed to 588 in 1966. The 1966 figure was remarkably small, however, when one considered the 4,171 non-Europeans in Australia as "limited temporary residents" who were supposedly eligible for naturalization after the acceptance of the March proposals,[73] and the comparatively large number naturalized in 1962, four years before Mr. Opperman's announced changes.[74]

Naturalization of Non-Europeans

Year	Australia		New Guinea	
	Naturalized	*Registered*	*Naturalized*	*Registered*
1962	662	47	120	—
1963	482	110	288	—
1964	398	112	224	1
1965	407	122	219	2
1966	588	196	87	—

The redefinition of migrant categories accounted for minor changes. Between 1956 and 1966 about 100 non-Europeans entered Australia as "distinguished visitors"; in the eight months after the revision of the policy 32 "professionally qualified persons" were admitted and an additional 102 applications were under consideration. Likewise, a new category, "persons having an identification with Australia," accounted for nine non-European migrants, during the March–October, 1966, period, who were formerly ineligible for residence status under the old regulations.

Taken together, the new categories were responsible for 47 non-Europeans and their 57 dependents in the eight-month period immediately after the March announcements.[75]

Another shift in the policy, which did not account for a numerical change but was potentially the most significant aspect of the liberalization, involved non-European students. Prior to the policy review, "private students were required to have spent a period of at least five years in their homelands before becoming eligible for re-entry under the then 'distinguished and highly qualified' rules." In March, 1966, this provision was deleted and the rules applying to "distinguished and highly qualified" were reworded on a less demanding basis. According to the Minister for Immigration, student "applications would be considered on their merits" and the Department "would expect the student to have given a period of substantial service in his own country" before re-entry would be considered. This could add a new dimension to the policy since 1,237 private students alone were admitted for the 1966 academic year.[76] A total of ten persons admitted initially with student status, who have been in Australia for a substantial period, and "whose qualifications are of no real value in their own country but are positively useful to Australia" were permitted to remain during the March–October, 1966, period.[77]

In most respects the announced policy changes did represent a slight numerical shift in the number of non-Europeans entering Australia and a potential increase of much greater proportions. But whether this will bring a significant change is highly debatable. Mr. Snedden, present Minister for Immigration, while acknowledging the limited number of non-Europeans in Australia, noted: "there is no doubt that our immigration programmes of the last two decades have been outstandingly successful. We must work with the object of making the programmes of the future equally so." [78] On another occasion he suggested: "the Federal Government would continue to restrict non-white immigration to avoid racial problems that bedevilled some other countries." [79] Mr. Opperman, the Minister who proposed the revisions, said "Asians that would be homogeneous in Australia are needed in their own countries." [80] This, as well as the fear of inter-racial strife ("if you make an error it is perpetuated"), were proferred as reasons for only moderate and very gradual changes. Obviously the Ministers directly affected by the revisions did not regard them as departures from the traditional policy. If anything the changes represented a mild response to domestic needs and the changing regional scene. Mr. Snedden pointed out: "While maintaining organic contact with the sources from which it principally derives, the Australian nation is building an orderly pattern against which our relations with allies, friends and neighbours will develop." [81]

If the announced change and its associated fanfare were designed to influence Asian opinion on the White Australia policy, as Mr. Snedden implied, their purpose was achieved. From March to July 31, 1966, the following work-load examples were recorded by immigration officials in non-European capitals.[82]

Post	Number of Inquiries Oral or Written	Applications Received		
		Number	Persons	Increase
Suva	1,056	62	218	substantial
Djakarta	206	2	4	substantial
Bangkok	2	—	—	—
Kuala Lumpur	80	48	31	marked
Singapore	not recorded	37	107	substantial
Tokyo	17	4	5	moderate
Colombo	not recorded	23	23	moderate
Nairobi	35	8	27	moderate
Hong Kong	101	9	23	moderate
Karachi	1,400 (approx.)	—	—	substantial

From the increase in inquiries and applications it seemed as if many non-Europeans were convinced that a "new policy" or perhaps a break-through in the established policy had been accomplished with the announced revisions. In fact, the overall effect of the new immigration categories and regulations was small. Mr. Opperman probably reflected the Government's attitude on future liberalization when he said, "Change will come about by a force of circumstances that does not exist now, not by Government design." [83] Or as Prime Minister Holt announced on his February, 1966, television broadcast, the review of the immigration policy "did not mean fundamentals of the restrictive policy would be changed." [84]

As noted earlier, it will not be before 1971 that a more accurate index of the policy's effect can be gauged; however, between March, 1966, and March, 1968, approximately 3,000 Asians were granted the right to become Australian citizens. This was almost as many as those acquiring citizenship between 1957 and 1966. But lest one consider this a very significant change, it should be pointed out that most of those Asians acquiring citizenship rights since 1966 were persons already in Australia on temporary permits and not recent arrivals. And the total of Asians who qualified for permanent settlement in the 1966–1968 period represented slightly less than one per cent of the more than 300,000 European migrants admitted during the same period.[85]

Although the Government has publicized this data in Asian states in order to create the impression that the policy was substantially altered, very few Australian politicians and their Asian counterparts would accept this interpretation of the widely heralded revisions.

3

Non-Europeans in Australia

Immigration reformers and supporters of the status quo can find in Australian non-European communities vivid illustrations of the problems as well as the successes of adjusting to Australian life. Likewise, those apprehensive or enthusiastic about immigration reform can find evidence for their respective opinions.

In 1968 there were approximately 40,900 non-Europeans in Australia. Approximately 19,800 were Australian citizens, either by birth or naturalization and 5,000 were granted residence status, but did not seek or qualify for citizenship. The remaining 16,100 comprised: 3,300 non-Europeans who were admitted for temporary residence; 800 visitors and a student population of 12,000.[1]

Whether an analysis of non-European residents in Australia can shed light on the absorption process of other non-Europeans is debatable, especially when one considers the possible differences in historical and socio-economic backgrounds. Still Australia's level of tolerance and potential for accepting more non-Europeans are at least partially indicated by her treatment of those already in residence.

Chinese adjustment to Australian society often presented no insurmountable obstacles. One could argue that most contemporary Chinese migrants, in particular, are usually well equipped for absorption into a new culture. And even when they are not so well-equipped, many are very often willing, indeed eager, to be Australianized. A widely circulated Australian anecdote illustrates this point.

Several years ago an Australian dance hall manager, annoyed by the allegedly boisterous antics of a few Aborigines, decided to bring suit against them. In order to present a more credible case the manager sought a witness who could corroborate his story. Since no witnesses were present on the evening of the incident he was willing to pay for this support. The first man he approached was a recent Chinese migrant. He explained the details and offered the migrant some money. "Yes, I will assist you," said the Chinese man, "but it is not necessary to give me money." "No money?" asked the manager incredulously. "You must really hate those bloody Abos." The Chinese man looked at the manager enigmatically and replied, "I thought all Australians hated the Aborigines. I just want to be a good Australian!"

This story seems to demonstrate the tremendous desire on the part of many Chinese to be accepted by Australians. The penchant for acceptance and desire to assimilate [2] are more apparent in recently arrived non-Europeans than they were among those who came earlier. This may, of course, be partly a result of the stress which immigration officials place upon maintaining a homogeneous population in Australia. But it is also a result of the outwardly successful assimilation of third- and fourth-generation Chinese who serve to embody the traditions of a new culture. Whether or not homogeneity is a valuable or even realistic goal of migration schemes remains to be seen. But the fact that many newly arrived and Australian-born non-Europeans have apparently accepted it as their own goal does help to alleviate the fears of those who assume that multi-racialism inevitably leads to tension and violence. Indeed, Chinese communities in Melbourne and Sydney are prime examples of how absorption is as possible for non-Europeans as it is for their favored European counterparts. Almost unwittingly these Chinese communities and to a lesser extent Asian students have become important factors in the struggle to liberalize the immigration policy.

A strong community feeling and consciousness developed among the Chinese who remained in Australia after the gold rush. These feelings were reinforced not only by the Immigration Restriction Act of 1901, but also by the insecurity which many migrants naturally feel in a new and hostile environment.[3] In order to find a vicarious family structure and a sense of security, Chinese social centers were very often organized by vocation. This separation—albeit partially a function of Australian antagonism—plus the active political role Chinese played in raising funds for the "national movement" at home, embittered many Australians. Chinese nationalism also reduced county and provincial loyalties and brought the Chinese together as an even more closely knit group within the Australian milieu, hampering, to a great extent, the smooth assimilation of first-generation Chinese migrants.[4] Legislation prohibiting Chinese migration and naturalization and hostility against Chinese customs and separateness also strengthened the very thing, i.e., clannishness, Australians wished to eliminate. Despite these drawbacks some Chinese made the necessary social and cultural adjustments for acceptability in the Australian community. But even with the emergence of a new generation of Australian-born Chinese who were bilingual and served as links between the host and the alien communities, westernization was, for the most part, slow.[5]

Chinese adjustment was partially accelerated by their acceptance of and entry into Christian churches, even though this sometimes meant the establishment of separate Christian churches, e.g., the Chinese Presbyterian Church. This partial accommodation reduced the use of Chinese names and the

Australian antagonism to the "cryptic Chinese religions." Increased absorption into Australian life resulted as additional forms of accommodation were accepted by each succeeding generation. As Dr. C. F. Yong argued:

> Given time, opportunity and favorable conditions, there is no reason to believe that Chinese could not be assimilated and could not co-exist with the Australians, rendering valuable services in market-gardening, cabinet-making, cooking, bush-clearing and in many other fields.[6]

If the Chinese community had been larger and had militantly pressed for either unchecked migration or more liberal migration policies, there might have been greater violence in these early years and an even more difficult period of adjustment. But this was not the case. Chinese leaders aimed for one primary migration goal: the right of domiciled migrants to bring their wives and children to Australia. However important this goal was to them, it still did not cause any major eruptions in the Chinese community.

Even though conditions had improved and communications with the Australian community had increased by 1920, most of the Chinese still lived apart in their own community. Each little Chinatown had its opium dens and gambling houses that were usually off-limits for the more respectable Australian citizens, despite their irresistible lure for some non-Chinese. Many Australians who sought refuge in these Chinatowns often took Chinese spouses. As a refuge for the downtrodden and dissolute, Chinatowns came to be regarded as areas of social blight. Even when the Government acted to ban opium dens and gambling houses and to administer strict health measures, "thereby eliminating the most objectionable features of the Chinese quarters," an Australian stereotype about these areas and their residents persisted.[7] To some extent this was overcome by Chinese children born in Australia who attended state schools and mixed with their Australian classmates. These children deserved much of the credit for the general acceptance accorded "John Chinaman" by 1930.

In Broome, a city almost completely populated by Japanese and Malayan pearl divers, relations between non-Europeans and Australians were notably harmonious. Moreover, the city was almost devoid of crime. The Governor-General's report on the pearling industry in the 1920's indicated, "Houses were left uncared for, with doors and windows unfastened, yet robberies and petty thieving were almost unknown. A police force of five men was found ample to control Broome's population of 2,700 and the surrounding district." [8] There has been no indication since this report of any appreciable racial strife in this town, despite its multi-racial character. Likewise, inter-racial relations in Darwin have been smooth, with only minor quarrels between the Aborigines and the non-European population. The extent of non-European absorption and acceptance is evident in the 1966 election of the late Harry Chan, the first Chinese mayor of an Australian capital city. After the election Mr. Chan said, "I believe what the people of Darwin have done about me shows Darwin to be the most racially unprejudiced place imaginable and, in its own way, strikes a blow in favor of a more realistic immigration policy." [9] In Darwin, where pride in racial relations is verified by an exuberant communal spirit, few residents think there is anything particularly unusual about a Chinese mayor in an Australian city.

By the beginning of World War II the largest Chinese communities in Melbourne and Sydney were well entrenched and accepted by the cities' residents. The war itself and Australia's sympathetic support of China accelerated the assimilation process. In a poll taken in 1948 many Australians regarded Aborigines and Chinese as "our local coloured groups." [10]

The Chinese are probably accepted because they are no longer considered a threat or a "mysterious and devious force" in the community. A history of industriousness, social rectitude, and a gradual willingness to accommodate, discredited the assumptions on which most Australian prejudices were based. Australian Chinese are generally willing to be westernized in costume, custom, and even beliefs. In 1930 there was only one non-Christian place of worship in Melbourne and by 1960 it had disassociated itself.[11] Melbourne Chinese worship a Christian God in Anglican, Presbyterian, and Methodist churches. In 1966, the Melbourne Buddhist Society did not have even one non-European member.[12] The Chinese community eschews oriental trappings usually associated with Chinese quarters elsewhere, e.g., San Francisco. There are no pagoda structures, little Chinese script on billboards, almost no exchange of Chinese words, and very few people in traditional Chinese dress. Most of Melbourne's shoppers are not even aware of the Chinese section two streets from their shopping center. Little Bourke Street, in the center of this district, is lined with Chinese restaurants, an import-export firm, one souvenir shop (selling more African and Indian artifacts than Chinese ones) and a Chinese social club. The proprietors of these shops think of themselves as Australian nationals, not Chinese. It is even dubious whether Little Bourke Street is a Chinese section or a center of Chinese business activity. The three thousand permanent Chinese residents and an equal number of students in the city are scattered throughout all the suburbs. In some ways they are thoroughly Australianized. The Chinese Youth League in Melbourne has its own Australian Rules football, cricket, and tennis teams.[13]

The Chairman of the Chinese Citizens' Society of Victoria, Ron Wing, claimed the Chinese resignation to Australian names, customs, clothes, etc., broke down communication barriers and contributed to better community relations. "When you stop being so different, people don't bother you any more," he argued.[14] Many Chinese elders have come to the realization their children are far less Chinese than Australian. But for the senior members of the community it is sad to see the Chinese New Year forgotten and the personal links with China severed. "They are not even very fond of Chinese food," said one of these elder citizens mournfully. Intermarriage with Australians, which, one reporter claimed, occurs twice as often as marriage with a Chinese partner, diminishes the use of the Chinese language and correspondingly accelerates the Australianizing process.[15] Only one school teaches the Chinese language in Melbourne: the Chinese Community Centre on Little Bourke Street. But only seventy-five students attend the center and many of them are Australians. Chinese political meetings are arranged, but they are usually poorly attended by the local Chinese residents. One businessman said, "I think most Chinese here would belong to more non-Chinese organizations than Chinese ones." David Wang, Chinese tradesman, noted that of the two or three hundred guests at his annual Chinese New Year Party in 1966, eighty per cent were Australian. In almost every way the Chinese customs, ideas, and outlook have merged with the prevailing Australian views. Even the ancient Chinese reverence for one's elders is breaking down. But despite some vocal disenchantment with this trend, Chinese residents argued, "You cannot go on enforcing the old Chinese rules when there are different ones all around." [16]

Politically, the Chinese population in Melbourne, although not very active, supported Senator McManus, largely because of the Democratic Labor Party's efforts to obtain a relaxed migration law. They also endorsed Mr. Arthur Calwell for his Labor seat, in spite of his strict application of the immigration regulations in the 1940's, because of his close personal association with the community. Liberalization of the immigration policy is not a provocative issue for most of the Melbourne Chinese. Many would like to see the laws further relaxed so families can be reunited, but this hope prompts almost no political activity. In one sense the Melbourne Chinese do not disavow their heritage: they still maintain the belief that in time wisdom will solve their problems.

Sydney Chinese are not unlike their Melbourne counterparts. Members of the generation now entering the work force are no longer market gardeners or fruit and vegetable proprietors but young men sharing Australian aspirations for comfort, wealth, and leisure. Dixon Street, the center of Chinese business, is composed of several fruit and vegetable stores, a few old warehouses, and several Chinese restaurants. But home could be anywhere and usually is. Most of Sydney's Chinese live in almost complete anonymity in any one of several Sydney suburbs. In this sense they are like any other Australians. In 1966 Professor of Mathematics Fred Chong, for example, denied he felt any identification with a Chinese community. Although he rejected mixed marriages and was glad a Chinese section existed, he avoided Chinatown and was not interested in Chinese community projects.[17] For most Australian-born Chinese the old Chinese bonds have been severed. They even reject new arrivals, about whom one well-established market gardener commented, "They come here and think they can do just what they please. They give all of us a bad name." The Australian Chinese Association has dissolved because of insufficient local support; the Chinese Chamber of Commerce, once a powerful business organization, has been reduced to perfunctory community relations chores, and the Chinese Women's Association and the Young Chinese Relief Movement limit their activities to social events.

There is still a minority of Chinese interested in the preservation of some traditions and rejuvenation of a lagging cultural commitment. One energetic Chinese resident has organized a "permanent Chinese centre" to attract all Chinese, whether local-born or not, interested in retaining Chinese traditions. But the project has several snags, not the least of which is community apathy, which has overcome the racial pride that was once a powerful force for solidarity. One Chinese businessman decrying the apathy said, "I think it is right you should have somewhere you can go and be Chinese and just not have to worry about being assimilated for a while."[18] Unfortunately, however, reestablishing a tightly knit Chinese community could regenerate prejudice and counter the successful assimilation of Sydney's many Chinese residents. Several Chinese are willing to take this risk. But as a very small minority they would have no easy task convincing the majority of Australianized Chinese to support a Chinatown.

A difference does exist between the Australian Chinese, Australian in every way but facial appearance, and Chinese Australians, who wish to maintain some association with Chinese heritage while residing in Australia. The large majority are Australian Chinese who are vehemently pro-Australian, although their reasons for this nationalism are not always the same. Mr. L. J. Channing, a part-Chinese Australian citizen, for example, is a vocal defender of Australia's right to determine who shall live within her shores. He contends that many escapees from Communist China who are arrested in Hong Kong because they do not possess an entry permit, have often been given refuge in Australia without the newspaper fanfare that usually accompanies a deportation case. He cites several occasions in which an Australian Minister for Immigration has tried to intervene in order to prevent deportation to Communist China. In Mr. Channing's view, Australia has acted more humanely in its implementation of immigration policy than Asian states. He has also noted that the relaxation of Australia's migration regulations would not serve to promote better relations with the people of Asia, "the majority of whom know very little . . . about Australia, let alone Australia's migration regulations." [19] Notwithstanding his own successful assimilation as well as that of many Chinese in Australia, he has argued that assimilation "is practically impossible where Asians are concerned because of the color of their skin. . . ." [20] Despite his Chinese appearance Mr. Channing considers himself an Australian citizen in every way. "People often ask me what do you Chinese think? or what is your opinion of Chinese food?, but I know little about Chinese people and I do not eat Chinese food. I am an Australian!" [21]

Another Australian Chinese, Dr. Tsiang, a well-established physician in an industrial suburb, has said, "Australia is the only place I know where Chinese people are assimilated after two generations." In Australia Chinese children go to school with Australians, adopt their language and customs, and even play the same games. "They are no different except that they look different." [22]

Even though they are part of the Australian community, a large number of Chinese Australians and other non-Europeans still feel insecure about their position, or perhaps they merely express their insecurity differently from those who have embraced every aspect of Australian life without discrimination. Some have not become naturalized and the fear of deportation still looms over them. Others feel that an anti-Communist crusade could be directed at their communities. Although many may want to maintain tradition, they fear the retention of Chinese customs would alienate them from Australian life. These groups are obviously more sensitive to the residue of racial prejudice and condescension directed at some Chinese residents. Intermarriage, still widely objected to by the Australian community, and the fear associated with the potentially enormous Chinese migration that persists in some sectors of Australia are factors spreading an uneasiness about Chinese identity throughout their quarters, even with the widespread and seemingly effective adjustment of many Chinese residents.

There are some Australian Chinese who have not become defensive and sensitive about their culture and can criticize Australia without a sense of guilt and betrayal. Despite outward appearances of assimilation, most Chinese do retain an uneasiness about their place in Australian society and their identity as citizens. Critical opinion recognizes that a desire to assimilate into a community which cannot tolerate cultural distinctiveness, leads not to self-respect but to self-effacement. Very often those who recognize this condition are among the few who can talk about discrimination and prejudice without self-consciousness.

Father Paschal Chang, a Chinese priest in Australia, argued that although intermarriage and assimilation were occurring with greater frequency, many Chinese still preferred to marry their own and live together. He maintained:

> the Australian Chinese fills a category of his own. He has relinquished his links with China, but he is still apart from other Australians.
> He knows from the immigration laws that Australia does not want him in the country. And he has been looked down upon in the past.
> No sociological study has been made, but I think you will find the Australian-Chinese has a complex.[23]

Many Chinese, noted Father Chang, are suspicious of the immigration laws. As the object of a discriminatory policy they are often embittered. He referred to the case of a Chinese cook who paid an Australian girl £300 to marry him so that he could remain in the country. But as soon as the facts were known, the cook was arraigned and chastized in the courts. This condemnation by the public was "no more than an expression of their [Australians'] biased prejudice." The tragedy in the case is "a reflection on the present policy of the Immigration Department . . . ," Father Chang contended.[24]

Another non-European in Australia, Mrs. Jyotikana Ray, said she was not at all eager to become a citizen of a country that had often been patronizing toward Asians.[25]

A Singhalese boy of mixed descent refused to attend his classes because while playing rugby on a Canberra school field he was abused by some of his white playmates with the epithets, "You little black beast" and "Nigger, nigger, get out darkie." [26]

Some Asians who have married Australians have been harassed by policemen and Immigration Department officials who often assume that mixed marriages result from non-Europeans who have contracted with Australian prostitutes in order to circumvent the law and remain in the country. Shortly after one particular mixed marriage the Immigration Department asked the newlyweds to appear for an interview in connection with the Chinese partner's application for permanent residence, "during which an official asked them if they had known one another long before being married. The implication was obvious —that ours had been a marriage of convenience," Lee said. "The whole manner of the questioning was so humiliating that we did not know what to do." [27]

In 1966 the Queensland Parliament was asked to repeal legislation under which any house where Asiatic women reside can be classed as a house of prostitution. The Justice Minister (Dr. Delamothe) called the legislation a form of discrimination left over from the days when Chinese migrants rushed to the Queensland gold fields. "With so many Asian students coming to Queensland the need for repeal was obvious," [28] he said. For over one hundred years the repeal of this legislation was a dormant issue, because the law was probably overlooked and perhaps unknown to Queensland's Chinese, but it still served as a reminder of Australian attitudes to Chinese residents generally.

Relatively few incidents of overt racial discrimination have occurred, but these have caused much concern in non-European communities. Fear of deportation may also be exaggerated out of all proportion to its actual occurrence, but these fears are reinforced by an immigration policy that seemingly discriminates against non-European migrants.

Foreign students comprise a temporary but nonetheless large and significant population of non-Europeans in Australia. In 1966 there were approximately 12,600 non-European students enrolled in Australian schools.[29] The Asian student population has been a matter of public debate since the initiation of the Colombo Plan in 1950. Some have argued that the government programs have been fraught with problems and have not engendered cooperation between the East and West, while others insist that non-European students have helped break down the rigid White Australia policy and encouraged affectionate ties between Australia and her Asian neighbors.

Most Asian students arrive in Australia thinking of their temporary homeland as "big" and "white." For many of them, these associations encourage a feeling of distrust that verges on trepidation. Very often they are rather pleasantly surprised to find that discrimination and prejudice simply do not exist on any meaningful scale. Said one student arrival:

> I had heard of the White Australia policy. It worried me. I thought people would despise Asians. But I was completely wrong.
> The Australian people are the friendliest I have met, friendlier even than Chinese.[30]

Harbans Singh Praser, an Indian from North Borneo (then a medical student in Melbourne), conceded, "there is hardly any color consciousness in Australia." [31] And Norman Harper, who has done considerable research in the area of non-European students in Australia, wrote:

> at no stage has racial prejudice had any appreciable effect on the reception of Asian students. Racial prejudice has been notable for its almost complete absence: only in the case of a tiny minority of landladies has it been at all evident. The Australian student body, at all levels, has warmly welcomed the influx of Asian students. Their contribution to the widening of the Australian horizon and the enrichment of Australian culture has been widely appreciated.[32]

At the University of Western Australia an orientation program and intensive English-language course has been initiated for Asian students in order to accelerate their adjustment to Australian life. The courses have provided foreign students with an opportunity to meet Australians and join in academic activities. Visitors usually comment on "the happy atmosphere which prevailed as young men and women from Malaysia, Hong Kong, Japan, Thailand, Vietnam, Pakistan, Indonesia, Tanzania and other countries mingled in these courses." [33] One observer of student activities has argued that students from Malaya "were helped as if they were brothers or sisters. . . ."[34]

Another effort to alleviate the loneliness which is a frequent complaint of non-European students in Australia has been the creation of student organizations. These students' societies have sponsored parties, debates, balls, etc., for Asian students. The first one, founded in 1950, Sydney University Chinese Students' Society, was organized exclusively for students of Chinese blood —Hong Kong, Malaysia, Singapore and Australian Chinese students.[35] By 1954 the student associations were reorganized on a national basis, e.g., Thai Students' Association. But many of these groups failed to remain cohesive and viable. In September, 1955, at the urging of the President of the Asian Students' Federation, an Asian Students' Council was inaugurated including all national, regional, racial, and international groups.[36] This council has been the most effective student organ for the formulation of Asian liaisons with the Australian community through activities such as Christmas parties for Asians and Australians. In April, 1956, it organized a "Suriya" in which Australian students presented Asian dances, music, and culture "to express their deep appreciation and friendship and hospitality" to their adopted student companions. The council has also established contacts with Rotary and Apex Clubs, sponsored a film dealing with Asian students in Australia, and produced a magazine designed to establish closer Australian-Asian student relations. "Friendship, understanding and mutual respect between Australians and Asians have been obtained as a result of the Council,"[37] noted one Australian student with pride.

Because Asian students do not represent an economic threat, they are generally welcomed by Australians who regard their friendly actions as a national gesture of goodwill. The fact that these Asian students are also prepared to spend a good deal of money in their host community makes them an asset in any Australian setting.[38] But perhaps the most important contribution

Asian students have made to Australia is simply their presence. In so many ways these students have unwittingly forced Australians to recast their views about Asian civilization. Before the influx of Asian students every Australian university followed the traditional English pattern. Sydney University made a significant departure in 1918 when it established a Department of Oriental Studies. But this was an isolated case. It was not until 1955, when the Government granted £14,000 to universities at Sydney, Melbourne, and Canberra to develop Indonesian and Malayan studies, that a notable change in Australia's educational outlook was discernible.[39] Now every university, even those recently established, offers courses in Asian history and culture. The Australian National University has research schools of Pacific Studies and Far Eastern History and a school for Oriental Studies.

Immigration reform organizations very often trace their origin to university campuses, and this indicates that the proximity of Asians and Australians often breeds respect rather than contempt. Australian students and faculty members in daily contact with Asians have spearheaded the drive for liberalization of immigration legislation. Although there was an undercurrent of discontent about "White Australia" on many campuses before 1950, there were no student demonstrations to compare with the massive indignation directed at immigration policy in the late fifties and sixties after the large influx of non-European students. For many Australian students the policy is manifestly insulting to "their campus friends."[40] For many faculty members the policy is a constant reminder of presumed Australian prejudice. Polite, serious-minded, inoffensive Asian students cast doubt on Australia's preconceived notions circulating since the gold rush. Without a concerted campaign or militant propaganda, these students have changed public attitudes. They just go about their daily tasks with a proficiency that many Australians admire. Every hard-working Asian student in an Australian university plays a part in liberalizing the immigration policy. Whether or not they realize it, many "Asian students are unofficial ambassadors helping to break down the artificial barrier of East and West." [41]

Although the presence of Asian students in Australia has an apparently good effect on erasing some prejudice and on stimulating understanding, it is very often a strain on the students themselves. The relationship between non-European students and Australia is very often tenuous, uneasy, and fleeting. The so-called adjustment of Asian students to Australian life is very often a rudimentary *modus vivendi*. The view that Asian students come to admire Australia very often neglects the hardships of university living in a foreign land.

One analyst of non-European students in Australia claims:

> The Asian student in Australia has, as a rule, no real desire to make a permanent change in his cultural outlook or in his national affiliation. In fact it would be a source of future problems if this were the case. He must maintain a membership in two societies without much swing in either direction.[42]

Adjusting to a life in a foreign country is difficult under the best conditions. When there are innumerable social forces operating against adjustment and an immigration policy that is an implicit rejection, the task of socialization is arduous indeed.

One of the non-European's first contacts in Australia is with the landlady. In the main the contact is congenial; the student's prompt attention to paying his rent usually creates a good first impression, but there is often a serious lack of understanding between landlady and Asian tenant. Young persons unaccustomed to cooking are often extravagant with fuel. Many who have servants at home tend to be untidy in their new surroundings. These characteristics usually irritate the landlady; on the other hand the Asian student is often irked by habits he considers unclean. The infrequency of Australian bathing, in contrast to South East Asians who usually bathe twice daily, is a constant source of friction. Landladies who sometimes restrict the use of the bathroom to alternate days, confuse and occasionally anger Asian tenants. And Australian households are often considered unhygienic by Asians from homes that were scrupulously cleaned by servants.[43]

Despite reports to the contrary, many non-European students do find condescension, if not prejudice, in Australian attitudes. At an education conference in Canberra, Mr. George Caiger, public relations officer for the University of New South Wales, said, "Australians tended to be sentimental, patronizing or suspicious of Asian and other foreign students."[44] It was also indicated at the conference that a high failure rate of Asian students cast doubt on their general academic ability and contributed in part to some Australian prejudice. Mr. Tylee, director of Swinburne Technical College, denied that Australians are prejudiced against Asians but noted that they do treat these overseas students as "poor chaps." Many Australians adopt the attitude that if you are from an undeveloped country you must be uncivilized. One Nigerian architect tells of an Australian who after learning he was an architect replied, "you ought to do well back in Nigeria." "It was said," the Nigerian claimed, "as though we had no architecture of our own." Afraid of being looked down upon many non-European students insulate themselves in their own social circles. One said, "we are afraid to mix with Australians. We retire into a corner where we can retain our own dignity."[45]

There are other Asian complaints too, ranging from misunderstandings with the Department of Immigration to language barriers and food adjustment. The major problem, however, is a social one. Dating patterns in many Asian societies are different from those in Australia. It is unusual for an Asian boy to date a girl unless he intends to marry her. The seriousness with which Asian boys date often upsets Australian parents and causes them to express their disapproval in the form of color prejudice.[46] Lack of companionship is a constant lament among Asian students and many use marriage as an escape from personal despair. Intermarriage, in fact, is increasing as the number of Asian students in Australia increases and the social barriers to dating remain entrenched. Most Australians still frown on the practice of intermarriage and are unlikely to accept their child's choice. Those Asian students who come from patriarchal or polygamous homes find it difficult to adjust to Australia's family customs; the retention of Asian ways in Australia is often a source of friction between the Asian husband and his Australian wife. On the whole, however, Asian spouses become part of Australian society and do not form a nucleus of Asian culture in their new home.[47]

Facing the immigration policy and its administration is most irritating for the Asian student. Despite his temporary residence status, the Asian student often considers the immigration policy, which relies on color as a test of assimilability, quite harsh. "It is a bit of a personal affront when you realise that you cannot stay here even if you wanted to," [48] said an Indian medical student. Many non-European students concede they are not interested in remaining in Australia, but they would like to be asked. "Because of the White Australia policy, many Asians are too proud to wish to stay on in Australia," [49] added another Asian student. Yet there is little doubt that at least some of the students come to Australia with the hope of staying on after the completion of their studies. The Federal Government contends that these students are badly needed in their own lands; to keep them in Australia would be to defeat the purpose of the educational exchange program. Non-European students find this argument hard to accept. In Hong Kong and Singapore, they claim, there is little opportunity and limited scope for university graduates. In Malaysia there is plenty of room for doctors, but the country is "saturated" with engineers and architects. Graduates are at times forced to work in clerical jobs because of the restricted job opportunities in their own lands. The Department of Immigration, argue Asian students, seems unconcerned with this dilemma. Students have charged that it categorically excludes non-European students from remaining in the country once their studies are completed.[50]

Obviously the Department has been severely criticized by many Asian students. The Overseas Students' Conference in 1965 passed seven unanimous resolutions condemning the Department's policies toward Asian students. Charges were made that the Department: "restricts the period of stay; discourages postgraduate studies; terminates visas with inadequate notice; restricts student marriages; controls courses of study; demands progress reports and interferes in private lives."[51] It was also alleged that the departmental actions were marked by "a lack of civility and highhandedness," and that officials tried to interfere in Asian-Australian marriages by enlisting the aid of Australian parents. Peter Heydon, Secretary of Immigration, denied these charges but admitted that misunderstandings do occur, especially with overzealous officials and insincere students. Mr. Heydon added:

> I do not say all students want to pull wangles to stay here, but an elected representative of the students has said on television that up to twenty per cent of those who come have as their main objective the finding of means to remain in Australia.[52]

The institutions which Asian students are sometimes asked to attend report to the Department on a student's record of attendance, deportment, grades, and progress. Since the Department has the right to communicate with parents and relate information dealing with the student's campus life, this report is often treated with contempt and suspicion by non-European students. The Department is reluctant to use its power to deport students but it does have this power, has used it upon occasion to refuse re-entry to so-called undesirables, and has elicited student discontent as a result.

Increased enrollment pressures in Australian universities indicate that greater competition will soon exist for the placement of students. Australia's university student population rose from 54,000 in 1960 to 96,000 in 1966.[53] At the current rate of population growth and an immigration rate of 100,000 per year (a very conservative estimate), "each state must plan for an increase of at least eighty per cent in university enrollments by 1970." This will double the enrollments since 1955. Between 1960 and 1965, when the crest of expansion occurred, 13,000 students—a number exceeding all students in attendance in 1939—were added to the university population. In 1955 there were 433 students per 10,000 people; by 1970 there will be over 500 students per 10,000.[54] More applicants and a virtually inelastic education budget make it necessary for most universities to restrict the admission of foreign students to a small quota. The University of Melbourne Medical School enacted an Asian student quota in 1956.[55] A similar quota was imposed at the University of Sydney in 1963, designed to favor New South Wales applicants and restrict the number of Asian students in all faculties to eighty-three.[56] Some Australian and Asian academics believe Australia has been "over patient and over tolerant in admitting Asian students." They argue it is better to expand aid programs than expand university facilities for Asians. Senator John Gorton, while Minister for Education, indicated in May, 1966, "that the intake of private Asian students might have to be restricted if it goes on increasing the way it is increasing at the moment."[57] He mentioned that the number of Asian students attending universities has grown at a faster rate than the general increase in the Australian student population over the last ten years, even though Asians represented only 5.5 per cent of the total undergraduates in 1966. This is a problem of increasing concern for many Australians even though some would argue restriction is not the best solution. Mr. John Ridley, president of the National Union of Australian University Students, argues: "restrictions on entry by Asians for study here would gain Australia nothing but widespread criticism throughout Asia."[58]

Many Asian students are becoming aware of the enrollment

pressure at Australian universities. The *Straits Times* noted, "Malaysian students in Australia should never forget that every place they occupied in an Australian university meant an Australian student turned away." It admonished "Malaysians, especially wealthy Malaysians, who want to while away time switching from one course to another," stating that there would soon be no room for them at Australian universities.[59]

What effect this increased pressure will have on the Australian population and visiting students is difficult to determine. At its worst Australians will resent having to educate non-Europeans while depriving their own children of university educations. This may have repercussions not only for the foreign students but also for future exchange programs. Undoubtedly the situation will place a burden on students whose adjustment to Australian life is already a difficult process.

Although there is evidence of successful non-European absorption into Australian life, there are enough extenuating circumstances to prevent its usage as a clear-cut argument for immigration reform. The extent to which different groups have assimilated varies from one community to another, but it is reasonably safe to assume that under the shadow of the White Australia policy complete assimilation for some non-Europeans is virtually impossible. On the other hand, the inability of Asians to assimilate completely cannot be used as an argument for a restrictive immigration policy, when the policy itself very often prevents their complete assimilation.

What the policy does, in effect, is deprive the Asian migrant of the feeling that he is welcome as a citizen in his new homeland. Implicitly the immigration policy through its emphasis on homogeneity defines Australia's goal for migrant absorption: conciliation to nothing but conformity. Very often this goal promotes an unrealistic desire to accept the new culture without reservations and reject any former association with the Old World, or forces the migrant to rely on his own race and enclave for security. Members of the first group usually become completely "Australianized" and divorced from their own culture, and they often compensate for their feelings of rejection by becoming vociferous supporters of allegedly discriminatory acts such as the White Australia policy. Members of the second group, who cling to the security of ancestral cultural patterns and traditional values, become the targets of those who claim non-Europeans are unassimilable.

Many permanent Chinese residents have altered their cultural patterns, including religious beliefs. They have entered into the societal network of groups and institutions, with the exception, in some cases, of their separate business quarters. They have intermarried, albeit the extent of intermarriage is indeterminate. They have reached a point where prejudicial encounters are rare. And they have virtually abandoned the values and identity of the Old World and adopted those of the New. By almost any meaningful sociological criterion they are thoroughly Australian.[60] But the constant reminder of an immigration policy which says they are not really wanted, often provokes self-conscious and exaggerated acts of national loyalty and denotes a basic insecurity about living in Australia. Members of this group are even embarrassed by recent Chinese arrivals and feel compelled to dissociate themselves through excessive criticism. There are notable exceptions to this pattern, including attempts to construct a Chinatown, resistance on the part of some Chinese parents to intermarriage, and a lingering respect for ancestral traditions, but these factors are precisely the ones that serve as a rationale for prejudicial behavior.

Temporary residents in Australia, particularly students, retain a strong association with their homeland and its traditions and are not as easily assimilated as permanent Chinese residents. In many cases they have been warned by family and friends of the dangers of complete acculturation. One reaction is a pride in one's birthplace that is exaggerated and defended beyond the bounds of propriety in a foreign land. Most Asian students are very much aware of the obstacles to permanent residence. The bars to naturalization affect student attitudes toward Australia as much as loyalty to their culture. With the retention of national loyalty and Australia's standards for assimilation, the Asian student usually opts to maintain a precarious accommodation between the old and new cultures. He wants to befriend Australians but he is afraid of being looked down upon. Faced with this contingency he very often retires within the orbit of his own ethnic group where condescension is avoided and cultural pride is embraced without fear of retribution. This behavior pattern facilitates living in a foreign land, and is usually the easier and less hazardous method of "cultural adjustment" for Asian students in a country that demands complete assimilation of its migrants.

University organizations and most Australian students have helped to make Asian adjustment to Australia as easy as possible, but as long as permanent residence for most non-European students is denied and a culture gap persists, adjustment remains a very difficult task.

It is not easy to assess the general effects of the White Australia policy on the assimilation process of non-European immigrants. On the one hand, the relatively small size of the Chinese communities and the avoidance of large-scale overt racial hostility probably accelerate the adjustment of some migrants. On the other hand, however, an immigration policy that implicitly rejects non-Europeans and serves as a symbol of national homogeneity often impedes assimilation. In the last analysis the policy may possibly be the cause of a disintegration it was designed to prevent.

4

Political Parties and the "White Australia" Policy

When former Prime Minister Menzies once answered some hecklers: "Like members of the Labor Party, and of all parties, I stand four-square for Australia's migration policy"[1] he reaffirmed the unified endorsement the policy has received since Federation. Recently, however, outspoken opponents of the policy have challenged this bipartisan endorsement. The challenge has not assumed major proportions in either of the parties, as the support of Mr. Opperman's March, 1966, proposals suggests, but firm opposition to the immigration policy as a politically rewarding decision is gaining currency. The D.L.P. (Democratic Labor Party) and the Communist Party have continually exerted pressure on the major parties to revise their immigration policies, and individual members of the two major parties have become active in reforming immigration policy from within in the last decade.

Although the Communist Party has been inconsequential electorally throughout its Australian history, except for the period between 1943 and 1949, and frowned on by politicians in both major parties, it has won some support from non-conformist churches by opposing the White Australia policy. The reasons for the party's position are different from those expressed by church leaders but it is ironic, indeed, that the immigration matter has brought Communism and religion together. This is perhaps the only issue on which the Communist Party and the churches agree. The party uses the immigration policy as part of its propaganda: "It [the White Australia policy] arose from the fundamental need and theory of the Australian capitalist class. It is imperialistic and chauvinistic in conception and content." [2] Communists have intimated that the "racialist policy" is part of the capitalist conspiracy to control the working class. By provoking hatred between white and non-white races, it is argued, capitalists have prevented working-class solidarity and have more easily accomplished their own selfish goals.

> Divide and conquer has ever been a capitalist weapon against the working class. They wanted also, to have the support of the working class for their reactionary "White Australia" policy. Nothing would have been more dangerous for the ruling classes than that Chinese and Australian workers should make common cause, as they are doing today, and instead of fighting each other join forces and fight reactionary employers.[3]

This Communist interpretation of the immigration policy has gained few supporters in Australia, but for some Asians, sensitive to Western traditions of superiority and aware of the exclusionist aims in the policy, it has reinforced their view of an exploitive white race bent on reducing non-whites to virtual slavery. Since Australia, generally rich, white, and complacent, lies so near to Asia, generally poor, non-white, and in ferment, Communists have been using their "anti-White-Australia" arguments effectively in Asia to excoriate the so-called reactionary self-interest of the Western powers.

The policy was expressed by Mr. R. Dixon, erstwhile Assistant Secretary and current President of the Australian Communist Party, in his pamphlet, *Immigration and the White Australia Policy,* published after World War II. Japanese oppression, he argued, made it crystal clear that Australia needed a larger population—a view now generally accepted by politicians. In order to augment the country's low birthrate the Government turned to assisted European migration. But, he claimed, this solution only exaggerated the racialism in the White Australia policy and put its basic assumptions into question by overseas spokesmen and "by the more farsighted among Australians." Mr. Dixon proposed a quota system to assuage Asian opinion and eliminate charges of racism associated with the immigration policy, and he emphasized a flexible economic situation as a prerequisite to non-European migration. Full employment, protection of migrant labor from "unscrupulous employers," and removal of barriers to trade union participation were the primary economic conditions for migrant adjustment in Australia.[4] It was Dixon's hope, and obviously the wish of the party, that the working class of Australia and the rest of Asia would be the policymaker in the Pacific. "Working class internationalism must replace the narrow isolationist nationalism that has so influenced Australian trade union thinking in the past." [5]

The Communist Party recognized the inappropriateness of a "White Australia" in the postwar era and assumed that the national interest could best be served by promoting mutual respect and equality with one's neighbors. "White Australia," the party line maintained, awkwardly interfered with a good neighbor policy. For this reason, it was alleged, the party opposed "all forms of racial discrimination" and encouraged the "abolition of the White Australia policy and adoption of a system of admitting migrants of all nationalities, based on the nation's capacity to absorb them into the community at the particular time without disruption." [6]

Within Australia those organizations working for reform have carefully avoided Communist sanctions. Most politicians and pressure group leaders believe that Communist endorsement would be tantamount to political suicide. Communist influence within unions and the A.L.P. (Australian Labor Party) has been egregiously unsuccessful on immigration reform, and it has even been suggested that if the Communists wanted to maintain their minimal influence in some Victorian unions, they would have to speak of immigration reform *sotto voce*. "Australian Communists," wrote James Jupp, "have been noticeably sectarian, extremist and negative." [7] This description helps explain the weakness of the party in affecting public opinion. As "extremists" in a predominantly conservative nation politically, Communists have been unable to convince unionists, heretofore opposed to immigration reform, that increased migration of Asians would not substantially affect labor's bargaining position with management.

The Democratic Labor Party (D.L.P.), which has its roots in an anti-Communist movement within trade unions, has adopted a position on the immigration issue similar to the Communist Party's. Since B. A. Santamaria, leader of the National Civic Council, established the position and was backed by the almost entirely Catholic vote of the D.L.P., it turned out to be similar to that of the National Civic Council and the Catholic Church. This partially explains why a labor party takes so liberal a view of immigration reform.

Top priority in the party program is given to "adequate defenses and the associated need to assist our non-communist Asian neighbours." [8] As long as Communist China poses a real or supposed threat to Australia, the party has pledged itself to work for a Pacific community of non-Communist Asian states whose purpose is to contain Chinese power. One manifestation of this Pacific community would be the relaxation of the exclusionist immigration policy. It is recognized by D.L.P. policy-makers that the immigration policy has "damaged the Australian image particularly throughout Asia and the term 'White Australia' has been well earned by us as a nation, though it is foreign to the general attitude of the great majority of Australians." [9] For this reason the party proposes "to welcome from amongst the other nations of Asia a proportion of new settlers capable of economic and social integration into the Australian community." It also has suggested the "adoption of children under five years of age into any Australian family irrespective of the country of origin." [10] It is high time, noted the Federal Executive of the party, for Australia to clearly indicate that its immigration policy would accept people on their merit and their capability of absorption into the community rather than by racial background.[11]

The D.L.P.'s relationship to the Catholic Church has influenced its anti-Communist ethos and apparently humanitarian attitude to immigration. But the D.L.P. even though implicitly a sectarian group is explicitly a labor party. Its first loyalty is the trade unions and, as trade unionists, some D.L.P. members oppose a more liberal immigration policy, arguing that relaxed migration laws can lead to deterioration of employee standards. This is not the dominant view, but it represents a segment opposed to National Civic Council and Catholic Church views. This factional disaffection with the immigration policy may explain why it is rationalized as a defense measure rather than a domestic consideration.

Since its inception the Australian Labor Party (A.L.P.) position on immigration has been a rigid application of the White Australia policy "strictly regulated so as not to impose an undue strain on the Australian economy." Recently modifications within the platform have been suggested and it remains to be seen whether the deletion of a phrase will have any effect on the party's immigration policy.

After World War II the policy was determined almost entirely by the Minister for Immigration, Mr. Arthur Calwell.

Calwell noted, "so long as the Labor Party remains in power, there will be no watering down of the White Australia Policy." [12] So long as Prime Minister Joseph B. Chifley remained silent on the issue and gave a free hand to the Minister it was tacitly assumed that Calwell represented Labor's view toward non-European immigration. Calwell worked to preserve the basic principles in the policy. He argued: "No matter how violent the criticism, no matter how fierce and unrelenting the attacks upon me personally may be, I am determined that the flag of White Australia will not be lowered." [13] He saw the immigration policy as an expression of national ambitions. It prevented the exploitation of the Kanakas as cheap labor; it preserved the "homogeneous character of the population"; it retained peace, prosperity, and an "unparalleled" standard of living; and it excluded the horrors of "man's inhumanity to man." [14] "A united race of freedom-loving Australians who can intermarry and associate without the disadvantages that inevitably result from the fusion of dissimilar races, a united people who share the same loyalties, the same outlook and the same tradition," [15] were advantages Calwell attributed to the White Australia policy. Yet there were those, he argued, who wanted to change the policy: "The ultra-conservatives and land barons would like vast pools of near-slave labor to make them richer; the Communists wish to bring about any condition of strife, poverty and mistrust in the community which would make good government more difficult. . . ." [16] As long as the "spirit of Blackbirders" lived on, Calwell would man the barricades against the attacks of reformers. He did little to conceal the racialism in his administration of the policy—a gesture accepted by all of his successors.

> It is true that a measure of discrimination on racial grounds is exercised in the administration of our immigration policy. That is inevitable in a policy which is based on the concept that the homogeneous character of the population, which settled and developed the country, shall be maintained.[17]

He argued that "Australia does not, however, stand alone in this regard. The dominant factor of United States Immigration Law [prior to 1965] is the preservation of the ethnic composition of the population of that country and that principle is inherent in the immigration laws of all countries. Non-Europeans as well as Europeans practise it." [18] This argument, according to his logic, was not a case of racial superiority and could not be offensive to Asians. It was an expression of Australia's sovereign right "to say who shall enter our shores and under what conditions they shall be permitted to remain." [19] As the administrator of this "right" Calwell allowed no leniency; he felt that an exception to the policy would vitiate the whole policy and endanger the survival of national traditions. This explained, in part, his intransigence in the O'Keefe and Gamboa cases, even when public opinion and the press reproached his actions. His sincerity and devotion to what he considered an ideal could not be questioned, and he even jeopardized his chances of retaining the floating-vote in the 1949 election rather than compromise his ideals. In a recent conversation, recognizing the inevitable shifts in the policy "brought about by defense and trade considerations," he argued: "Asians present a menace to our society. Australians are fearful of foreigners. They have xenophobia. And they do not want their rhythm of life disrupted. Because of this, the established policy is still the best one." [20]

Even Labor Party members, e.g., Dr. H. V. Evatt, Deputy Prime Minister after World War II, who emphasized a foreign policy based on friendship with the newly emerged nations of South East Asia, were adamantly dedicated to the principles of "White Australia." This policy, Evatt noted, was "absolutely basic to the economy and politics of the country." [21] Since every self-governing state has a right to determine its own composition and provide for national security, there could be no strong objections to a policy that provides for them, he claimed. This prima facie agreement with Calwell did not alter his opposition to Calwell's "injudicious administration" of the immigration policy.

Evatt was disenchanted with Calwell's actions as well as the resolution of another party member calling for an apology to the Philippines after the Gamboa incident, but the Parliamentary Labor Party still endorsed Calwell's implementation of the policy. In keeping with traditional attitudes, Calwell received additional support from the Australian Workers Union (A.W.U.) which defended a rigid enforcement of the Immigration Restriction Act.

To increase the population during a period of declining birthrate, and silence Asian claims to Australia's empty spaces, Arthur Calwell initiated an assisted European migrant program.[22] But at no time did he deviate from his original non-European immigration position. When Calwell was party leader in 1962, the Australian Natives' Association (A.N.A.) *Advocate* published his list of reasons for the A.L.P.'s maintenance of the White Australia policy.[23]

(1) Because the same social-economic reasons that justified its adoption in 1901 demand its continuance today.

(2) All other countries have immigration laws similar to our own and claim the same right as we do to determine whether or not immigration will be permitted and, if so, on what conditions.

(3) All other countries claim the same right as we do to determine the composition of their populations, and that means to exclude those we do not desire to come and live among us.

(4) All immigration laws are illiberal, but Australia is no more illiberal in this respect than are most Asian countries. Indeed we are more liberal in our immigration laws than almost any other country.

(5) The claim that the "White Australia" policy gives offence to Asians and Africans and other coloured people is nonsense. The vast majority of these people have never heard of Australia either. The argument is a manufactured one by those who want to destroy the policy—in stages.

(6) No significant figure in Asian or African politics has ever advanced this argument, but the P.M. of Malaya (Tunku Abdul Rahman) has said he does not object to the policy

Political Parties and the "White Australia" Policy 85

because it is not offensive and is intended to protect Australia from being swamped.

(7) The advocates of the so-called quota system have no clear ideas on what they want. The present system whereby traders can ultimately become permanent naturalized citizens, and wives and husbands of Australian citizens can enter permanently, and students can come temporarily, is preferable to any quota system.

(8) Some who urge a quota system want to use it as a wedge to create another Singapore, another Fiji, or to reproduce something of the tragic situation in the United States. These are the dishonest advocates. The honest ones cannot see that ten or even a hundred people from each of the thirty old and new Asian and African nations will have no effect at all on the unemployment situation in those countries, or appease any wounded national pride anywhere. And we of the Labor Party deny that any exists in any Asian or African country. All quota advocates see no dangers, economic or social, in a multi-racial society. We do.

(9) Those who want to allow Asians and Africans to enter Australia in limited numbers, or on the same terms as Europeans, suggest that educated or skilled persons be admitted. Such people are the very ones that Asia and Africa can least afford to lose, or would want to leave their homelands. The duty of such people is to their own and if they wish to avoid their obligations and go elsewhere they are escapists and deserters. This is particularly true of those Asian students in Australian universities who wish to break their bond and forget their obligations to help build their own nations. These are the last people Australia should wish to welcome.

(10) Every responsible body of Australian opinion favours the retention of our immigration laws, and none more so than the Returned Servicemen's Organizations representing those who fought in two world wars to keep Australia exactly as it has always been, and exactly as it always ought to be.

Mr. Calwell reasserted his position in a speech delivered in Melbourne in 1966. Although he departed from his prepared text on the issue of immigration, due to what was termed a "hostile crowd," the original text had the following statements:

> Australians are descended, to a predominant degree, from people of English, Scotch, Irish and Welsh origins. That predominance should not be disturbed.
> Labor believes that our policy of assimilation and absorption is the only sensible policy for Australia to pursue.
> It is determined to continue to oppose, for many obvious reasons, any attempt to create a multi-racial society in our midst. We can and do absorb migrants from Asia as well as from Europe and we shall continue to do so, but a policy that avoids the tragedies of Ceylon, Fiji, Indonesia and Singapore— to give but a few instances—is one to be supported. It must have the support of all Australians, young and old and whether born in this country or not, who are mindful of their heritage and the need to maintain and improve their living standards and social conditions.[24]

While Calwell represented the majority position in the party, there has been an undercurrent of increasingly vocal intra-party dissent on the immigration issue. In 1960 the Associations for Immigration Reform were first organized and several members of the A.L.P. actively participated in their membership, but even earlier, in 1959, before formation of the Associations, six branches submitted motions critical of the White Australia policy to the Victorian A.L.P. Conference, and the Western Australian Branch made a motion to substitute the words "restricted immigration" for the term "White Australia." The Conference motion was defeated but only by twenty votes to sixteen.[25] When the Associations were formed three members on the Victorian Association for Immigration Reform (V.A.I.R.) committee were A.L.P. members and in Western Australia, Mr. J. Henshaw, a member of the A.L.P. State Executive, was on the planning committee of the Association for Immigration Reform.[26] By 1961 the "Old Guard" in the West Australian Labor Party, represented by Mr. F. E. Chamberlain, reputedly warned immigration reformers, particularly Reverend Keith Dowding, that membership in the Association was incompatible with loyalty to the party. A *Bulletin* correspondent explained Mr. Chamberlain's actions, not as a reflection of his opposition to immigration reform, but "as a means of ridding himself of an influential rival in his home State." [27] Whatever the motive, Mr. Chamberlain "persuaded the State executive to outlaw the Reform Movement"—a move that was inconsistent with the State Executive's protest against the deportation of Thomas Palmer, a Eurasian seaman.[28] The next move was made by Reverend Dowding, who organized a successful rally against the ban. However, when the controversy was taken to the Federal Executive "the ban was implemented eleven votes to one." [29] Most of those party members affected by the decision chose to remain in the A.L.P., but they denounced the action as "unworkable and perhaps impossible to carry out." [30] A prominent member of the House of Representatives affected by the ban, Dr. J. F. Cairns, said he would "continue to work for immigration reform within the A.L.P." But not all Immigration Reform members agreed with Cairns' decision to leave the Association. Mr. Henshaw and Reverend Dowding "seemed inclined to stand out and face expulsion" [31] from the party. Since Dowding's moral sensibilities as a Presbyterian minister were affected he chose to endorse the Associations for Immigration Reform. The reformers remaining in the party had some success fighting for their cause: in 1963 the six Victorian delegates to the party's Federal Conference supported deletion of the ban from the party's platform and in 1965 this was accomplished.

Because of the split within the party on the immigration issue a Migration Review Committee deliberated on resolving disputes and formulating one consistent stand toward "White Australia." But the intra-party cleavage on the issue was manifested even in the Committee representation. After a meeting in 1961 the Committee, while maintaining the term "White Australia" in its policy statement, added the following phrase as a palliative to reformers: "the policy was not a racial policy nor did it carry any suggestion of racial superiority." [32] After several meetings in 1962 the Committee reported its inability to reach any further agreement: "no finding can be made which would reflect the unanimous opinion of the Committee." On one aspect of the party's immigration position, however, there was unanimity: "No changes must be made in the Party's migration programme, which would in any way undermine or jeopardize the economic and social standards of Australia." [33] Different approaches to non-European immigration, recommendations to delete the phrase "White Australia" from the platform, and alterations in the substance of the policy were discussed. But the two sides represented at the Committee came no closer to agreement.

The Victoria Association for Immigration Reform (V.A.I.R.), a non-partisan body composed mainly of Labor voters, sent deputations to the A.L.P. in the hope of proselytizing its members on the "White Australia" issue. In a prepared statement issued in 1964, V.A.I.R. representatives declared that controlled colored migration presented no threat to living standards. Furthermore, it was suggested that the A.L.P. as the "reform party of Australian politics" should be in the avant-garde of immigration reform. "It would be in keeping with the A.L.P.'s express concern for minority groups to assist people in some of the world's overcrowded areas." [34] This notice probably did not affect the attitude of the Federal Executive, but the combination of adamant reformers within the party and pressure exerted externally in the form of Immigration Reform statements and evidence, e.g., Australian Gallup Polls, of a changing political climate on the immigration issue, had to be considered in the party's immigration policy decisions.

Another Immigration Review Committee with some of the most reputable men in the party was organized in 1965 to make recommendations about policy shifts and respond to the factional disputes associated with immigration. The Committee was chaired by Mr. R. W. Holt, the Vice-Chairman was Mr. F. M. Daly, and the other members were Mr. F. E. Chamberlain, Mr. F. Collard, Honorable D. A. Dunstan, Senator Fitzgerald, Mr. C. T. Oliver and Mr. F. E. Stewart. Mr. Calwell, then party leader, was invited and Mr. Whitlam, then deputy leader, actively participated in most of the discussions.[35] The participants were equally divided among advocates of liberal reform, the status quo, and a change in the policy's nomenclature but not its substance.

At the first meeting they decided that immigration policy should be divided into two parts—racial and general. Daly was given the responsibility of preparing a paper presenting the pros and cons of liberalization of the racial aspects and recommendations for possible revision. His report initially reiterated most of the arguments for maintenance of the established policy, which were published in the A.N.A. *Advocate* in 1962, but his additions to this report may be summarized as:

> 1) The Australian economy has demanded "special selection of migrants and planned growth";
> 2) In case of war, Australia could not afford "pockets of differing races being either neutral to the national welfare or hostile";
> 3) Lifting the restrictions would mean more Chinese migrants—"as is well known, this Chinese migration is a particular worry to Asia today";
> 4) A change in policy would have a serious effect on election results as was the case with Patrick Gordon Walker in Great Britain;
> 5) Since assimilation is virtually impossible, congregation in certain areas is inevitable;
> 6) Treatment of Aborigines is not a recommendation of ability to assimilate non-Europeans successfully.[36]

His arguments providing a basis for policy change were:

> 1) Morality—Europeans are not superior;
> 2) Australia would benefit from Asian contacts;
> 3) A bad image of the nation was created;

4) "No harm would accrue if the intake was not too large and suitably chosen";

5) The policy was insulting to Asian neighbours and it correspondingly reduced Australia's influence in international bodies.[37]

Daly's own opinion was affirmed by references to the racial conflict in the United Kingdom, the United States and South Africa as well as questions which contested Asian objections to the policy. The linchpin of his argument, however, was the absence of racial strife in Australia: "If for no other reason, and of course there are many, the very fact of our freedom from racial hatred and strife should be enough to convince people of the value of the policy and the need to maintain it." [38]

The report suggested eliminating the term "White Australia" from the platform while preserving the principle, laid down since Federation, of maintaining a predominantly homogeneous population. The word that caused the most controversy was "homogeneous." Reformers argued that "homogeneous" was offensive to non-Europeans already in Australia. Moreover, it is incompatible, they argued, with "a vigorous and expanding immigration programme." Their argument was politely but coolly accepted and the word was dropped from the policy statement. In the recommendations submitted by Daly, ministerial discretion was endorsed as an administrative principle rather than the alternative Asian quota system. The report also suggested: the categories for entry be reviewed; the period of residence for non-Europeans' naturalization be the same as that applying to Europeans; student visas be carefully scrutinized for possible transfer to migrant visas or some other category, and cover only a twelve-month period subject to a check on student performances; tourist visas clearly state that the holder cannot transfer to a migrant visa.[39]

The Committee unanimously approved the recommendations, but approval largely meant compromise. Reformers won with the deletion of "White Australia" from the platform and with it any suggestion of racialism in the party policy. The Conservative "Old Guard" assumed a greater victory since the substance of the policy had not changed, albeit the offensive wording was discarded. Recognition of a *modus vivendi* achieved the result. Reformers knew that only limited change was practicable; conservatives, put on the defensive by the continuous pressure of the reformers, thought of the "new policy statement" as an affirmation of their basic principles without any major concessions to their adversaries.

At the August 3, 1965, A.L.P. Federal Conference, Don Dunstan, who later became Premier of South Australia, rose to his feet and presented the report on behalf of the Immigration Review Committee. He then moved: "That Clause XXI—Immigration of the Platform be deleted and the following inserted:" [40]

> Convinced that increased population is vital to the future development of Australia, the Australian Labor Party will support and uphold a vigorous and expanding immigration programme administered with sympathy, understanding and tolerance. The basis of such policy will be.
> (a) Australia's national and economic security;
> (b) the welfare and integration of all its citizens;
> (c) the preservation of our democratic system and balanced development of our nation; and
> (d) the avoidance of the difficult social and economic problems which may follow from an influx of peoples having different standards of living, traditions and cultures.

The resolution was seconded by Mr. Calwell and the motion carried 36 to 0. The decision was heralded as the end of the A.L.P.'s "fifty-seven year old White Australia policy" and Mr. Dunstan suggested it was prompted by the changing Asian scene. "Conditions had now changed, particularly in Asia where living conditions had greatly improved" and the rationale for the policy was inappropriate,[41] noted Dunstan. Mr. Daly was reported to have assured the Australian Citizenship Convention delegates ". . . that the decision of the A.L.P. to drop White Australia from its platform was no more than a change in wording."[42] A Queensland Labor M.P. suggested that the declaration "be amended to provide for 'adequate settlement of migrants regardless of race, color or creed.'" By doing this the A.L.P. could make clear that "it was not just making a verbal change in its policy for political purposes, while still opposing the entry of colored migrants." However, this amendment was rejected at the A.L.P. Federal Conference after Mr. Dunstan said, "in some instances race might be a factor an Immigration Minister should consider when assessing the suitability of a migrant for integration." The Chairman of the V.A.I.R., A. M. Harold, said "that the A.L.P. conference had decided upon more than a mere change of name for the White Australia policy—it had voted against the practice of a color bar."[43] However, the New South Wales President of the A.L.P., Mr. C. T. Oliver, noted, "there would be very little alteration to the position that applies now" under the new policy statement.[44] Opinions of the A.L.P. decision varied to the extent that it elicited the feeling the policy statement was either obscure or so cautiously neutral it served to reinforce the preconceived ideas of whoever examined it.

The deletion of the phrase "White Australia" from the A.L.P. platform did not solve the intra-party schism over the immigration issue. At the Australian Citizenship Convention, January, 1966, Mr. E. G. Whitlam, then the Deputy Leader of the Opposition and later its leader, urged a more liberal attitude toward the permanent settlement of non-European students in Australia. He also suggested that skilled Europeans and non-Europeans be allowed to settle on an equal basis. "Discrimination exists in the fact that we actively promote immigration at the same time as we restrict it,"[45] he noted. The only way to remove the stigma of "White Australia," he said, was to "remove any of the social aspects of discrimination" as far as possible, while avoiding social and economic problems which may result from the influx of peoples with different standards.[46] Daly, who appeared to accept these remarks as a challenge to the A.L.P.

policy, said the party "was against the introduction of non-European labor, even though the policy had been reworded to remove the term 'White Australia.' " He added, "It would be virtually impossible to keep non-Europeans in Australia from congregating in certain areas of cities and they would become particularly hard to integrate." [47]

The same differences prevailing at the Citizenship Convention often flared up in parliamentary debates on immigration issues. Then sides were not drawn so clearly by partisan loyalties. Younger men on both sides of the House often endorsed more liberal administration of the immigration policy, while older members were usually intransigently opposed to change. Mr. Hayden, thirty-four in 1966, is an example of the younger parliamentary reformer who vigorously opposed the "discriminatory" administration of the immigration policy. He thought the Government was reacting hysterically to the "coloured horde":

> It is apparent in the Government's foreign policy that it has a fear that "they" are going to flood Australia and take over the country. It is never made clear who "they" are or how "they" are going to get here—which is very convenient. We never hear who "they" are but it is a very convenient if unprincipled way of exploiting the emotions of the people in an hysterical manner.[48]

Mr. Jones, A.L.P. representative from Newcastle, then forty-nine, felt that multi-racialism could not be peacefully enacted. "I do not believe that I can be shown one country in the world where a multi-racial community has been a success." [49] He argued that Australians, particularly the idealistic reformers, must "face the facts of life. People of different colours just do not mix." [50] Ignoring A.L.P. reformers he concluded, "the Australian Labor Party's policy does not envisage a multi-racial community in Australia." [51] Calwell supposedly chastized Hayden privately for what he considered imprudent remarks. He allegedly reminded Hayden that Mr. Jones had stated the majority opinion in the party and if he had "anything to do with it, it will remain that way."[52]

The two most influential older members of the party who have broken with their generation on immigration policy are Dr. J. Cairns and party leader Mr. G. Whitlam. Whitlam claims that liberalization could have political capital as an election issue. In addition, because student programs enable Australians to have more contact with Asians, and shifting trade agreements have brought about more concern with Asia, it is logical for Australians to be willing, even desirous, of further policy shifts. Cairns, who believes the policy is racial, an insult to Australians and exceptionable to Asians, wrote:

> The only aspect of migration that is really on our conscience is the White Australia Policy. We do refuse people permanent residence in Australia because of their colour alone. The White Australia Policy might have been justified in the nineteenth century, but now it must be ended.
> And it is not just use of the phrase "White Australia" that must be ended: it would be the sheerest humbug to ban the words and, in practice, retain the policy. Both our use of the phrase and our application of the policy have harmed our relations with Asia and we cannot allow that harm to continue.[53]

As long as Calwell remained the party leader there was little chance for immigration reform. But with Whitlam as leader a new direction for the party's immigration policy is imminent. It will probably be toward further liberalization, and the strategy may involve an attempt to outflank the government position on this very sensitive issue. Consistent with this apparent trend, Whitlam assigned Mr. Cameron (a reformer) to immigration issues in his "shadow cabinet" and by-passed the obvious choice, Mr. F. Daly, an avowed conservative on non-European immigration.

Even though immigration has been a bipartisan issue for most of Australia's history, recent developments have made it much more difficult to predict whether it will remain so in the future. If the A.L.P. is convinced that immigration reform can be politically profitable it has the impetus and a new leadership to implement intra-party reform on its immigration policy.

Liberal and Country Parties at times criticized Mr. Calwell's administration of the White Australia policy but during their years of government they have maintained essentially the same position on non-European migration. Mr. (now Sir) Percy Spender, representing the Liberal Party in 1956, said: "There can be no compromise on the White Australia Policy." [54] A counterpart in the Country Party noted that his party "was absolutely firm in maintaining the White Australia Policy and would in no circumstances consider abandoning it." [55]

During the 1940's and 1950's Menzies unreservedly endorsed the White Australia policy. He based his endorsement on the maintenance of Australia's homogeneous population. By limiting migration to people who could assimilate easily, that is, Europeans, homogeneity would be preserved, he thought. He realized that the policy would be challenged by the United Nations and several Commonwealth members, but he argued that friendship with the United States and Great Britain would neutralize potential Asian criticism. Menzies palpably preferred to avoid testing the bond of loyalty in these friendships. He felt a sensible administration of the policy would satisfy most Asian objections to it. "All cases of aliens resident in Australia should be considered not as if the law allowed no human discretion, but in the light of the circumstances of each case," [56] he said. Another way of engendering goodwill in Asia, thought Menzies, was by adjusting Australia's foreign policy to the immediate dictates of Asian needs. They would not bite the hand that feeds them, he reasoned. As a manifestation of his basic philosophy, aid programs were initiated and increased, the policy was administered more humanely, and alliances with the United States were consummated.

Consistent with Menzies' promise to administer the policy

more humanely were several changes in administrative practices in the 1950's and 1960's. Mr. Holt, Minister for Immigration, announced in 1956 that non-European spouses would be eligible for citizenship and in 1957, that non-Europeans resident in Australia for fifteen or more years would be eligible for naturalization. The 1956 reform statement was followed by an apparent explanation of Menzies' motives:

> I feel that this decision will be welcomed . . . as evidence of our determination to maintain our traditional immigration policy but to see to it that good sense and humanity are exercised in the administration of it.[57]

In 1957, Minister for Territories Mr. (now Sir) Paul Hasluck announced that naturalization would be granted to Chinese residents in Papua and New Guinea "since the territory could be regarded as their only home and they had proved themselves to be good citizens."[58] And in 1958 Holt's successor as Minister for Immigration, Mr. (now Sir) Alexander Downer, announced the abolition of the dictation test.

> Its clumsy, creaking operation has evoked much resentment outside Australia, and has tarnished our good name in the eyes of the world. The Government, therefore, proposed to abolish it, and to substitute in its stead the neat, simple expedient of an entry permit.[59]

From 1959 through 1964 further changes, perhaps less dramatic, applying to the naturalization of unmarried children and the position of persons of mixed descent, were approved by Menzies' Government.

Some members of the Liberal-Country Administration felt that the Government could make more far-reaching modifications. But Menzies, who directed "a tight ship," refused to consider these recommendations and often proclaimed his wholehearted support for traditional policy. While dissension over this issue existed, it did not cause much intra-party bitterness and, if occasional arguments did ensue, they were usually squelched by Mr. Menzies. It was not until Menzies retired and the Holt Government enacted several immigration reforms in 1966 that the public learned of Menzies' flat refusal to consider similar reform proposals in 1964. The late Holt Government gave Liberal adherents greater opportunities to express their views.

Young Liberals have been outspoken in their desire to change "White Australia." In March, 1966, the Chairman of the Victorian Liberal Party Council, Andrew Peacock, was twenty-seven when he initiated a proposal suggesting:

> That the Federal Government be requested to . . . allow those persons of non-European race (excluding students and visitors) who have been admitted to Australia to become eligible to qualify for permanent residence and naturalization. . . .[60]

Senior members of the party usually advocate imposing severe restraints in order to avoid social and racial disturbances. The fear that racial tension is a concomitant of substantial Asian migration is sufficient cause for the rejection of liberalization proposals. Furthermore, some believe that the advantages of a homogeneous population outweigh speculative benefits to culture from multi-racialism. Sir John Latham has written, "It is prudent, in the interests both of Australians and of immigrants, not to incur the risk of creating another festering sore of racial hatred."[61] Mr. W. C. Wentworth, another party stalwart, said, "it was better for us from every point of view to maintain Australia as a white people rather than admit people of other races."[62] And the late Mr. Holt, as Prime Minister, noted, "the political leaders of Asian countries recognize the value of a strongly growing homogeneous Australia rather than one divided by a plethora of minority elements contributing to national weakness."[63]

While accepted on an official level, the more conservative view that Australia should retain its homogeneous population is rapidly losing government adherents. This is partially the result of liberal elements working within the party, but it is also due to the influence of reputable opinion that regards population homogeneity as an anachronism. As High Commissioner to Great Britain, former Minister for Immigration Sir Alexander Downer made this point at a lecture on "The Influence of Immigration on Australia's National Character":

> I have long felt myself that as our population increased, as our people became better acquainted with the nations of Asia so Australia could afford to relax her restrictive policy—not to the extent of changing its Anglo-European basis—but to a point where a yearly influx of non-Europeans would be admitted as a matter of course.[64]

Many Liberal Party members were impressed because Downer seemed to represent a change from his earlier statements as Minister for Immigration. At the Commonwealth Luncheon in December, 1959, Downer said: "We seek to create a homogeneous nation. Can anyone reasonably object to that? Is not this the elementary right of every government, to decide the composition of the nation? It is just the same prerogative as the head of a family exercises as to who is to live in his own house." [65]

Another indication of changing opinions toward immigration goals are the recent Department of Immigration pamphlets dealing with entry rules for non-Europeans, which carefully include the words "preserving a homogeneous population" in the middle of a complex paragraph almost completely obscured for the casual observer. On every previous pamphlet the Department's goal of homogeneity has been included in an underlined statement on the first line of the front page. Correspondingly, Mr. Opperman, Minister for Immigration from 1964 to 1966, said in an address to the Youth and Student Seminar on International Affairs:

> Our primary aim in immigration is a constantly developing community which is generally integrated, substantially harmonious, and usefully industrious. Without prejudice to that primary aim, the policy and the rules and procedures by which this aim

Political Parties and the "White Australia" Policy 99

is achieved cannot remain static and will be redefined from time to time, as Australia grows and the world changes.[66]

A "flexible" stand, periodically reviewed but rhetorically in substantial agreement with the "traditional policy," has been the Liberal-Country Parties' method of satisfying immigration traditionalists and reformers in the party. Mr. Heydon, Secretary of Immigration for three Ministers, skillfully interpreted the immigration policy so that a confluence of advocates for change and supporters of the status quo has been established. It is significant that Mr. Heydon came to his post in Immigration from External Affairs, where disenchantment with the immigration policy existed for a considerable period before Heydon's appointment as Secretary of Immigration. This appointment is rumored to be a tactical effort at reestablishing harmonious relations between the departments and avoiding situations that embarrass representatives of External Affairs or interfere with their foreign policy decisions. At times, however, Heydon's ability to coordinate policy has been hampered by the views of the Minister for Immigration.

Since the Minister for Immigration has enormous latitude in administrative matters, his own views can influence the Government's attitude on immigration. He can rely on the advice and discretion of his Secretary, but in the case of Downer, for example, there was active participation of the Minister in most decision-making. Some of Downer's critics argued that his captivity in a Japanese prisoner-of-war camp during the war affected his attitude (perhaps unconsciously, noted quasi-psychologists) to all Asians. But there is little evidence to substantiate the charge. And it could be argued that the contention expressed some reformer dissatisfaction with Downer's unwillingness to establish new immigration precedents.

In a discussion of Japanese war orphans and their possible migration to Australia, Mr. Downer said:

> A bid for the children is a bid for the mothers. And by the time such an operation was carried out, we would have a small

colony of Japanese migrants in Australia. As long as I am Minister for Immigration, that will never happen. I make no bones about that. . . . If you are going to consider the principle for Australia taking the responsibility for a lapse of that nature by its ex-servicemen you will not be able to stop at Japan when you consider the history of this country in the sixty years of this century. . . . The Government is not prepared to make a specific exception in this case unless there are individual cases which require the most particular or sympathetic attention.[67]

He argued that the entry of illegitimate Japanese children "would enunciate a new principle altogether, not merely in international relations, but certainly in the immigration policies that have hitherto been accepted by all sides of politics since the federation of this country." [68] When Mr. Opperman was given the Immigration portfolio in 1964 some critics maintained that he was even less equipped than Downer to draw fine distinctions or argue the Department's cause effectively. It was true that Opperman was far less outspoken than Downer and much more reliant on the advice of his staff. But this apparent disadvantage proved to be advantageous for the sympathizers of reform within the Department of Immigration. Heydon, for example, had greater freedom to initiate new proposals and relax the current administrative practices, within the limits of the existing policy. It also gave him the opportunity to win goodwill from immigration reformers and defend the trend of recent immigration decisions to overseas visitors. He managed his role skillfully; both opponents and proponents of the policy felt sure that Heydon understood their positions. Non-white visitors to Australia, such as the late Tom Mboya of Kenya and Era Bell Thompson, a reporter for *Ebony* magazine, who discussed immigration policy with Heydon left Australia seemingly less critical.

Holt announced several Cabinet changes in December, 1966. Appointment of a new Minister for Immigration, Mr. B. M. Snedden, led to much speculation. Why was Opperman replaced after his fairly successful performance? Why was Snedden chosen as his successor? The answers provide some clue to the future immigration policy. Opperman's three-year performance did include modifications in the policy, but it was an uninspiring ministry during this period. His handling of the Locsin and Prasad cases won little sympathy for the Government outside Australia. It was generally believed within government circles that Opperman had few creative ideas to contribute to the policy and was an awkward interpreter of the Government's position. The choice of Snedden and his retention by Holt's successor, Prime Minister Gorton, probably coincides with a decision to liberalize the policy gradually while maintaining the rhetoric of restriction. Snedden did not have a liberal reputation as Attorney General, but he is well prepared to explain apparent contradictions in the Government's decisions. If the Government decides to expand dramatically its annual intake of non-European permanent residents and simultaneously adhere to the traditional principle of rigid restriction, the talents of a former legal adviser would be useful.

In his Master's dissertation, A. C. Palfreeman contended:

> To prevent criticism by the Parliamentary opposition—criticism which may damage both the government's domestic position as well as the nation's foreign policy, the government has been careful to ensure that it cannot be accused of laxity in administering the policy, nor indeed of any undue harshness. It has been more important to guard against the former than the latter because a more flexible administration of the policy made up part of the Liberal election platform in 1949 and has therefore been more of a target for the opposition, which can interpret it as a "thin edge of the wedge" in the traditional policy.[69]

Eliminating "undue harshness" in the administration of immigration policy is no simple chore. After being chided by Opposition members in 1962 the Minister for Immigration admitted in a House debate that immigrants were rejected because they were more than twenty-five per cent non-European in appearance.[70] In August, 1966, an English couple was refused assisted passage to Australia because an immigration officer at

Australia House had allegedly remarked the woman looked Asiatic.[71] A family of Singhalese burghers, the Vanderputts, were refused admission in 1964 because of their non-European appearance. Mr. Heydon explained the Department's action in the Vanderputt case as one ramification of the immigration policy.

> In general only those applicants who can be regarded as being substantially of European origin may be permitted to settle in Australia.
> Unfortunately Mr. Vanderputt and certain members of his family were found to be unable to satisfy the requirement to which I have referred.[72]

Department officials gratuitously admit that color is a criterion of assimilability. This is not considered a racial attitude but a practical consideration of Australian feelings for non-Europeans. Heydon rationalized these feelings as a function of racial tension throughout the world.

> Feeling against non-Europeans has increased rather than decreased in the past five years because of racial difficulties in Britain and Rhodesia, and especially because of the breakup of Malaysia.
> Australians are nervous about minorities, not only dark minorities but Southern Europeans with lower living standards who form ethnic colonies in our large cities.[73]

Recognizing the difficulties involved in accepting non-Europeans (perhaps overestimating them), the Government retains to some extent the criteria of skin pigmentation, bone structure, facial characteristics, etc., but it systematically attempts to evade the use of these standards and to eliminate other administrative practices and party statements that can be construed as racial and unduly harsh. This may explain the Country Party decision to drop the phrase "White Australia" from its platform in 1965. The change underscored the shift in official thinking and perhaps the desire to be consistent with Liberal Party policy, which had the phrase removed a few years earlier.

The immigration policy has not been a major area of contention between the parties. Indeed, it is probably the one political issue on which an undeclared, but well-understood, truce exists. Younger, somewhat more idealistic members of both parties do not accept this *modus operandi*. They argue on the practical side that a more liberal public opinion has made immigration reform politically feasible.

The D.L.P. and the Communist Party, for very different reasons, employ immigration reform as an indication of their opponents' reactionary philosophy or anachronistic approach to politics, but it is doubtful whether either of these parties win voter endorsement because of their immigration statements. An exception is the penchant of the relatively small Melbourne Chinese community to vote for D.L.P. candidates, presumably because the party endorses liberalization of non-European immigration policy.

The A.L.P. has had the extremely difficult task of modifying its views while the opponents of immigration reform control the party apparatus. Union delegates at party conferences have been loath to discuss immigration reform. Arthur Calwell, as party leader, frequently proclaimed his loyalty to the "policy that has served us so well since Federation." Reformers within the party counterbalance their uncompromising opponents by adopting an equally aggressive stance on this issue. Associations for Immigration Reform have had much greater influence with several Members of Parliament in the A.L.P. than with Liberal Party representatives. If the Labor Party has modified its policy at all—and opinions on this vary—it is due to a compromise of competing forces, with the anti-status quo group continually applying a prod to obtain even moderate reform. This party condition could change dramatically under Whitlam's leadership, but the Federal Executive supported by the majority of party members is still opposed to major modifications.

The Liberal and Country Parties have cautiously used the immigration issue to maintain coalition harmony and public support. Only "extremists," argued one Liberal Party member, disapprove of our migration policy. This is palpably untrue, but the gradual shift in administrative practices accompanied by the loyal recitation of traditional principles gives opponents and proponents of the policy some cause for support. Menzies' strategy of defending the policy and gradually modifying its administration has been employed by both Holt and Gorton and will probably remain the government position in the near future. The only factors that can upset this balance are: a more liberal position adopted by the Labor Party which the public countenanced in an election; a Minister for Immigration who decides that further liberalization is necessary and "practicable"; a radical change in foreign affairs or international pressure that dictates a policy shift; and a change of leadership in the Liberal-Country Party coalition in which a reformer who gains control feels the political climate has shifted sufficiently to accept a major break with the traditional policy. None of these actions seems remotely probable at this time. The A.L.P., in an attempt to regain political support, will probably not rely on immigration reform, albeit Whitlam can conceivably use the issue to demonstrate the party's reform impulse. Second, the Minister for Immigration, with the exception of Calwell, has not been "his own man" since World War II. He does have a tremendous degree of discretion in individual cases, but the Prime Minister and his Cabinet determine policy and are not prepared to surrender this authority. Third, foreign policy and international pressure, although they influence immigration decisions, do not solely determine Liberal Party policy. Most party members still believe there are better ways of aiding Asian states than permitting their citizens to migrate. Migration of several millions, they argue, would not solve overpopulation in Asia, but it could cause insuperable problems in Australia. Therefore, it is considered best for the Government to provide aid to Asia but to maintain the essential features of the policy. Lastly, it seems very unlikely that a reformer can gain control of the Liberal Party leadership. The leadership position, as is the case in most political organizations, is usually obtained by the person least offensive to all the factions in the party. An immigration reformer does not fit that role.

It is also unlikely that the political climate will change enough to effectuate major policy shifts in the party platform. Although public opinion has become more liberal on this issue, it will not, at this time, be a determining factor in voter preference. Even in those few cases where immigration reform is considered an essential consideration there will be a greater likelihood of Liberal Party rather than A.L.P. support because of the Liberal Party's less offensive historical posture on immigration. In 1966 the Liberal-Country Party Government avoided immigration as an important campaign issue and, standing on its record when the subject was mentioned, won by one of the biggest landslides in the history of Australia's federal elections. With that kind of success there is no reason to assume a radical government shift on a relatively unimportant political issue. As long as the nation's political climate remains more concerned with other issues, e.g., the war in Vietnam and conscription, and the electorate is reasonably satisfied or unconcerned with the Government's immigration policy, there is not much chance of an overhaul or a major liberalization of policy.

5

Pressure Groups: Immigration Reform Versus the Status Quo

A democratic government supposedly represents the will of the people. Determining this will is usually the job of decision-makers. But the crude choice between two sets of leaders to decide policies affecting the national interest very often leaves gaps in the system. Pressure groups often help fill this gap by serving the ideals of a particular group of people, united by economic, social, religious, or political beliefs, and exerting influence on decision-making public officials.[1]

Pressure groups have been actively involved in challenging or endorsing the White Australia policy since the end of World War II. In the mid-1940's Methodist and Presbyterian churches attacked the racial implication of the policy. Archbishop Mannix, representing the Catholic diocese, advocated a quota system in order to remove the stigma from the existing policy. The Australian Council of Churches asked the Commonwealth Government to consider reform. National Catholic Rural Movement officials and the Australian Junior Chamber of Commerce advocated policy review. And in the 1960's two groups were organized for the expressed purpose of eliminating racialism in the policy: Student Action and the Associations for Immigration Reform. Conversely, the Australian Natives' Association (A.N.A.) was opposed to reform. In 1950 the Federal President of the organization said, "The White Australia Policy must cease to exist if exemptions to its provisions were allowed to operate." [2] And in 1954 the Secretary of the Association announced, "The permanent entry of even a small quota of these people into Australia would be a step towards national suicide." [3] The Returned Servicemen's League (R.S.L.) held views virtually identical with those of the A.N.A. before 1962. "We must assist every worthwhile attempt to build up Australia with good types of white people," was its defense of all the particulars in the White Australia policy.[4] In 1962 the phrase "White Australia" was deleted from the R.S.L. policy statement but the League still acted as a countervailing force against further modification. While these organizations are only a partial representation of all the pressure groups interested in the immigration issue, they do indicate the deep feelings and widespread interest engendered by the policy.

It is difficult to determine which of these organizations has had the greatest influence and which, if any, is responsible for liberalization of the policy or maintenance of its basic principles. A few groups can make their attitudes known through representatives on the Immigration Advisory Committee, albeit the Committee does not actually have the power to shape policy shifts. One group, the R.S.L., has had direct access to decision-making machinery through an ex-servicemen's committee of Cabinet, the Minister for Repatriation and on occasion the Prime Minister. Nonetheless, it is impossible to estimate accurately the degree to which the League has influenced immigration policy. R.S.L.'s special position might actually put it in jeopardy of angering those who have granted it direct access. It becomes encumbent on the leadership, according to this argument, to practice restraint on issues not directly related to repatriation. Department officials have asserted that policy changes were not affected by most pressure group activity,[5] but the inability of pressure groups to affect the policy strategy directly, does not diminish their role on the issue of "White Australia." Conditions for shifts in the policy, the manipulation of public opinion, and the receptivity of legislators to changes are often determined by pressure group activity. Sir Alan Watt noted: "Political parties are very conservative on this issue because of their traditional devotion to the policy. If there is change it has to come from the people to the Government, not the reverse."[6] If change does occur in this way what role, techniques, and rhetorical arguments do pressure groups adopt as spokesmen for factional attitudes?

Between the two world wars the R.S.L. continually pressed the Commonwealth for increased defense expenditure and military preparedness. However, even more important to Australian security, in the organization's view, was the maintenance of the White Australia policy. "White Australia" was equated with Australian security and xenophobic feelings took the form of opposition to any non-British migrant group.[7] After World War II returning soldiers increased the R.S.L. membership and concomitantly its ability to exert pressure. G. W. Holland, Federal President of the R.S.L., worked to obtain the League's direct access to the new Menzies Government in 1950. By early 1952 he was able to report:

> the Prime Minister has agreed that the sub-committee of Cabinet . . . will . . . be available for discussions with me on behalf of the Federal Executive in respect of all matters affecting ex-servicemen. . . . Other organizations' approaches will be through Ministers as usual.[8]

The League became "the only public organization with direct access to Federal Cabinet"—and this occurred at the same time the Australian political system was concentrating decision-making power at ministerial and Cabinet levels. Because of the R.S.L.'s privileged Cabinet position, it had an integral role in the decision-making process—an unprecedented position for a pressure group.[9] But its position did not necessarily mean that its opinions on "White Australia" gained government acceptance. It only illustrated the possible advantage obtained by its role "on an executive which effectively dominated Parliament."[10] One could maintain, with some validity, that the League could gain more by recurrent lobbying of parliamentarians and parties than by employing its special Cabinet position and risking the anger of those who had granted it.[11] League opinion on the issue of White Australia has not always received government approbation. In such cases, however, hostility has rarely been directed at the League itself, since its demands were made at the Cabinet level and were not therefore subject to public opposition.[12] Long after the Government was officially opposed to the racial intent in the immigration policy a League representative said, "No matter what we call it, unless we have a restricted immigration policy we could eliminate our own race."[13] Since the mid-1950's the attitude of the League has moderated, although it has maintained the belief that "firmness was necessary for enforcement." Historical forces shifting the assumptions on which the policy was based only slightly affected opinion in the League. Five years after naturalization of non-Europeans was approved by the Government for the first time, the R.S.L. still argued "that no change will be countenanced in the White Australia policy."[14] This view was represented in the Cabinet as well as on the Immigration Advisory Council. When Minister for Immigration Downer addressed the annual Congress in 1960 he said the contributions of R.S.L. leaders on "the Immigration Advisory Council has given the Government the benefit of the views of this important section of the community on the development of the national policy of immigration which have been of inestimable benefit."[15] He might have added that the "benefit of R.S.L.

views" had not been influential in shaping his department's policy.

Nonetheless, considerable evidence indicates a close association between the Department of Immigration and the R.S.L. Every annual R.S.L. conference since 1960 has been attended by either a high-ranking official of the Department or a migration officer of one of the states.[16] In 1961 the R.S.L. Congress noted with misgivings the current agitation to amend the fundamental principles of Australia's established immigration policy and recommended to its leadership that it:

a) Unequivocally reaffirm the adherence of the League to that principle.
b) Investigate the possibility of the League itself or in collaboration with other organizations countering this propaganda by informing the Australian public of the real dangers involved in the change advocated.[17]

Downer promised the League his assistance in countering the propaganda of immigration reformers. "When the Immigration Advisory Council had finished examining the same problem, he would send the League its findings as a guide."[18] On another occasion Downer assured the membership that he and his department were "imbued with the same beliefs" as the R.S.L. and "that in the immigration policy and programme, we shall seek people whose character, skills and outlook will strengthen Australia's development as a democratic nation in keeping with our British heritage."[19] On another occasion Mr. Armstrong, then Acting Deputy Secretary to the Department of Immigration, congratulated the League on "the help and cooperation" given the Department in the formulation of its policy.[20] Due to the minor pressures from within and considerable pressure from without—in the form of government representations—the R.S.L. deleted the phrase "White Australia" from its platform in 1962 in order "to remove the racial intent" in its immigration policy. In its place was substituted the phrase, "The maintenance of a vigorous and progressive selective immigration policy."[21]

However, the virtual exclusion of non-Europeans was still considered the *sine qua non* of the policy. And some officials "had difficulty restraining their impatience with the 'unholy alliance of do-gooders, some influenced by Communist organizations and others by religious organizations,' " who worked for modification.[22] But it was agreed that "White Australia" as "an offensive and unofficial term," not included in the Constitution and "not applicable to the Australian Immigration policy," [23] had to be removed. The principles inherent in the League's policy remained unchanged. In 1961 the National Headquarters of the R.S.L. sought assurances from the Commonwealth Government "that all possible steps would be taken to implement" the policy without modification and "as set out in its Constitution." [24] After the term "White Australia" was deleted from its platform, the R.S.L. continued "to strongly oppose any move to bring into Australia any mass migration of Asians." [25] To implement this policy the leadership advocated "the most stringent screening procedures with intending migrants to this country." [26] The policy and its underlying attitudes have not changed appreciably since 1924, when "White Australia" was first put into the R.S.L. platform, but the rhetoric of exclusion has been altered radically. R.S.L. leaders have developed their public relations and recognized the international forces at work to eliminate racialist policies. This explains why "White Australia" was revised to "Restrictive Immigration Policy," and "keep out undesirable types" became "a vigorous and selective" policy. Mr. Keys, National Secretary of the League, said, "we are willing to accept anyone we can absorb. Ours is not a racial policy. It is progressive but restrictive." [27] But what is a progressive policy? Is it not determined by the degree of restriction? The League's rhetoric under closer scrutiny is too often sheer obscurantism. In its standing policy statement the R.S.L. affirms its desire "to refute at every opportunity propaganda designed to destroy this policy." [28] Its presentation has changed, but the R.S.L. endorsement of the established immigration policy and opposition to reform remain intact.

One of the most nationally conscious pressure groups is the Australian Natives' Association (A.N.A.), which was founded almost one hundred years ago. It played an influential part in Federation and used its prominent position to further acceptance of the White Australia policy which, the leadership maintained, was based on loyalty to the "national character" and its British heritage. The Federal President of the Association wrote: "Our Association would oppose further liberalization of the policy, if it in any way threatened to destroy Australia's present homogeneity of population or national character." [29] For him the policy could be equated with the Australian ethos and the historical experiences of the past sixty-five years. "It [White Australia] was born of experience and warnings which our forefathers heeded." [30] Considering the White Australia policy as a manifestation of nationalist sentiment corresponded very closely to Labor's parochial attitude to the policy during the 1940's. As Minister for Immigration, Mr. Calwell had opinions remarkably similar to the Association's. Both felt exemptions to the policy would destroy it, and once the Liberal Party came into power in 1950, the A.N.A. voiced its resistance to the announced liberalization. Holt's reversal of some of Calwell's decisions were denounced along with government proposals to modify the policy provisions.[31] Mr. McGoll, Secretary of the Queensland branch of the A.N.A., inveighed against the anticipated changes by stating: "Our Australians fought and died . . . to keep their country free from dictators, coolie labor, cheap goods and low standards." [32] But after the Government enacted changes in 1956 and 1957 the A.N.A. tempered its resistance to modification, though it continued to oppose further liberalization through its frequent representations on the Immigration Advisory Council. The Federal President noted in 1966 that the A.N.A. supported "the established immigration policy and the manner in which it is being at present administered." At the same time, he suggested, it had mobilized all its efforts to oppose "the insincerity and inconsistency of those who are endeavouring to break down and destroy this policy." "Our Association," he wrote, "draws attention to the dangers of 'a liberalizing policy.' No degree of liberalization would satisfy so-called Immigration Reformists, nor would it assist in raising the standards of living in overseas countries."[33] The Association, by its own admission, based its immigration policy on several arguments:

> 1) It wants to avoid a repetition of Chinese migration 1850–1880, introduction of Kanaka labor in Queensland and "the difficulty of Asians &c. to integrate into our community life —as is also demonstrated in Fiji, Natal, United Kingdom, the U.S.A. . . ."
> 2) It does not want to import the racial problems of Rhodesia, South Africa, the Congo, Kenya, the United States and the United Kingdom.[34]

The first argument alludes to past episodes of strife in a multi-racial Australia, and the second attempts to support the first with its references to social conflict in other societies. This understanding of history and the fears associated with multi-racialism buttress the need A.N.A. members feel for a continuous vigil against policy reform. It is this intransigence that the reformers have interpreted as "racism," but complete acceptance of this argument would be a glib and naive description of the A.N.A. attitude. The conclusion that Australian security can only be maintained by adhering to the tenets of "White Australia" is perhaps an unnecessarily chauvinistic concern for the welfare and progress of Australia. The President suggested that Australians—the reference here undoubtedly included the A.N.A. membership—"are not 'race bigots,' nor 'color fiends,' nor 'arrogant superiorists.' We are proud of our country and we evaluate our success by the support our national policy on immigration continues to receive so generously."[35] Concern for the national aspirations is the A.N.A.'s most frequent appeal and greatest source of inspirational support. By associating the nation with the traditional immigration policy the A.N.A. can denounce as disloyal any immigration reformers. Likewise, its devotion to the "national interest" obscures its role as a pressure group. "We do not attempt to be a pressure group," observed the Federal President, "we seek to promote the welfare and progress of our country. We appeal to a pride in our country and by our actions extend the Friendly Society principles to national understanding." [36] It appears from this statement that pressure group activities and promoting the national welfare are mutually exclusive. Since "pressure group" has been a pejorative in Australia, the A.N.A. prefers to think of itself as a national body interested in the public welfare as opposed to a narrowly defined factional organization interested in special pursuits. It is this kind of presentation that has accounted for its relatively prominent position in the community and has made its views on the immigration policy credible.

Support for the policy as a determinant of Australia's high living standards comes from the A.W.U. (Australian Workers Union). Steeped in the history of "White Australia" this organization has used its influential position in the A.L.P. to maintain the status quo. Its arguments have combined a gratuitous altruism with a more credible self-interest. Unionists argue that the Government, even if it were inclined to liberalize the policy, would be attracting to Australia the very people Asia could least afford to lose—tradesmen, skilled workers and technicians.[37] Fundamentally, however, the policy was, and continues to be, endorsed for economic reasons. Unionists claim Asian laborers would lower working standards and wages irreparably, damage worker morale and lead ultimately to racial conflict. "To flood this country with unskilled Asian labor, would only disrupt our economy, and add to the unemployment that already exists . . ." [38] said one union official. Automated machinery, which has displaced unskilled laborers, raises the question: How can we allow unskilled Asians into our country, when the unskilled laborers already here are in jeopardy of losing their jobs?

However, not all unionists agree with this opinion. C. H. Fitzgibbon, Federal Secretary of the Waterside Workers Federation, which removed a rule excluding Asians from its membership in 1949, said:

> Personally, I would say we have to realize sooner or later that we must accept the fact that there should be some controlled immigration of Asian people, perhaps based on a quota system so that there is no drop in our living standards.
>
> The situation is such in Australia today that controlled immigration would pose no threat whatsoever; they would be assimilated into our trade union and award structure without trouble.[39]

Leaders in the Federated Ironworkers Association and the Railwaymen's Union have also cautiously suggested a more humane and flexible approach to immigration. Barriers to immigration reform in unions, once impregnable, are apparently weakening, and even T. Dougherty, General Secretary of the "strongly discriminatory" A.W.U., has modified his stand. "Times have changed now. Any Australian who does the ostrich act now is a bloody idiot!" [40]

Organizations calling for reform denounce the policy mainly on humanitarian grounds but few have sought, until recently, reasonable alternatives to it. It would be spurious to describe Australian churches as pressure groups on most political issues but the alleged violation of Christian principles implicit in a White Australia policy makes immigration a question of direct concern for religious leaders. Since Christians everywhere have admitted the inclusion of heathens of every tribe and nation in the gospel plan of salvation it was rather remarkable, churchmen noted, "that the alien may enter Heaven, but may not enter Australia!" [41] Almost all of the churches in Australia have to varying degrees opposed the immigration policy at one time or another.

In the last three decades the Methodist Church has vehemently castigated the racial discrimination in the policy and the "authoritarianism" in its administration. A specific section of the *Methodist Church Statement of Policy on Social Issues* notes:

Prejudices based on race, colour, nationality or religion should have no place in the attitude of the Christian towards the problem of immigration.

Australian immigration policy should be stated and administered in a way that leaves no room for a charge that there is discrimination on these grounds.[42]

By far the most vocal person in the Church on this issue is Reverend Alan Walker. From World War II to the present, Reverend Walker has attacked immigration policy in several ways. He has said that it is a "denial of Christian principles" and it is "deepening the world's colour conflict." [43] He has also noted that the policy is a threat to Australian security rather than a defender of it. "If Australia persists in a policy which must alienate sympathy among our neighbours, then war one day will surely come." [44] Australian immigration policy has also been a constant embarrassment, claims Reverend Walker, and as an adviser in the Australian delegation to the United Nations in 1949, he brought the harshness of the immigration policy to the attention of the international body by citing nine deportation incidents.[45] A quota system was the solution to this dilemma, argued Walker in the 1940's and 1950's, but by the early 1960's his position, no doubt influenced by continual debates and the views of the Associations for Immigration Reform, had changed. Instead of a quota system, he and the Methodist Church desire "the Government to accept the principle that Asians should be admitted to Australia on the same basis of Inter-governmental agreements as now applies to the admission of Europeans." [46] His disenchantment with the policy may have been expressed differently but it has not wavered throughout the years. As a result, he has become suspicious of supposed changes. When asked about Mr. Opperman's liberalization, he replied: "It is difficult to say whether recent proposals have liberalized the administration of the White Australia policy or whether they are a disguise for a continuance of the policy." [47] In his opinion, "Government policy is lagging behind public opinion on this question but it will eventually express the mind of the electorate." Walker believes constant pressure exerted by opinion leaders shifted public opinion toward modifications: "the consistent witness of the Church over a period of fifty years has gradually created a climate of public opinion which is right for change." [48] Another Church official, however, attributes changing attitudes less to the Church's effort to present its views in the mass media, than to the successful integration of Asian exchange students.[49]

From 1946 to the present the Anglican Church has continually reiterated its objection to rigid policy administration. It has appealed, on at least one occasion, for the implementation of the policy according to the principles in the Declaration of Human Rights.[50] At the 1962 inaugural meeting of the New South Wales Association for Immigration Reform, Bishop J. S. Moyes noted several "mythical" assumptions on which the policy is based—fear of migration and intermarriage. However, he observed "that they [non-Europeans] have a social self-respect just as much as we have, and that they are not anxious nor even willing on any large scale to intermarry with people of another race." Focusing again on Australia, he drew critical attention to the hypocrisy of a Christian nation with a basically racialist immigration policy and to the rhetoric of isolationism which could not be squared with the interdependence of nations in the contemporary setting.[51]

More recently Archbishop Strong argued that if Australia is earnest in its desire to play a constructive role in Asia it has to admit more migrants from that area.[52] One week after this address the Anglican General Synod unanimously decided to ask the Federal Government to double the annual intake of non-European migrants to 1,500 for a trial period. Dr. Charles Price, who moved the resolution, suggested "it was better to keep pressure on the Government and get the number increased gradually." [53]

The Presbyterian Church, in opposition to the immigration policy, denounced Mr. Calwell's policy administration in the

1940's and argued that the admission of non-Europeans at that time could have been more equitably "controlled by legislation rather than by personal decision of the Minister." The Church also viewed the policy as a strategic obstacle in the conflict against Communist propaganda. How can Australia categorically exclude Asians from its shore, ask church leaders, and still attempt to win their friendship and support? The Immigration Chaplain claims that recent changes in the Church have been designed "to present a more liberal image of Australia . . . in the eyes of Asian neighbours. . . ." But it appears, he has written, as if these changes represent "no significant departure from the general policy which is to maintain a homogeneous population." [54]

Assembly resolutions and recent communications to immigration authorities indicate the Church's desire to exert continued pressure for further liberalization. Australian Citizenship Conventions, organized by Commonwealth Immigration Officials, have become platforms for the Church's point of view and for urging reform, however indirect, of the Government's attitude.

Official Baptist opinion is devoted to the complete "opposition at all times to any barriers of race and color." This attitude applies to Aboriginal affairs as well as immigration. But the Church has couched its views in such general terms that humanitarianism—an admirable religious goal but not necessarily a political catalyst—is its principal argument for modification. This is in keeping with the Church's "belief in separation of Church and State, their different areas of responsibility and authority . . ." and its avoidance of "either open or hidden pressure upon the Government" to modify the policy.[55] It should be noted that Anglican and other churches have assisted in Aboriginal welfare, for instance, Tranbie College in Glebe (an inner-Sydney suburb), where Aboriginal students on scholarships or from country areas may stay so that they can attend day and evening classes in secondary and tertiary institutions, learn skills, and work in the city.

The Foundation for Aboriginal Affairs, established in Sydney in 1964, is a voluntary, non-sectarian and non-political organization of Aboriginals and Europeans to promote the welfare of Aboriginal people. Through its activities the Foundation stimulates Aboriginal endeavor. In 1968, 2,564 Aboriginals sought help from the Foundation. While this Foundation is not directly related to immigration policy it is an expression of the increasing community efforts to eliminate charges of racism directed at Australian life. However, official church opposition to the established policy may not be indicative of lay opinion. The General Secretary of the Congregational Union of New South Wales has suggested "that a fairly substantial proportion of our ministers (probably a small majority) would favour the progressive liberalization of the Policy, even abolition of it, but . . . it is not likely that a small majority of our lay people would hold the same view." [56]

Many Protestant churches leave issues such as the formulation of immigration policy to the Australian Council of Churches (A.C.C.), which possesses means of accumulating much more accurate information than its member churches. The A.C.C. has long advocated a progressive liberalization of the White Australia policy. Its statements apply Christian principles to the concerns of the national interest in order to press its claim for modification. "How can a nation seek its own ends without regard for the feelings and aspirations of other people?" is the kind of hypothetical question often raised by A.C.C. officials.[57] Although it has not affirmed any loyalty to a political party and on some political issues remains neutral, the A.C.C. considers itself charged with a responsibility for moral problems. It is for this reason that the Council, deploring the administration of the policy in several deportation cases, e.g., Gamboa, suggested a government-appointed Commission to judge deportation appeals.[58] Most of the Council's suggestions have been moderate proposals to eliminate racial intent without eliminating restrictions. Periodic communications to the Prime Minister, activity at Citizenship Conventions and its role as spokesman for Australian churches on the immigration reform issue manifest the Council's interest. However, the A.C.C.'s passionate opposition to "White Australia" when it was unusual to take that position and its present "non-conformist" attitude to the war in Vietnam lessen the Government's regard for many of its policies, even though the Council no longer presents a united radical front. The representation of many different churches in this body has led to divisions which obscure its aims. Many of its press releases and other public pronouncements are an effort at compromise between dissidents and are, by no means, representative of the more radical sentiments of non-conformist churches within the Council. In the past ten years it has become clear that the A.C.C. is not in the vanguard of reform. It accepts "radical opinion" only when it has become publicly acceptable. When the A.C.C. formally adopted 1,500 migrants as its annual non-European immigration standard, it merely echoed the long-standing suggestion of "radical" religious leaders and immigration reformers.

The Roman Catholic hierarchy was ostentatiously silent on the immigration issue right after the war. Its silence led many people to assume the Church endorsed the policy. During the 1950's two factions—one led by Archbishops Mannix and Duhig and another which sought its inspiration from Dr. Rumble—brought the Church's position to the surface. The former maintained "that the total exclusion of Asians from Australia should be abandoned and that we should admit a sufficient number of the different races to dispel forever the myth of racial superiority inherent in the so-called 'White Australia Policy.' " [59] Dr. Rumble's group countered "that White Australia was more a national and political than a moral problem," [60] and for this reason it endorsed neutrality on the matter. A statement issued by the Australian bishops in 1951 indicated at least a temporary victory within the hierarchical policy board for the immigration reformers:

Nor will the necessary justification [for Australia's survival] be found in any false assumption of racial superiority which too often underlies the so-called White Australia Policy. In fairness, it should be admitted that there is merit in the economic argument which has been used to justify this policy—that the mass migration of Asian peoples to Australia might be used by sinister forces to establish a cheap labour market to the detriment both of native Australians and of the newcomers. The absolute exclusion of Asian migrants has little relation, however, to this economic argument and can hardly be justified.[61]

More recently reformers can claim victory primarily because of successful Christian proselytizing in the East, the disparity in wealth between most Asians and Australians, and the realization that a state problem with moral implications is not divorced from the Church's purview. Catholic spokesmen now insist that "all racialism be eliminated from Migration Policy." [62] This should be done, it is asserted, not only by changing the name of the White Australia policy, but by changing the policy itself.

> For, as long as exclusion remains the guiding principle for the exercise of the Minister's discretionary powers, and colour and blood are deciding factors in the refusal of permanent residence to non-Europeans, no amount of foreign aid, dodging behind economic and cultural considerations or verbal humanitarianism can obscure or change the fact that White Australia is a racially discriminatory policy.
>
> In the absence of an effective international judiciary, Australia cannot be forced to make this change. But the national conscience remains bound by the natural international law to abolish the White Australia Policy.[63]

In November, 1963, twenty-six prominent New South Wales citizens, including Church leaders, urged the Government to allow more non-European migrants into Australia. They argued that politically minded Asians and Africans "are more likely to be concerned about the content of our immigration policy than the name used to describe it. . . . It is time to show the world that

Australians are able to view the fact of racial difference with a due sense of proportion." [64] Similar statements were issued in Victoria and Western Australia.

Vocal student outbursts against "White Australia" could be observed in university organizations which fomented policy opposition in 1961. Asian presence on Australian campuses as a result of the Colombo Plan seemed to make the White Australia policy a more lively issue. At the University of Melbourne "isolated criticism became mass action" in the late 1950's. Both the Students' Representative Council and the National Union of Students recorded their opposition to the immigration policy. But the National Union, as a constitutionally apolitical organization, felt any motion formulated on immigration would be contrary to its aims. It, therefore, did not mobilize any political action but it decided "to canvass, collate and publicize" university opinion.[65] In a plebiscite conducted among Melbourne students in the late 1950's, seventy-seven per cent favored a major change in the policy.[66] This reaction, however, was only a forerunner of an active, reasonably well-knit, and extremely vocal Student Action movement organized specifically to protest against the immigration policy during the 1961 federal election campaign.

One sympathetic follower of the Student Action movement claims that its driving force did not stem from a moral revulsion with the White Australia policy but from intra-Labor Party decisions at Melbourne University in June, 1961. Bill Thomas, president of the university A.L.P. club, distraught with the choice of leaders in the A.L.P. Victorian Federal Executive, sought to exert pressure on the A.L.P. hierarchy through his political base on the campus. Realizing that the growth of the A.L.P. club was limited to those sharing similar political views, he decided to build a student action front by coalescing many university groups around a moral issue—the White Australia policy.[67] "This was one way," said an activist in the organization, "to attract middle class girls who enjoy political protest without alienating them from their parents' money." From its inception the A.L.P. club controlled Student Action. Several Melbourne student clubs including the Liberal Club, Student Christian Movement, Newman Society, Rationalist Society, Fabian Society, Nationalist Society, Athenian Society, Political Science Society, Debating Society, and Public Questions Society voluntarily joined or were recruited for the A.L.P. club's protest movement.[68]

At a lunchtime meeting in the third term of 1961, representatives from each of these clubs formulated a motion and called a mass meeting of students. It was suggested that the immigration policy be made an election issue and students demonstrate so that "White Australia" would not be overlooked by politicians running in the federal election.[69] The motion which passed unanimously was later adopted at Royal Melbourne Institute of Technology, Monash University, and Swinburne Technical College. Student organizers were chosen from each institution as representatives on a central committee which met at Melbourne during the examination period.[70] John Johnson, "Bill Thomas' handpicked choice," was given the post of Student Action President.

Huge throngs of students who filled all available seats and standing room in the Public Lecture Theater at Melbourne University on the second to last Friday of the third term indicated the popularity of the movement. On most resolutions relating to the White Australia policy the audience enthusiastically concurred, but a resolution obliging all members of the Committee to declare their political allegiance was defeated. Members of the A.L.P. club legitimately claimed they would be expelled from the party "if it was discovered they actively campaigned against their party's declared views on immigration." [71]

Subsequent meetings at Monash and the Royal Melbourne Institute of Technology did not attract crowds as large as the Melbourne conclave. But the organizational apparatus for the group was completed at these meetings and arrangements made to raise funds from businesses, churches, and staff members in order to print handbills, make signs, and hire halls for the movement.[72]

By this time the election campaign had reached full swing, fifty thousand handbills had been printed, several thousand "facts and arguments" about the policy had been mimeographed, and a large segment of Victoria's university students were available at only a day's notice for public demonstrations. The first handbill distributed was entitled "Time For A Change In Migration Policy," a statement which drew heavily on the ideas of the Immigration Reform Group (I.R.G.) and the Associations for Immigration Reform. It recognized the rapidly shifting public opinion on the issue of non-European migration and the continued "racialist policy" pursued by the Government. In order to erase the stigma of racialism and the insult implicit in a policy that "suggests we harbor illusions of racial superiority," Student Action recommended that the Government "maintain control but bar colour bar." [73] These recommendations indicated that the Student Action Committee was less concerned with creating viable alternatives to the immigration policy than with excoriating the racial intent in its administration and publicizing this to the uninformed public. Prior to the election and even after the results were announced Student Action distributed a myriad of written statements which attempted to apprise and often shock the general public. These arguments, usually well documented, often proved extremely embarrassing to the Government. On one occasion an Australian official at an immigration recruitment center in Southern Europe wrote to the Student Action Committee and related the criteria employed by Australian authorities for migrant selection in Rome, Genoa, Trieste, Naples, Messina, and Spain.

A criterion for initial acceptance was that the applicant had to appear not more than twenty-five per cent non-European in appearance and this the selection officer necessarily judged on facial characteristics, skin color and to a lesser extent bone structure, eyes etc. Skin color was often given as a reason for low assimilation potential even if the applicant appeared less than twenty-five per cent non-European and common in the selection reports were comments such as: "Far too dark,"

"Obvious Moorish blood," "Could be taken for Asian," "Fuzzy-wuzzy hair—look like South Sea Islanders." . . .[74]

This statement and a public letter were sent to the major parties before the election. In the letter the Committee wrote:

> Australia's present policy is immoral because it discriminates against certain people solely on the basis of skin colour; it is foolish because it insults our neighbours, embarrasses our friends and lowers our national prestige.
>
> In a world which is very conscious of colour discrimination a "White Australia" policy cannot be sustained.
>
> We urge each of the major parties to indicate how it proposes to prevent our immigration policies doing further harm.[75]

Student Action not only denounced the Menzies-Downer position on racialism, it continually reissued statements by Calwell which expressed his devotion to the White Australia policy; a policy, he noted, which kept "Australia exactly as it has always been, and exactly as it always ought to be." Moreover, pointed out Committee leaders, Calwell as the Labor leader showed no sympathy with Darwin trade unionists who went on strike over the threatened deportation of two Malayan pearl divers who had spent numerous years in Australia working in one of the country's "vital industries."

The decision to deport the pearl divers provided Student Action with its first collective activity. About one hundred students turned up, some five days before the examination period, to greet the two divers and a Darwin editor, Jim Bowditch, who was acting as counsel and defender. At a public meeting held a few days later several resolutions denouncing the deportation order were passed by the Student Action Committee.[76] Now that the students had a cause their demonstrations could be directed at a definite action—revocation of the deportation order.

When it was learned that Mr. Menzies planned to give his Federal Campaign speech at Kew Civic Hall, Student Action organized a massive demonstration in front of the auditorium.

With faces blackened, students sat on the steps and sang to the tune of "Michael Row The Boat Ashore":

> Old Bob Menzies he ought to know, White Australia,
> That the divers they shouldn't go, No more White Australia,
> Let's be human, Let's be bold, White Australia,
> A new world rises from the old, No more White Australia.[77]

Placards were prominently displayed during the demonstration with such slogans as: "Menzies Orders Racist Deportations, Where Is the Opposition?"; "Mind That Tan, They Might Deport You"; "Deport Downer Not Divers"; "Control Yes, Colour Bar No"; "Australians Not Colour Conscious, Migration Policy Is"; "White Australia Policy Equals Apartheid"; and "White Australia Policy, Good Enough For Our Grandfathers, Not Good Enough For Us." During his speech Menzies, interrupted by shouts, referred to his detractors as "ill-bred children," "this rabble," and "allegedly educated boys and girls." He told his audience, "These are not representatives of the universities. They are just a collection of ratbags." To one interjector Menzies said: "You have the beard of a man of forty and the mind of a boy of four."[78] Menzies' quick wit disarmed many students and illustrated his ability to score heavily off his opponents, but his remarks also gave Student Action the kind of publicity it desired. The front page of almost every Australian newspaper carried a story on the rally. Most of the newspapers dismissed the movement as a student prank but at least two, the Adelaide *Advertiser* and the Melbourne *Sun,* cautiously published the "student point of view."

One nasty incident which developed after the student demonstration was an alleged altercation between W. J. (Bill) Thomas and Mr. Opperman (soon to be Downer's replacement as Minister for Immigration), in which Thomas claimed to have been struck. Thomas issued a writ for assault which was allowed to lapse,[79] but this incident gave Student Action additional newspaper coverage and some sympathetic reportage.

At Calwell's campaign policy address another much less disruptive rally was conducted where demonstrators asked why the Labor Party did not present an alternative to the government immigration policy and why Calwell endorsed the government position on the Malay divers. He ignored these interjections and went on to announce A.L.P. support for a more equitable Aborigine program—even student detractors applauded him enthusiastically.[80]

Newspapers and politicians continued discussing the Student Action Movement and its potential political role. Detractors accused the movement's leaders of embodying every political ideology between the Democratic Labor Party (right wing) and the Communist Party (left wing). And the two major parties became embroiled in intra-party disputes over issues raised by Student Action and the strategies that should be employed in answer to them. Most politicians objected to Student Action and deplored its methods. They were particularly upset by reports of rowdiness and disruptive actions, despite the fact that the Student Committee printed orders for all demonstrators to "be orderly" and avoid "heckling on irrelevant issues," and even informed the police of the anticipated route of any demonstration.[81]

Condemnation was not confined solely to politicians. One observer wrote:

> It is strange that university students, who are regarded as persons possessing a high standard of education and knowledge, should be so ignorant as to conditions in Asia and unaware of the fact that there is no mass outcry in Asia against Australia's immigration laws.[82]

Another critic of Student Action, who deplored the arguments used by student leaders, claimed they "lived off the cream" and had "no real troubles to plague them . . . due, ironically, to the White Australia Policy itself."[83] Still another questioned the loyalty and motives of its members.

If they honestly sympathise with the misfortunes of coloured peoples, let them devote themselves to assisting in areas where coloured people are trying to emancipate themselves. Their present attitude is merely exhibitionism. They are trying to proclaim a righteousness they do not possess.[84]

Support for Student Action came from unexpected quarters. *The Times* of London, while it called student ideals "sometimes wise and sometimes foolish," was generally satisfied with the students' political action and saw them as a force that "will soon affect Australian parties and parliaments."[85] Dr. Jim Cairns (M.H.R. for Yarra), a former member of the Victorian Association for Immigration Reform, proclaimed his complete sympathy with Student Action.[86]

After the 1961 election ambiguity about the role of Student Action grew, but it soon became clear that Thomas intended to develop a network of Student Action fronts throughout the states as a permanent protest movement. Despite his efforts, the movement might have petered out except for a series of well-publicized deportations which revived interest and Student Action. In the beginning of the year the Government refused to give political asylum to three sailors and decided to deport them to their homeland, Portugal—an allegedly fascist state. Student Action rallied against the Government's decision. The issue in this case was obviously not the White Australia policy, but deportation provided an issue to illustrate the arbitrary power of the Minister for Immigration and the political effectiveness of Student Action. Student Action marches were organized in Brisbane and Melbourne simultaneously and Bill Thomas, the coordinator, went to Brisbane to establish a new branch of the Student Action front. The same techniques used in the past were employed again: distribution of pamphlets, marches, songs, and the ubiquitous banners. The banners had the usual allegations condemning Downer: "Portuguese Fascists Love Downer"; "Dictators Love Downer Deportations"; "Downer's New Exports:

Malayan Divers, Portuguese Sailors"; "Downer Does It Again—Australia's Name Blackened."

In the spring of 1962 a virtual storm erupted over the deportation of a Chinese market gardener, Willie Wong, to Mainland China. The clandestine manner in which the case was handled, reports of divergent views within the Department, fear that Wong would be executed as soon as he was forcibly removed from Hong Kong, and the alleged delivery to a totalitarian state of a "political refugee seeking asylum," aroused the Student Action Committee.[87] Not only did the Wong case elicit a spate of newspaper criticism, it uncovered again what Student Action leaders referred to as "the underlying racialist sentiments" of the immigration policy. The Student Action Committee circulated reports that Downer, by this time nicknamed "Dither Downer," tried to stop the publication of the story because Willie Wong was not the first Asian he had deported to Communist China.

A demonstration protesting the deportation of Willie Wong followed with the usual posters, jeers, and the vocal ensemble of the Student Action song:

> There are mean things happening in this land
> Though you're in the human race,
> We'll check the colour of your face,
> There are mean things happening in this land.
>
> Have you heard Mr. Downer make his stand?
> Though the divers want to stay,
> He'd send them back, for they're Malay.
>
> If you're black it seems you've got no right
> While the bureaucrats sat and lied
> Democracy got kicked aside.
> If you're black. . . .
>
> There are mean things happening in this land,
> Black men working night and day,
> They can't get a white man's pay,

> Mr. Menzies, he is white like driven snow,
> Yes with gladness and with pride
> He stood up for Apartheid.
>
> There are mean things happening in this land,
> Black or yellow, white or tan,
> Lord, a man is just a man,
>
> An end to hate and fear thru' out this land,
> Let us walk beneath the sun,
> Knowing that all men are one,
> Then, we will have a strong and peaceful land.[88]

Student Action claimed that Wong was "forced" to sign "voluntary compliance" papers he did not understand. It objected strenuously to the authoritarian attitude of the Minister and described the case as "the latest manifestation of the White Australia Policy." [89] Downer, livid with anger at the fuss created by the deportation, allegedly cried: "I would rather have a migration office in Edinburgh than in Kuala Lumpur," [90] no matter what the students argue.

The primary purpose of Student Action was accomplished: the supposed racialism of the policy was exposed. It was done not through the conventional political channels but by creating new rules of action. When the press and the politicians ignored what Student Action considered an example of "White Australia," members painted their faces black, carried placards, and brought the issue into the streets. The demonstrators had been appropriately described as "the shock troops of the anti-White Australia forces." [91] If the Immigration Reform Group comprised the thinkers, Student Action represented the activists. It was a student group of widely divergent views united to alter "White Australia" by forcing the issue into the federal election. When its actions made headlines and its views penetrated political organizations, its job was done. The end of Student Action as an active immigration reform body followed the sudden accidental death of Bill Thomas and the graduation of many of the group's leaders, but its methods and exuberance continued to be employed by student leaders with other causes.

The Immigration Reform Group (I.R.G.) was formed in Melbourne and was led by Kenneth Rivett and J. A. C. Mackie (now a lecturer at Melbourne University), both of whom had traveled in South East Asia. Organized initially as a study unit, I.R.G. began with only a few participants aware of the administrative practices in the Department of Immigration. All were agreed, however, that the policy needed study and probably revision. In order to facilitate this study membership in the group was limited. Mackie wrote:

> The question of the membership of the group is rather delicate at this stage. We should cast our net as widely as possible in attracting anyone who supports modification of the White Australia policy, but it seems wisest to begin with a small private meeting and to appeal for wider participation only after we have agreed on our basic objectives.[92]

Each of the twelve men and women in the original group [93] was assigned study of a particular aspect of the policy. They met regularly for a six-month period discussing each member's findings, making recommendations, and seeking complete verbal agreement on every issue. They also wrote to those organizations in favor of liberalization (churches, Apex, etc.) and sought their advice on reform procedures and criticism of their demands.

In 1959 "something like a deadlock as regards the next move" existed. It had become obvious that Macmahon Ball's 1948 prophesy of the demise of the White Australia policy within a "decade" * had not been borne out and a concerted effort for a policy shift was necessary. Public opinion was moving in the direction of liberalization, but the form liberalization should take was

---

* Professor Macmahon Ball has pointed out that he meant "decades," not "a decade." *The Sun* (Melbourne), November 12, 1967.

undecided. "Token quotas," a solution widely discussed in the 1950's, was rejected by both reformers and supporters of the policy. By study and discussion it was the group's aim "to break this deadlock, partly by feeding in new constructive proposals, but partly also by restating *and widening* the arguments used in favour of change." [94] It tried to determine "the likely flow of Asian immigrants if Australia 'opened the gates' to the possible flood; the economic effects of a large inflow; the possible effects of even a smaller flow if the migrants concentrated in particular occupations." [95]

When ideas were sufficiently crystallized, the group decided to produce a pamphlet amplifying the research. The main reason for the pamphlet, it was alleged, was to publicize policy that had been liberalized by stealth and make proposals pursuant to this issue. In April and June, 1960, *Control or Colour Bar?* was published and distributed. I.R.G. members, skeptical about its ability to sell, had only one thousand copies published at first. These sold in the first week; in all the pamphlet sold a surprising eight thousand copies. In 1962 the pamphlet was expanded into a book, *Immigration: Control or Colour Bar?* which has so far sold approximately six and a half thousand copies.

Although the I.R.G. was above all a study group "not committed to any particular policy as regards Asian migration," it did give rise to a series of Associations for Immigration Reform, all desirous of implementing the proposals set forth in *Control or Colour Bar?* Although each branch Association adopted its own formal statement of aims, there was very little difference among them, and even less difference from proposals in *Control or Colour Bar?* When the New South Wales Association was formed in June, 1962, it adopted the following goals:

(a) To change Australia's Immigration Policy so that it will, in practice, neither exclude nor appear to exclude people on the basis of their race or colour.

(b) To increase awareness that the present policy is morally wrong, and that it weakens Australia's impact in the councils of the world by the fact that it bears the taint of racial exclusiveness.

(c) To secure an Australian Immigration Policy based on the following principles:
    i The social and economic benefit to Australia from absorbing immigrants, taking into consideration the needs of other countries and the claims of humanity, will be the main determinant of our level of intake.
    ii Migration from any country will be limited by the need to avoid harmful economic competition, to prevent undesirable concentrations of racial groups in particular employments, to avoid housing congestion, and to ensure a reasonable degree of integration with the Australian community.

(d) To ensure that Australia shall announce its willingness to negotiate bilateral migration agreements with friendly governments.[96]

    These goals carefully avoided the endorsement of either the military or the conventional economic arguments for large-scale immigration. The military argument has raised "the whole question of attitudes to war in general and the Cold War in particular. Moreover, it is dubious just how far immigration would contribute to Australia's military strength in the sort of conflict that would seriously tax that strength, i.e. full scale war." Several of the conventional economic arguments, particularly the one suggesting that migration will raise living standards, have also been subjected to serious challenge by P. H. Karmel, W. B. Reddaway, and other notable economists.

    These immigration reformers were by no means "radical or irresponsible rabble" unaware of the issues or the political and social problems involved in altering the policy. Their proposals recognized the need for housing provision, occupational balance, social workers, and even political courage. But it was continually stressed that a revision in the policy involved no great reversal of recent immigration practice. "The Government must remain the master of its own house in this respect under a restated policy . . .";[97] it could control year by year the overall volume of immigration and the volume from each country. The Secretary of the New South Wales Association for Immigration Reform wrote:

> Associations for Immigration Reform say frankly that they are prepared to see Australia pay some regard to the country of origin and even the race of the would-be immigrants, partly because race sometimes corresponds to true cultural difference and partly because it would be folly to change Australia's racial balance too quickly.[98]

It was decided that an annual intake of 1,500 non-Europeans allowed to settle for an experimental period of five years would best meet the objections to more radical proposals and simultaneously recognize the difficulties of migrant integration.[99]

The Associations for Immigration Reform represent a relatively small number of Australians, but they have been remarkably active and quite successful in dissemination of their opinions. Press releases, letters to the editor, guest speakers, publications, and debates have been used to counter arguments of staunch antagonists of immigration reform. They have sent speakers to Churches, Apex meetings, and even R.S.L. headquarters, and have sponsored conferences in every state. They have published "White Australia: Time for a Change?"; "Immigration Reform: Where Do We Go From Here?"; "My Experiences in Australia" (an address by an Indian academic); "A Case for Reform"; and "Immigration Quarterly," a broadsheet of news and opinion published for some years by the Western Australian Association for Immigration Reform.

Just prior to the 1961 federal election, the Victorian Association for Immigration Reform (V.A.I.R.) issued 6,600 copies of a publication entitled "Why Does White Australia Matter?" In it they advised the Government to make "a frank avowal that there is no objection to Asians (or other non-Europeans) just because of their birth."[100] The pamphlet, a synopsis of *Control or Colour Bar?*, was used by Student Action as "the authoritative statement on reform," even though there was no formal connection between the two groups. Members of the V.A.I.R. committee, such as Chairman A. M. Harold (a member of a leading legal firm), barristers, ministers, and prominent politicians were among the most active citizenry challenging underlying racial preferences in immigration.

It is difficult to evaluate accurately the influence I.R.G. and the Associations have had on the Government, on other groups concerned with immigration, and on public opinion. Membership is seldom as high as 200, and the problem of keeping Associations in existence in less populous states [101] makes it difficult to exert effective pressure on the Government. Nonetheless, they have persuaded individual politicians and more influential reform groups, e.g., churches, by using an educative, almost missionary, approach for their conversion task. Immigration Reform Associations "have tried to make up through strategic shrewdness for what they lacked in numbers and material resources. . . ."[102]

The Associations' efforts to liberalize the White Australia policy has led some observers to credit them with announced changes in the formal policy after 1960. Donald Horne writes, "If reform of immigration policies proceeds calmly these Groups are entitled to much of the praise."[103] "Any change in this opinion is almost certainly the result of the devotion and energy of the immigration reform associations," notes an *Australian* editorial.[104] On the other hand, several government officials have dismissed the efforts of the Associations to bring about reform.[105] And even leaders of the reform movement have noted that the Associations have not been organized long enough and do not have a large enough membership to impress the policy-makers directly.[106]

Even without a direct line to government circles and no representation at the Citizenship Convention or the Immigration Advisory Committee, their ideas have been accepted by individuals in all three bodies. It is no coincidence, for example, that the Anglican General Synod and the Australian Council of Churches have decided to pledge their support to an annual intake of 1,500 non-Europeans for permanent residence. It has also been suggested that the Associations have influenced the thinking of more powerful organizations which have given "needed support and encouragement" to progressive elements within the Department of Immigration.[107] In attempting to defend the current trend in the policy and opting for increased liberalization these immigration officers have had support from the reform groups.

On the question of influence, Kenneth Rivett states that "utilitarian considerations (using 'utilitarian' in the philosophic sense)" were made "the sole standard of appeal," and he believes this widened the support for the proposals in *Immigration: Control or Colour Bar?* [108] Recognizing the recent change in the Government's attitude and illustrating an awareness of political bargaining, he has argued that reform groups should not be militant at that time (1967). With many of their proposals already enacted and one of the most important—migration of 1,500 non-Europeans for permanent residence—soon to be considered as a permanent aspect of policy, the Associations do not want to jeopardize their influence by creating new demands just as the old ones are about to be satisfied. This does not imply that the immigration issue is closed. It is still recognized that race determines very largely the acceptance of many immigrants to Australia. But it suggests that pressure exerted on the Government during a period of experimentation puts it in a defensive and somewhat proscriptive position and increases the likelihood of reform associations losing favor with their political contacts. Their efforts, if the prescribed changes are enacted, would

> focus on investigating how successful the Australian community was proving in integrating non-European migrants at each occupational level. The findings of such investigations might largely determine whether, at a later stage, the Associations would press the Government to liberalize policy more rapidly.[109]

The Immigration Reform Group aimed at informing the public about the discriminatory aspects of immigration policy, and as an educational group it has helped liberalize public opinion. The Associations have played a special role in offering to "initially sympathetic" individuals "a fully reasoned and substantiated argument, not only to answer their own doubts (if any), but also to help them to meet the quite penetrating objections which are sometimes raised." [110] Through education, debate, and discussion both the Associations and the I.R.G. have done something to challenge policy defenders and make them reappraise their arguments.

The National Civic Council, a pressure group which combined an anti-Communist appellation, a Pacific community ideology, a Christian loyalty, and a personality cult, is in the vanguard of immigration reform. Although its effectiveness is limited to its narrow denominational and political base, its "guru" and spokesman, B. A. Santamaria, reaches a large segment of the Australian community through his television commentary and *News Weekly* publication. The Council's views on most issues are consistent with those of the Democratic Labor Party (D.L.P.). It has been gratuitously admitted that Council members are usually D.L.P. voters and Catholic congregants, albeit one Council member has noted a recent D.L.P. reticence to adopt several Civic Council reforms.[111] The Civic Council has employed several arguments for a more liberalized policy:

(1) Australia needs people for its own economic development;
(2) Australian foreign policy and defense needs are constantly impaired by a policy that is offensive to its neighbors;
(3) Christian principles are inconsistent with a discriminatory and exclusive policy;
(4) the future welfare of the nation would be best served by allowing Asians to migrate.

In addition, Santamaria, who envisages forcible Asian entry to Australia if the continent remains underpopulated, argues:

> Irrespective of the morality of the so-called "White Australia" policy, this overwhelming contrast of population in Australia and in the countries to our near north, makes it impossible to preserve, into the indeterminate future, a purely European race in Australia.[112]

The right of twelve million to hold a continent as large and rich as Australia has prompted him to demand government encouragement of Asian migration to Australia. He has also suggested that the assisted migrant program be extended to all suitable Asian migrants as well as the Europeans already covered by the program.[113] Santamaria's followers contend that for Australians population is everything. As long as hostile absorption remains a very real threat, the Government, note Council officials, must take every possible step to increase population. Since the birthrate is quite low by international standards and European migration in large numbers is becoming more difficult to sustain, Asian migration is proffered as the only solution to the population dilemma. "Are we so benightedly racist in our attitude that we would rather destroy the reproductive base of our own population than admit easily assimilable Asians into our country?"[114] asks Santamaria rhetorically.

Santamaria has noted that there are discriminatory strains in some segments of the Australian population that may interfere with migrant adjustment. In order to eliminate this kind of discrimination, he prescribes an education program that would eventually lead to the public's adoption of "what the learned call 'cultural pluralism.'"[115] If by cultural pluralism, notwithstanding its many definitions and nuances, Santamaria means insulated national and racial clans, it is a more extreme solution than either assimilation, which implies the rejection of Old World ties and the complete acceptance of the new culture, and integration, which assumes the maintenance of some cultural traits associated with the motherland but presupposes contact with Australia and its people.

National Civic Council and Santamaria's attacks on the

immigration policy, while usually rational and pragmatic, have appealed to emotional and religious impulses as well. In 1962 Australian newspapers publicized a story about one hundred unwanted war babies—children everyone wanted to forget. These were the children of Japanese mothers and Australian occupation soldiers. It was reported that many of these children were living in conditions of abject poverty, while most of the Australian fathers, who had returned to their homeland, did not want or were unwilling to recognize a responsibility to them. They preferred to forget while the half-caste children, not completely accepted in their own land, suffered. The issue made headlines in most of the Australian newspapers and was debated in the House. The Government's refusal to admit the children to Australia brought Santamaria into the public discussion. In his opinion rejection was based entirely on the White Australia policy.

> To maintain this sacred cow, we, as a nation, refuse to recognize our responsibilities to children of our own nationals. This is a flagrant scandal.
> It is written that Our Lord Jesus Christ said: "Suffer the little children to come unto me for of such is the Kingdom of Heaven." The Japanese children are fortunate that the Kingdom of Heaven at least, has no White Australia Policy and that entry into it doesn't demand a visa.
> When are the politicians and bureaucrats who reside comfortably in the ivory castle of Canberra going to wake up? These are not just Japanese children. These are half-Australian children. They are not just social and political factors. They are people.[116]

From pressure groups that organize stunts such as Student Action to churches unobtrusively seeking change through moral persuasion, the immigration policy is continually meeting new challenges and is periodically revised. For some groups the price of revision comes too high—they are dedicated to retaining what is vaguely considered the national consciousness and maintaining a so-called standard of living. "Though the status quo is only a web of past decisions the groups whom it favours represent it as something more," [117] wrote Peter Westerway. This statement validly applies to groups defending the status quo. They have called immigration policy "the national ethos" or "our way of life" even when that policy has undergone major postwar revisions. Since 1960 the R.S.L. and several trade unions have modified their positions. The tide of history is against them and it has become increasingly evident that either they change, however slightly, to keep in tune with the prevailing sentiment or they bargain away their effectiveness as pressure groups. Some of these organizations keep a relatively high membership and prestigious position, even though they intransigently oppose modification, but this is for reasons unrelated to its immigration arguments. The Natives' Association, for example, probably has more influence because of its generous pension plans than because of its immigration program.

Because groups seeking change in the policy are generally the intruders or opposed to the status quo, they are in far fewer positions of power and have almost no direct contacts with government officials. Nonetheless these pressure groups have conducted themselves with moderation—Student Action being a notable exception—and within the guidelines created by "the Establishment." Perhaps this explains their relative success in affecting public opinion. While representing their own attitude they have stressed a concern for the "national welfare" and demonstrated this through a thoughtful analysis of the immigration policy avoiding extremes. At no time have they advocated unrestricted migration or abandonment of government controls— two propositions that would undoubtedly mobilize the Opposition.

The reform movement has been affected by the stream of recent historical events. A postwar foreign policy that is more concerned with events in South East Asia and a trade policy that curries favor with Japan cannot be constructively developed with an immigration policy that categorically restricts and implicitly insults Asiatics.

Influence for change has been indirect since most politicians, even those who recognize the historical trend, have either rejected or avoided association with the reformers. The Associations, formally banned by the A.L.P., were considered a political liability. Nonetheless, the publicity these groups have received and the widespread distribution of their publications has resulted in a persuasive though circuitous communication with politicians. Their endorsement by churches affords the reformers a moral as well as a political front. It has become increasingly difficult for politicians to accuse the reformers of irresponsibility when the churches act for reform, and congregants are also Association supporters. Gradual change in official and public opinion aided by a thoughtful presentation of revision proposals has increased acceptance of reform. They must constantly compromise, avoid offense, and persuasively illustrate. "Only when the political climate is suitable do politicians act" is a political axiom of the utmost importance to reformers. Reformers must affect that climate. Unfortunately any appraisal of pressure group success is complicated by the personal beliefs and individual will of politicians and the variegated daily events that influence public opinion. With this amalgam of competing and unpredictable forces it is impossible to say with any assurance who or what has "influenced" or "caused" a shift in government policy. But as long as the immigration policy is offensive to reformers and glorified by their opponents, a struggle for change will continue.

Part Two

6

Public Opinion

Public opinion is the expression by a large group of its perceived impression of a controversial point.[1] Since many situations are not experienced by respondents, their opinion reflects their conceptual associations with an event. This explains why so many Australians were once opposed to non-European migration even though there were so few non-Europeans in the nation and almost no contact between them and the white population—and why public opinion on White Australia has become consistently moderated since World War II, even though the non-European population has not changed appreciably.[2] What has changed is the Australian's image of Asians.

Opinion not based on personal experience is generally more resistant to change than opinion arrived at through individual deduction, because most often it is presented early in life and uncritically accepted on faith. And like any childhood values, it tends to perpetuate itself by preventing the individual from embarking upon investigation that might call its validity into question. Thus, individuals who believe that whites and non-whites cannot live together harmoniously support an immigration policy which ensures that the tension "inevitable" from racial mixing cannot occur.

No opinion, however, is immutable. Most beliefs change from generation to generation and, whether positive or negative, they very often become less intense. More dramatic changes occur on rare occasions when individuals are forced to analyze their beliefs in the face of contradictory evidence. But most often this evidence is simply not available.

Australian opinion about non-European immigration is to a very large extent derived from the experiences and beliefs of early settlers who lived in social and economic conditions remote from the contemporary scene. In the past century opinion derived from this historic source has not been effectively challenged either by government leaders or by the existence of non-Europeans in the country. It has not been proved wrong because it has not been tested, and, even with signs that opinion is becoming more liberal, most Australians will make no real effort to change non-European immigration until circumstances force them to examine their beliefs.

Public opinion is manifested in a variety of ways, through polls, articles in national journals, newspaper editorials and private expressions of the distinguished, as well as the "man in the street." If an indication of opinion at a given time is to be determined, it seems necessary to sample a cross section of all of these public opinion barometers.

In 1947 Professor O. A. Oeser and Dr. S. B. Hammond reported on a Unesco study concerning Australian attitudes to different race-nation groups (see page 147).[3]

The chart reveals a hierarchy of race-nation acceptability in Australia, with the exception of the Chinese who are regarded somewhat differently because of their favorable reception in parts of the country. It was "overdetermined," claim the authors, "by Australian cultural tradition derived from an English back-

Race/Nationality	Keep Out	Let a Few In	Allow Them to Come	Try to Get Them to Come
U.K.	0.9	1.8	25	72
U.S.	3	12	48	37
Irish	6	22	45	26
Swedish	4	20	45	31
French	5	20	60	14
Balt	12	37	39	12
German	23	32	28	17
Jew	39	31	26	4
Italian	38	35	23	4
Russian	57	25	16	2
Chinese	26	42	23	8
Indian	45	39	14	2
Negro	68	23	9	0

ground." The level of acceptance was largely determined on the basis of: [4]

    a) similarity to the Australian way of life
    b) proximity to Great Britain
    c) share in English stock and history
    d) capacity to assimilate in Australia
    e) myth and legend about racial affinity.

Non-Europeans on the chart were perceived as a threat to Australia's development and unique cultural heritage. In most cases Australians argued that non-Europeans "do not fit in" or "are not like us." Many Australians regarded coloreds, because of their generally lower standard of living, as a threat to labor-employer relations. Oeser and Hammond claim this was partially explained by a working class "depression syndrome." Those whose social mobility was static or lower than their parents showed a higher than average hostility to non-Europeans.[5] In most cases hostility was a reflection of insecurity rather than a concern with the attributes of a migrant group. It was a function of self-interest operating as simple prejudice or as a "scapegoat reaction." Acceptance of migrants, according to the evidence, ultimately rests on their ability to serve the present interests of society without threatening entrenched labor positions.

The major exception in this race-nation classification was the Chinese migrant. In a poll conducted in 1948 by Oeser and Hammond respondents clearly favored Chinese to Italian migrants.[6]

Race/Nationality	Keep Them Out	Let In Only a Few	Allow Them to Come In	Try to Get Them to Come
Negro	77	13	7	3
Jew	58	25	13	4
Italian	45	34	17	4
Greek	32	42	18	8
German	30	34	22	14
Chinese	25	44	22	9
Irish	16	19	40	25
English	2	7	28	63

The exceptional position of the Chinese in the hierarchy of national groupings was attributed to the easy assimilation of the Melbourne Chinese community. In a separate questionnaire prepared in 1964, but following closely the voting list used in 1948, seemingly different results were obtained (see page 149).[7]

It would appear from this poll that attitudes to the Chinese changed markedly from 1948 to 1964. Arthur Huck, who accumulated the evidence, explains the change as a "softening" attitude toward Germans, Jews, Italians and Greeks rather than a drastic shift in attitudes toward Chinese. "This makes the relative position of the Chinese appear worse overall. . . ."[8] Since fifty per cent of the respondents were in favor of limited Chinese entry and seventeen per cent were positively favorable,

Race/Nationality	Keep Them Out	Let Only a Few In	Allow Them to Come In	Try to Get Them to Come
Negro	47	36	14	3
Chinese	33	50	15	2
Italian	23	31	38	8
Greek	18	37	38	7
Jew	17	29	45	9
German	5	19	46	30
Irish	4	13	51	32
English	2	6	37	54

only one in three voted for exclusion. In 1948 Oeser and Hammond found that one in four voted for Chinese exclusion.

In an Asian preference scale, ranked in "exclusion" order, Huck determined a clear preference for Indians and a clear non-preference for Indonesians.[9]

Race/Nationality	Percentage
Indians	2.79
Malays	3.17
Pakistanis	3.51
Filipinos	3.62
Chinese	4.34
Japanese	5.03
Indonesians	5.52

Although there can be manifold explanations for the results, Huck attributes them to a "recent political/military image." India with its good press and Commonwealth background is preferable to Indonesia, a state that confronted Australian troops in West New Guinea and Malaysia. The relatively low score for China is obscured by the apparent Australian willingness to accept Chinese from Hong Kong and Singapore and an unwillingness to accept those from Mainland China. Communism is clearly one crucial factor in this preference but the presumably "British tradition" of Hong Kong and Singapore is another overriding concern. An Australian predilection for English-speaking and British-oriented migrants applies to non-Europeans as well as Europeans. Huck concludes that the change in China's political posture from 1948 to 1964 partially affected the respondents' answers but it did not affect them significantly. Most Australians were not opposed to Chinese migration, a conclusion that was not substantially different from the one in the 1948 poll, even with the dramatic shift in historical perspective.[10]

The similarity between the 1948 and 1964 polls with regard to the acceptability of Chinese migrants is not duplicated by the Australian attitude to non-European migration in general. From 1943 to 1965, if the Australian Gallup Poll can be considered an accurate guide, Australians became increasingly tolerant of non-European migration. A considerable shift in public opinion occurred in this period. In 1943 almost one in every two respondents was categorically opposed to non-European migration, while in 1965 approximately one in every six was against non-European migration. The trend toward non-European acceptance was not even halted during the 1960–1961 recession, a fact that immigration reformers argued "is the clearest proof of how strongly the tide of opinion is flowing" (see page 151).[11]

In a February, 1967, Australian Gallup Poll Australians indicated they were inclined to accept an increase of non-European migration. At least six out of ten approved the 1966–1967 increase to an alleged 1,000 non-European migrants a year.[12]

Only three years earlier an Australian Gallup Poll revealed that though six out of ten Australians then favored "allowing some Asians with skills to come and live in Australia permanently," the actual intake they had in mind was very small (see page 151).[13]

There is also an indication that Australians have accepted the Opperman proposal which reduced the naturalization period

Australian Gallup Polls

Year	No Non-Europeans	Limited Entry	Unrestricted Entry	No Opinion
1943	51	40	—	9
1944	53	35	—	12
1948	57	35	4	4
1950	54	39	3	4
1954	61	31	—	8
1956	51	42	—	7
1957	55	36	—	9
1958	45	44	—	11
1959	34	55	—	11
1960	33	59	—	8
1961	32	57	—	11
1962	30	64	—	8
1963	34	58	—	6
1964	22	73	5	—
1965	16	71	6	7

Australian Gallup Poll 1963

Number of Acceptable Migrants	Percentage of Respondents
100	26
500	18
1,000	15
more than 1,000	7
no idea	34

for non-Europeans from fifteen to five years. The respondents were asked, "How many years should Asians live here before becoming eligible for citizenship?" [14] (See page 152 for results.)

The Australian Gallup Poll figures impressively indicate the direction of public opinion. But there is still a substantial minority of Australians devoutly interested in the preservation

Period for Naturalization	Percentage
1-4 years	2
5 years	63
6-10 years	7
15 years	8
no naturalization for Asians	6
no idea	14

of the "pure" White Australia policy. In a 1963 poll—the same year the Gallup Poll showed thirty-four per cent opposed to non-European migration—Alan Hughes, a research scholar at the Australian National University, conducted a survey of Melbourne voters and found forty-seven per cent of the respondents interested in retaining the policy without modification.

In the results of the Hughes poll there was no significant difference between those over and those under forty-five.[15] This result is contrary to the assumption young adults are for reform. It is also an apparent contradiction of the Gallup Poll series. In the 1964 Australian Gallup Poll of respondents aged 20-49, nineteen per cent were in favor of prohibition, seventy-three per cent for a limited number of non-Europeans, and six per cent for unrestricted non-European migration; whereas in the fifty and over group, twenty-eight per cent were in favor of prohibition, sixty-six per cent for a limited number, and three per cent for unrestricted entry.[16] These differences are significant. However, an N.U.A.U.S. (National Union of Australian University Students) Poll in 1964, does not bear out the substantial difference between the university student opinion on easing the policy restrictions and that of the general population as measured in the same year by the Gallup Poll.[17]

	Australian Gallup Poll	N.U.A.U.S.
Prohibit non-Europeans	22	13
Ease the policy or limited entry	73	69

But it is clear that fewer university students are in favor of a color bar than respondents from the whole society. When polls restrict their replies to only those aged 16 to 25, substantially younger than the total population in the Australian Gallup Poll, N.U.A.U.S. and Hughes surveys, there is a considerable difference in the results. In a survey conducted by Australian Sales Research Pty. Ltd., nearly eighty per cent of those aged 16 to 25 supported Asian migration to Australia.[18] If this random sample of 771 young Australians accurately portrays their age group attitude, pressure for a fundamental change in the immigration policy may be imminent.

Public opinion poll results have not changed dramatically since World War II but there has been a continual shift in the direction of liberalization. And this trend, if recent accounts can be projected into the future, should continue. Using public opinion as an argument for the retention of the immigration policy or as an indication that change will result in "political suicide," has become a specious argument, if the polls examined here have any statistical validity.

Consistent with public opinion polls, journals and popular magazines have also liberalized their views on the White Australia policy over the years. By the 1950's only a few popular Australian publications adamantly retained the view that "White Australia is still a must." For example, the *Truth* abused those "who would stand by and see this nation become streaked with black, brown and brindle . . . [the White Australia policy] is frankly racial because those who wisely laid it down meant it that way."[19] It did not rationalize the grounds for the policy by citing economic or political reasons. By its own admission the policy was an attempt to prevent "a country of mixed races such as southern United States."[20] In 1908 *The Bulletin,* one of the nation's most prestigious magazines, adopted the motto, "Australia for the White Man." As recently as 1960 it attacked university students and churchmen for their misguided values and in its editorials it often argued that Australia should not receive non-European migrants at all.

> It [*The Bulletin*] takes pride in the fact that it had some influence in getting that policy adopted nationally and accepted universally for well over half-a-century. It believes that the policy has been necessary for the well-being of Australia and that the mass of the Australian people of the present day are better off because of it.[21]

When the late Ezra Norton, an "Old Guard" defender of "White Australia" and controller of *The Bulletin* and the chain of *Truth* newspapers, left the industry, *The Bulletin* and several other newspapers confronted no major obstructionist who might impede a change in their editorial positions. Today, not one major newspaper or journal in Australia favors a rigid White Australia policy. Even the term "White Australia" has no currency in these journals. The Sydney *Mirror* formerly owned by the Norton chain has become an ardent supporter of immigration reform and has even defended the rights of non-European migrants whom some reformers were reluctant to champion, e.g., the Prasad family. In another dramatic change, *The Bulletin* dropped its old motto and some of its former loyalties. This change did not represent an immediate about-face, but it did indicate some chinks in a once solid editorial armor.

> To put it as a matter of expediency this is the kind of insult that Australia can no longer afford. We are a small Power living a secluded life by virtue of the American H-bomb. In our more cheeky days we were an even smaller Power living a secluded life by virtue of the Royal Navy, but almost everyone in a non-European skin at that time was being kept in some kind of order by someone in a European skin. Now the allies—who keep us safe from Communist danger—can perhaps continue to do so only if they can keep most of the people with non-European skins on our side.
> If, in the middle of this, we start flapping the colour of our

skins at everyone we become meddlesome, troublesome and downright absurd. Those of us who spend our time sprawling around on beaches are more than a little off-white anyway, lighter than most Africans, but darker than most Asians. Even in the winter we mostly range from pink to lighter brown. Surely we can stop this nonsense about skins.[22]

The Bulletin maintained there were still reasons for restricting non-European migration, not the least of which was the preservation of a "European culture," but its adherence to a purely "White Australia" was at an end.

This is not an atypical portrayal of Australian newspaper and periodical opinion. From conservative to radical there is the acceptance of some non-European migrants, albeit the number and the degree of flexibility vary. Most newspapers and journals are disenchanted with the present policy administration but in most cases, aside from general prescriptions for "relaxation," there have been few alternative suggestions. Since the concept of a quota system fell into disrepute in the early 1960's, newspaper opinion has relied on the immigration formulas of the Immigration Reform Group or has admonished against a policy that "reeks of naked racial discrimination" and interferes with Australian relations. The Adelaide *News,* for example, endorsed the recommendations of the I.R.G. and noted:

> Some degree of integration with Asia is inevitable in the long term. Unless Australia makes a sincere attempt to achieve this integration on its own terms and in its own way, it might come more violently.
> Can this nation remain forever a stronghold of the white race in a sphere where non-white races overwhelmingly predominate, meanwhile building hostility in the neighbours around us?
> The White Australia policy makes nonsense of all efforts on a diplomatic, cultural, and social level to win friends and customers for Australia in Asia. It is a pill too bitter for any Asian to swallow.[23]

The *Canberra Times* contended that several thousand non-Europeans passed through Australia's alleged barrier without major criticism and the admission of more Asians "would hardly be noticed." It accounted for the vocal opposition to a change as "a dispute about symbols." "For many Australians, 'White Australia,' together with bushrangers, diggers, mateship, jackeroos, shearing and Gallipoli, is an important component of the Australian national mystique."[24] The *Australian* argued that "intelligent opinion" and the demands of industry require a dismantling of restrictive immigration policy. "Industrious and inventive, skilled Japanese immigrants would be an asset to the development of Australia . . . and they need be no threat to the nation's main labor force."[25] In an article supposedly representing the editorial view of the *Catholic Worker* a request was made "not to let the Policy die by gradually liberalizing its application over a period. It should be openly repudiated and then the implementation of the new policy should be prudently gradual."[26] A "satisfactory" evolution of policy liberalization was recognized by the editors of *Round Table,* but they urged that this gradual solution should continue to be employed rather than one that attempts to immediately satisfy "the *amour propre* of Asian countries which have recently become independent and are jealous of their prestige," or "student sections of their populations, who will doubtless be sure they know all the solutions of all the problems."[27] The editors of *Crux,* the journal of the Australian Student Christian Movement, wrote:

> This country, which proclaims and expresses its independence, vigor and confidence in many fields, is not going to be damaged by controlled immigration from new sources. Rather, such immigration will enrich our national life (which is already beginning to welcome such contact as it already has with Asia through Asian students) and will take away from us an international stigma, and that defensiveness and discomfort which we rightly feel concerning our present relations with the world.[28]

One of the reasons for the publication of *Nation* was its editorial opposition to the White Australia policy. It expressed opposition "on grounds of national self expression and morality," but it emphasized above all the "enlightened self-interest" of Australians. "We . . . need Asian migrants to increase our understanding of neighbouring countries, and we need to promote their confidence in us" the editors argued. Racially isolated in the South Pacific, Australia is, willy-nilly, a representative of Western life, and in order to play the role effectively, the editors concluded, Australia has to acknowledge a "common humanity" with Asians.[29]

Writers, academics, and public men have agreed with the attempt "to bring Australia closer to her Asian neighbors," but there is dissension over the judiciousness of a modified immigration policy. Some believe it would not affect the condition of non-Europeans one iota, while it could cause insuperable racial problems for Australia. Others maintain that a strategy of good neighborliness could best be pursued through an aid program without an alteration in the migration policy. Still others contend that the term "White Australia" and its publicity and not the administration is what offends Asians. And lastly, a vocal group laments Australia's "inability to handle her own racial problem," e.g., Aborigines, and claims non-European migration would only exacerbate existing racial tensions. These spokesmen represent the defenders of the status quo. They are by no means united as a group; their only bond is the general objective of preserving the established policy, in some cases with slight modifications.

Sir John Latham argued that the Versailles and Asian Relations conferences held in 1919 and 1947 respectively accepted the resolution that each state has the right to control the composition of its own population "by means of restriction on immigration from any . . . other communities."[30] Non-Europeans realize, he noted, that the acceptance of a small number of migrants is not going to improve their economic condition. Nonetheless, these non-Europeans could vitiate the

European civilization Australians wish and are entitled to preserve. The desire to defend national standards is why Japan imposed restrictions on Chinese and Korean migrants. In view of the racial tensions around the world is not a policy of exclusion prudent? he asked. And, if "a man can have many friends without inviting them all to come into his home," why cannot this same principle be applied to Australia? Latham maintained that:

> Our policy is not based on color prejudice or racial superiority. . . . It is based on a recognition of real differences and a recognition of racial intolerance that may occur if the Policy was further relaxed.[31]

N. Bede Nairn, member of the history faculty at Australian National University, has defended exclusive immigration in much the same way as Sir John Latham. Australia wants its immigrants "to accept its basic values and it has a right to this," he notes. "When Australians defend this position they are not racialists and are not insulting colored peoples, they are merely seeking to retain those Christian and Western values associated with nationhood. To deny them this right is to deny them national values."[32]

Field Marshal Sir William Slim, a former Governor-General, believed immigration to Australia should be confined to white people. "If you dilute the population too much Australia can no longer be a bastion of Western civilization in the southern hemisphere."[33]

Some unionists, although they also reject the notion of racial discrimination, have argued that Asian migration, "unless carefully controlled," would inevitably lead to pockets of "black slavery." J. T. Lang, as the spokesman for this position, has maintained that the same forces responsible for "starving Chinese . . . chained to lathes and existing as bundles of skin and bone" could be unleashed again if the immigration policy were relaxed. The "slave masters" of another age would reappear and undo the efforts of union organizers who fought for higher wage standards. Legislators, acting in good but misguided faith, would soon be haunted by their altruistic attempt to appease Asian opinion.[34]

Sir Raphael Cilento, noted doctor, barrister, historian and commentator on most issues, agrees with unionists who endorse a restrictive policy. The policy, he contended, prevented "the whole land from sinking to the coolie level of living of their colored competitors. . . ." Furthermore, he added, Australians must be vigilant against "the mindless mob . . . , sentimental do-gooders, sensation hungry beatniks, bottle blondes (of both sexes) and the avant-garde eggheads" who would change policy and import the very evils now excluded.

> It [the immigration policy] resulted in a standard of living that is among the highest in the world and that has never been threatened—until now—by the rising tide of color that nearly submerged it. Australia's greatest danger is not from invasion by foreign arms, but from invasion by foreign germs which would be brought in by indiscriminate Asian migration.[35]

Mr. Ross Gollan, a columnist on the *Sydney Morning Herald,* beseeched Australians to be wary of the "sweet logic" of immigration reformers. Their contention is no different from the people who applauded appeasement after the Munich conference. He saw immigration reformers as contemporary appeasers of Asiatic criticism and felt that once appeasement is accepted it cannot be stopped; it only encourages further demands. "You cannot hold the pass that is vital to this country's survival by selling a part of it, even on a reversed instalment plan which over-hopefully predicates a very small deposit and no further real payments." [36]

Both Sir Alan Watt and Sir Wilfrid Kent Hughes, while urging a modest immigration reform, suggest other ways of assisting non-Europeans besides the promotion of a liberal migrant program. Sir Alan Watt cited with pride Australia's aid and technical assistance program in Asia which has mollified many objections to immigration laws.[37] Sir Wilfrid based his support for assistance programs and a strict migration policy on the "problems of assimilation" and "the social and economic consideration" of non-European migration.[38] W. D. Borrie, Professor of Demography at the Australian National University, noted that no territory in Australia has the resources to absorb "more than a minute fraction of the annual increase of Asiatic population." If Australia wants to do a service for Asians, he continues, it should "move resources to people not the reverse." [39]

Although Professor Borrie does not back the status quo, he has pointed out that "White Australia" can be defended in racial terms because Asian states have not dealt effectively with minority enclaves within their own countries. This argument has not lessened Asian distaste for the policy, however. Most non-European dissatisfaction with Australia's immigration laws stems from the belief that they are racially exclusive and imply racial superiority even if designed to prevent racial enclaves. Sir Frederick Eggleston insisted that the inability of Asians to differentiate a racial from a national policy is due to the publicity which has created a false impression. Publicity has done more damage to Australia's reputation than the policy itself.

> Australia always has been, and still is more lenient in her policy than the United States. The difference is that American action is taken as a matter of course by the people of that country and is not ventilated in the press, whereas, in Australia, criticism has a political basis and is made without a knowledge of the circumstances in each case, in ignorance of Australian policy and in ignorance of the policy of other countries.[40]

Sir Alan Watt, in an effort to assuage the offensiveness associated with the policy called for a change in its descriptive title, a "public burial" of the expression "White Australia," and said, "The very phrase 'White Australia,' though in no sense official, haunts the Australian diplomat in Asia trying to build up goodwill." He proposed two courses as a way toward the eventual disuse of the expression: 1) rejection of the expression by Commonwealth political party members and 2) "recommendation by leaders of those parties to all mass media of communication never to use the phrase in future." [41]

Prominent Australians seeking maintenance of the status quo probably fear racial unrest as it has developed in other multi-racial societies, such as Fiji, the United States, the United Kingdom, South Africa, Rhodesia and Kenya. Their fears are usually predicated on empirical evidence but they also contain strains of "cultural superiority," national insulation and a "fear of the next man's reaction to coloured migrants."

H. L. Harris, well-known academic, wrote on the national aspiration for homogeneity:

> We do not want anybody who looks, speaks or thinks very differently from ourselves. In fact, although we seldom admit it, we want people who are almost if not quite indistinguishable from ourselves or will rapidly become so. Those who are born here of Australian, British or European parents meet our original specifications quite satisfactorily. Those who are born in the British Isles, fairly well. Those who are born elsewhere in Northern and Western Europe or North America, acceptably, but not many others.[42]

Reg Coombe, stipendary magistrate from South Australia, founder and President of its Good Neighbour Council and member of the Immigration Advisory Committee, argued that racial tension was "the most poignant argument against rapid increase of non-Europeans in our population." After examining the conditions in the United States and South Africa and recent British immigration laws he concluded that "no sane Australian would risk a problem such as that if it can be avoided." [43]

Sir Alan Watt reiterated this point by saying: "I would not take any action which in my judgment might reproduce not merely situations which exist say in the United States and South Africa but even such situations as exist in places like Ceylon and Malaya." [44]

Strategy and objectives are problems for distinguished Australians supporting liberalization. No one of renown is clamoring for unrestricted non-European migration and very few still argue for quotas—although this was not the case in the 1950's—but there is disagreement over the number of migrants that can be accepted without concomitant problems and the reasons for their entry. Should Asians be admitted because Australians should encourage good relations for economic and strategic reasons? Should restriction, allegedly based on race, be eliminated because it is morally indefensible? If the policy damages Australia's image abroad should it be changed? Should military alliances dictate migration policies?

Professor Gordon Greenwood was an ardent supporter of a quota system in the forties and fifties and recently defended a more moderate immigration posture. In his opinion, inadequate information about the policy and, particularly, about Australia has created a false impression in Asian states. If Australians relax the policy, he contended, and explain the geographic limitations of the country there will be almost no valid objections.

> Every effort should be made to explain that any judgement of the potential population-carrying capacity of Australia that is based solely on the size of the country is certain to be erroneous. What is important is to stress the limitations imposed by physical conditions, to make known the conclusions of the geographers who believe that thirty million would be the optimum of population Australia could conceivably support. In the light of such information, the charges of a dog-in-the-manger attitude so frequently levelled against Australia lose much of their validity.[45]

Australia's place in international affairs and her stance on issues of vital concern to Asians have become major questions since World War II. After the war W. D. Borrie wrote, "Any population policy for Australia, whether it refers to fertility or immigration or to both, cannot be related only to the Western world." Technological developments have "forced Australians to the realization that they constitute primarily a Pacific nation and that every question of national policy must now be considered in relation to their near neighbours. . . ."[46] For this reason he now advocates a policy that will engender cooperation rather than ill-feeling.

The Marshalls, seizing on the issue of Australia's Asian reputation, recalled the effective way the Japanese used this affront of immigration exclusion during World War II. "It is probable, indeed most certain, that but for this insistence on the theory of 'white' superiority, Japan would have been far less successful in her 'co-prosperity' propaganda."[47] Professor Heinz Arndt, Professor of Economics in the Research School of Pacific Studies at the Australian National University, said nothing Australia does in assisting Asians can overcome "the tremendous amount of unnecessary damage . . . done to Australia's relationship with Asian countries because of the immigration policy."[48] Even union spokesmen such as Laurie Short (Federal Secretary of the Federated Ironworkers Association) and Dr. Lloyd Ross (Secretary of the N.S.W. branch of the Australian Railwaymen's Union), uniformly opposed to policy revisions in the past, maintain the policy should be administered so as not to give offense to Asians and instead actively encourage better relations with them.[49]

In her effort to avoid criticism, Australia has endorsed domestic sovereignty on many racial issues injuring, perhaps irreparably, her international reputation, wrote W. Macmahon Ball. If Australia is sincerely interested in "mending these fences," he contended, it should "make its policies on race a more faithful expression of the feelings and beliefs of the Australian people."[50]

Some distinguished Australian reformers believe that many Australians associate "national homogeneity" with race. Peter Samuel, correspondent for *The Bulletin* and ardent reformer, wrote, "As long as the White Australia policy exists we share the illusion that racial difference is important."[51] Many reformers argue this attitude is what should be eliminated. J. A. C. Mackie and Dr. K. Rivett contend that racial difference is an important aspect of immigration policy. They hold that "it is irrelevant that Asian governments have immigration laws similar to ours. Unlike the Australian [Asian governments] do not actively encourage immigration and, at the same time, exclude almost every would-be immigrant of different skin colour." [52] As long as Australia's immigration policy maintains a principle of racial homogeneity reformers will find it exceptionable.

Douglas Brass, columnist, has suggested that Australian military presence in Asia is the height of hypocrisy. While Australian diggers allegedly fight to defend the rights of Vietnamese, these same Vietnamese cannot, with rare exceptions, express this right by emigrating to Australia. It is about time, he noted, "the Government . . . acknowledge that if it is all right to fight alongside Asians it is all right to live alongside them." [53]

Recent attempts by the Department of Immigration to eliminate supposedly racial aspects of immigration policy have appeased many of the dissenters on this issue. But academics, writers and many public men still harbor an antagonism to immigration policy easily elicited by one miscalculation, one *cause célèbre* or one government slight. Feeling runs high; it is not very far from the surface in the best of times.

"Man in the street" opinion, while it cannot be gauged accurately through random samples, does indicate some prevalent moods even if their intensity is unknown. One characteristic Australian response to the issue of White Australia is the reliance on the nation's culture and history. Racialism, in this sense, is a manifestation of cultural and national pride. In the last century a desire to retain Anglo-Saxon purity was related to a "White Australia" prejudice; but the continuation of this belief has been fomented by the nation's homogeneity, isolation, idealization of its "unique way of life," and proximity to Asia's poverty-stricken millions.

One segment of Australian opinion is the "oil and water do not mix" theorists who probably represent a small portion of the general public. In the Australian context, however, the difference between racialism and nationalism is often obscure. Many policy supporters who claim "Asians will destroy our national ideals" often couch racial antipathy in more acceptable terms.

The average person who expresses an opinion on immigration policy or takes the time to submit a letter to his local newspaper usually feels strongly about the issue. His emotional response sometimes reveals intense deep-seated hostility, or even prejudice, which often prevents him from a rational examination of the arguments surrounding the matter. For example, a Queenslander, offended by the "increasing" Asian migration to Australia, did not conceal his blunt racial feelings toward non-Europeans.

> The white race may not be the best to belong to, but I like it. We may not be the smartest, but I would bend over backwards to preserve it.
>
> If man has the right to breed his stock, a Clydesdale with a Clydesdale, a Jersey with a Jersey, why then should the white parents be classed as bigots by insisting on the preservation of the white race?
>
> Even now the inroad of intermarriage is beginning in Australia, the ever increasing numbers of marriages between Asians and white Australian girls is apparent by the number of mixed couples seen on the streets of Sydney.
>
> The increase in the number of Asians in Australia is also alarmingly dangerous.
>
> The challenge is survival: survival of the white Australian race.[54]

Another letter argued that social relations between whites and non-Europeans is "not natural."

> One has only to look at the birds and animals in the bush, there is not one lot that inter-mixes with the other, it is not natural yet we have crackpots in this country who want us to breed up half-castes, three-quarter castes ... and what have you.[55]

The fear of miscegenation between Europeans and Asians is widespread in Australia. One worried Australian wrote "his mates" about South America as a place where "the evils of miscegenation" are visibly apparent:

> There [South America] the people are a mixture of Negro, Indian (Asiatic), and European. They are also the most unstable, irrational, cruel, and altogether uncivilized people in the Western half of the world. Would you have Australia "diversified" to the standard of Bolivia?, of Columbia? As individuals, the South Americains [sic] can be very nice people. But as a mob, they are a trifle inhuman.[56]

Some Australians recognize racial prejudice as a consequence of a strong feeling of national identity. Because, they maintain, "the Australian character has not changed," realism demands the continuation of a restrictive immigration policy. Australians, according to this argument, will accept only those "people who are related . . . ethnically, and who share a common culture, the same Christian ideals and have much the same history."[57] "How," asked a self-described dinkum Aussie, "can we ever be sure that Asians will fit into the Australian Way of Life—i.e., that they will understand and accept the fundamental importance of beer, sex and footy?"[58]

Concern for national identity is often extended to "if you let in a few they will swamp us" (thin edge of the wedge). One Canberra resident suggested that Marshal Ky's visit to Australia in 1967 presaged the end of restrictive migration. He claimed that Mr. Ky was "the forerunner of others who will come later, each with his own claims upon Australian hospitality. . . ."

> The admission of a few thousand migrants from South Vietnam (the first of whom would probably be young refugees) would be followed logically by equal quotas from the Philippines, Japan, South Korea, Formosa, etc.
> By natural increase, our new migrants would within one generation pose formidable problems.

> With the increasing popularity of the pill among our own people, and the natural increase of people who are noted for their prolific reproduction, we will have conferred upon our children forced acceptance of minority status.[59]

A Broome pearling master explained the same view much more succinctly: "Give them [Asian migrants] an inch and they would take a mile. They would infiltrate right throughout the country. There would be no stopping them once they were here." [60]

More pragmatic Australians claim a restrictive policy prevents racial tension. "It stops the problems at the outset, rather than getting them in and then you have got the problems and then you will never get rid of them." [61] Another protagonist of this position wrote:

> To open the migration gates and to subject Australians to the shocking racial disturbances that regularly make the headlines from other parts of the world would be the greatest act of folly, and those responsible for it would warrant the condemnation they would surely receive.[62]

Racial tension around the globe has had a profound effect on Australian opinion. Many Australians are frankly afraid of thrusting their children into a racial confrontation in the schools or of facing antagonism from a racial enclave. Faced by the possibility of these occurrences one academic wrote: "one wonders if even selected immigration of very intelligent and able people with different racial backgrounds is desirable." [63] Rigid policy advocates argue that the exclusion of colored people has avoided the racial disputes which seem to occur with regularity in many civilized Western nations. As a nation devoid of racial strife, wrote one university student, "Australia should not allow itself to be deluded that its immigration policy is in any way the concern of other nations, or that it is a question of morals when in fact it is not." [64] A fearful parent argued that ghettos in a multiracial community and the corresponding friction attendant on their appearance are inevitable.

> Is it not natural that immigrants, either European or Asian would congregate together where they speak the same language and have some common interests.
> Should you go to live in, say, India, would you not look for British people who spoke your language to live amongst? With any material number, colonies are inevitable.
> Can you name one white country with any appreciable number of Asian population [sic] where there has not been friction and riots? [65]

Another argument employed by seemingly altruistic, yet at times misleading, Australians is based on encouraging international goodwill. Migration of talented and professional Asians—"the very people most needed for their own nations' development"—will lose Asian friendship from the nations who need these people at home. "Should we rob the non-European world?" asked a staunch supporter of strict immigration laws. He continued:

> I cannot see how, as Christians, we can possible [sic] do this. I cannot quote figures, but: I do know that the ratio of Doctors to heads of population in almost all non-European lands is only a fraction of the ratio that stands in European countries. The same applies to all professions and trades. To take even such a low percentage as 1% of, say, Indonesia's Doctors or train drivers, clerks or Agricultural scientists, is to hold back that countries [sic] progress.[66]

Perhaps the largest and most widely represented group of status quo defenders is composed of laborers worried about cheap labor and farmers careful to point out Australia has little fertile soil. One farmer said:

> Despite its size, the Australian continent is in many areas uninhabitable, and the highly populated coast strip is already rapidly reaching saturation point. We may well say, "populate the interior . . . develop the north," etc., but so far neither the Federal or the State Governments have offered any encouragement to do so. . . .

To throw open their gates to illiterate masses is a different proposition. The resultant economic effect could be disastrous and we would be struggling to stay on our own feet let alone support unfortunate people unable to help themselves.[67]

Another partisan asked: "do we choose our immigrants from the illiterate, land-hungry masses when Australia has a shortage of good agricultural land, and trained farmers who cannot find farms?" [68]

Intolerance is not isolated in Australia; and intransigence is not uncharacteristic of Australians. "I sometimes despair," said Dr. Darling, Chairman of the Australian Broadcasting Commission, "of a supposedly educated democracy which seems so much to dislike hearing any criticism of itself." [69] Yet despite the traditions associated with the White Australia policy and the emotional attachment with which some people regard it, many Australians have become highly critical of its "inflexibility, immorality and out-of-date principles."

> Our leaders do not seem to realize that a new climate of opinion is arising throughout Australia, the article of faith has been taken off the shelf and dusted down, and is now coming under scrutiny. There is more than a trace of hypocrisy and self-righteousness in our attitude to what is happening in, say, South Africa and the United States, if we are not prepared ourselves to accept and work for a true multi-racial society in Australia.[70]

According to reformers, conservatives consider the policy a "sacred cow" leading them to misinterpretations of racial incidents abroad. Some contend, noted an immigration reformer, that the "second-class citizenship" of American Negroes "should serve as a lesson to us to keep colored races out of Australia and thereby avoid racial problems." But this view overlooks "the tremendous improvement in their [Negro] status within American society in a relatively short time." [71] A colored minority is not necessarily confined to an inferior position if the Government actively combats discrimination and creatively plans for migrant absorption. Riots in Watts, Detroit and Notting Hill make headlines in Australia, but the underlying reasons for these racial outbursts are often ignored, reformers argue. In their view riots in a multi-racial community are not inevitable.

> The time-worn arguments about uncontrolled migration, depressed living standards, minority communities and racial conflict simply do not apply to the policy being urged by the Immigration Reform Groups who aim at a controlled, planned and non-discriminatory policy.
> Firstly, we must recognize that all areas of the world where racial discord exists are areas where there is marked economic exploitation by one race against another, and in all of these cases this exploitation has its origins in the expropriation of territory by one of the races, uncontrolled immigration from depressed areas or deliberate importation of cheap labor under the slave or indenture systems.[72]

"There is no danger of social strife arising from an Australian multi-racial immigration policy if we adopt . . . control."[73] Control over numbers and research into the problems of migrant absorption are concomitants of a more liberal immigration proposal. "If a policy was implemented which welcomed from among the other nations of Asia a proportion of new settlers capable of economic and social integration into the Australian community, such fears [of racial tension] would prove as unreal as those which were once voiced about European immigrants."[74] A student defended this position: "there were no racial riots at Sydney University mainly because we are equal to the Asians. This means that arguments based on analogies with South Africa and Notting Hill are of doubtful validity."[75]

Some of those opposed to established policy find it morally reprehensible and scientifically fraudulent. As long as race is a criterion of acceptability, note reformers, the immigration policy will be held up for international scorn. "Must all people entering Australia possess a skin of a certain light color?"[76] "Most

Asians," said another reformer, "now regard Australians as having racial superiority complexes." [77] The reformers seem convinced Australia is harmed from within by implicitly condoning the idea that people of different races can never live together harmoniously and Australia's foreign relations must suffer because the policy is plainly offensive to Asian states. They stress the value of Asian migration for Australia's development: "An influx of newcomers certainly would change some aspects of Australian living, but I think the benefits would far outweigh the disadvantages." [78] Migration to the United States serves as an illustration of the positive effect of diverse races and cultures on a national character.

> The United States did not adopt a selective policy when that country was first opened to Japanese migrants and recognized that an unskilled, hardworking Japanese was, in all respects, a desirable future citizen. Senators, scientists, judges, engineers, artists, business executives—all proud descendants of those original truck farmers on the West Coast and in Hawaii—provide living proof that a free society does not demand you continue to hoe the family cabbage patch just because that was all your grandpa could find to do.[79]

More pragmatic reformers contend that with Australia's growing financial and trade interests in Asia the immigration policy is an obstacle to economic self-interest.

> there has got to be a drastic reversal in the policy as far as White Australia is concerned because our markets are in the Asian and South East Asian areas . . . we have to look to South East Asia for future trade (with the implication of the Common Market), and I think that we have got to establish more friendly relationships with these people, and we cannot do it if we continue with the policy as it is at present.[80]

This same point was put another, more urgent, way by a reformer who claims "that the policy creates ill-feeling among Asians and Africans . . . at a time when this country may be forced to seek new markets in Asia and Africa because of the effects of the Common Market, maintenance of the policy may seriously imperil our future." [81] A sixteen-year-old bank clerk supports reform because: "Asian workers are needed if Australia is to expand her industries to compete with overseas trade." "We need more migrants to populate the country"; "with the falling birthrate in Australia we badly need more migrants"; and "it [Asian migration] will help to open the undeveloped parts of the country" illustrate other reasons for reform.[82]

An academic, critical of restricted migration laws, argued that exclusion accentuates racialism. In his view Australian self-interest is served by liberalization. "The racialism," he wrote, "of insular people is a brute fact."

> The real question is whether one should attempt to overcome racial barriers in a shrinking world or to preserve, by force if need be, comfortable breeding cages for human sub-species unable to withstand fair competition in a crowded world.[83]

Many Australians who profess unreserved endorsement of a rigid policy are, in fact, unwitting immigration reformers who would be willing to make "exceptions" or willing to vouchsafe an "honorary Caucasian status" to certain non-Europeans that are "like us." At a recent discussion conducted by a university researcher the following conversation transpired: [84]

> Mr. P.:
> Well I would think that we should preserve White Australia policy. . . . That is not to say that there are some, perhaps some Asians-Asiatics—that would—would not perhaps be permissible. From my view, I think that if we need to build up the country population quickly we may have to accept a sort of a quota of perhaps Asians, but they are not really coloured in the sense that I was thinking about: I mean they are and they are not.
> Chairman:
> In what way are they not?

Mr. P.:
> Well I mean I am thinking the—that dark coloured people are—present problems, but there is less trouble with—even where intermarriage occurs with say, Malaysians and people like that.

Chairman:
> How about Malaysian Indians? When you say dark people are you thinking of Africans?

Mr. P.:
> Well I was thinking about negroes, of course.

Whatever side he takes the Australian citizen's opinion is often zealously maintained. Since the national character is so integrally bound up with immigration policy, and patriotism for some is an expression of support for "White Australia," there are times when an immigration issue will elicit an undue emotional reaction usually uncharacteristic of Australian opinion. One relatively recent incident illustrates this point well.

A visiting Professor of History from Yale University, Robin W. Winks, remarked in a 1963 public interview he "would like to see 50,000 Negroes in Melbourne." This transplantation, he maintained, with all its possible difficulties, would contribute to Australia's cultural future, a future that "will depend to a large extent on a satisfactory mingling of races." Furthermore, he contended that "with all the difficulties we have encountered in the United States because of our mixture of races, I believe it has also been one of our greatest assets in speeding our cultural and political development and in providing a constant stimulus to our national vitality." [85] Almost as soon as these statements reached the front page of most major dailies, a public outcry erupted.

Minister for Immigration Downer described the statements as "foolish, short-sighted and productive of social problems and internal strife." He said, "no Australian Immigration Minister could do a worse disservice to his country than to consider seriously the suggested settlement of 50,000 Negroes here." [86] A

Sydney Morning Herald editorial cynically criticized "so brash a visitor as Professor Winks," who was so "seemingly naive" about Australian culture.[87] In response to Professor Winks' comments and other criticisms of Australia made by an American visitor, one woman, with xenophobic ardor, wrote "that the criticism of Australia was infantile, presumptuous, condescending, insulting, absolute rubbish." She concluded, "it all adds up to this: We're quite happy with what we've got."[88] An Australian, vacationing in England, was so distraught with Winks' statement he sent a letter directly to the professor expressing his anger:

> what do you mean we should admit ten thousand Negroes into Australia each year. [*sic*] We are proud that our country is British and it is a White Man's Country, we don't want any niggers here. We have seen what has happened to our Mother Country England, where they have allowed hundreds of thousands of niggers into the country, now in a few years time, there will be millions of them, it will be like Haarlem [*sic*] in America, a black Man's paradise. If you want to get rid of some of them, send them to Africa.[89]

Still another angry Australian wrote to Winks: "Amazement over your effrontery is only equalled by the fact that an ill-informed dolt like you should hold a professorship. If you know such a bloody lot why not go back to U.S.A. and show your elders how to handle the Negro situation. . . ."[90] A poetic reaction came too:

> But perhaps he'd been dreaming in
> forty-odd winks,
> When wisdom's asleep and the baser
> man thinks.
> Asleep was all knowledge of racial
> suppression
> Practised by whites 'fore and since
> the Depression—
> Two and half centuries of grovelling
> slavery,

> Imbibing choice facets of Yankeeland
> knavery,
> Then a century free in a so-called
> democracy
> Which Black Muslims label just white
> man's hypocrisy.
> Treatment of Abos by us rather stinks
> But fifty thou. negroes! Wake up,
> dreamer Winks.[91]

In a student survey conducted in response to Winks' suggestion one professor at Adelaide University rather critically remarked: "I regard this [Winks' remark] either as an irresponsible remark or a deliberate one indicating a complete lack of human compassion." [92]

While the larger segment of public opinion seemed to regard Winks' comments as indiscreet at best, and "bloody" insulting at worst, there were individuals who welcomed the implied criticism of Australia's cultural homogeneity. A reformer noted: "the substance of his remarks merits our serious consideration. It is not only for the sake of 'cultural vitality,' but for many other reasons also, that Australians should now be taking an earnest look at the policy. . . ." [93] A sympathetic listener wrote: "I agree that its solution [the racial question] and more especially the tribulations on the way, will enrich the country in a way we can't comprehend." [94] A clergyman concurred with this opinion: "I am sure your words could do us good if only we have the grace to hear and heed them." [95] And an expatriot academic thought of the comments as "delightfully provocative." Furthermore, he suggested,

> you could not have said it in a more appropriate city than stuffy, patrician Adelaide. I have now been absent from Australia for two years and I am frankly staggered to hear the average Australian speak of their ethnic groups as if they were sheep or worse. I would like to think that this is due, in large

part, to narrowness of mind born of isolation rather than bloody mindedness.[96]

What was completely ignored both by those censuring and those supporting Winks, was the context in which his controversial statements were made. As a student of Commonwealth affairs Professor Winks had discussed Australia's immigration policy in Malaysia and Singapore and was informed by numerous nationals in both states of the policy's presumed effrontery. This Asian view of Australia's immigration policy accounted for, at least, some of his opinions. On the hypothetical matter of "50,000 Negroes in Melbourne," Professor Winks was trying to illustrate with a "dramatic example" that Australian cultural life would benefit as a result of ethnic heterogeneity. He was not, in fact, suggesting the importation of 50,000 Negroes or, for that matter, only Negroes; he was merely noting that any culturally diverse group, probably Asian, and especially if injected at an earlier date could have added cultural vitality to the nation. However, as he noted, the public was misled by his "metaphorical usage," and a statement which was designed primarily to provoke an examination of government policy opened a Pandora's box of emotional disputes.[97]

That the public, newspapers, and the Minister for Immigration should become so concerned about one remark (Winks described it as "a direct answer to a direct question") casually made by a temporary visitor, regardless of his academic credentials, attests to both the tenacity and anxiety connected to immigration policy. Professor Winks pointed out, "I boggle at the thought of Attorney General Robert Kennedy feeling sensitive enough to personally chastise every visitor to the United States who passes derogatory remarks on our racial policies. . . ."[98] It is apparent that in the Australian setting it is unlikely that an examination of immigration policy can be conducted without simultaneously seeking a form of national catharsis on the issue. It seems equally apparent that feelings on immigration have the potential to run high, even though there are rarely instances that lead to their public expression.

Despite what seems to have been an extreme reaction to the Winks incident, protagonists and antagonists of policy revision do not have widely divergent opinions. Neither side is for "a rigid color bar" or "unrestricted non-European migration." Both groups want controls; the only matter of crucial difference is the degree of control. Reformers argue in favor of more Asian migrants, while the status quo satisfies others. Since the present number is quickly approaching the desired short-term goal of immigration reformers, the supposed issue between the groups concerning immediate policy may be, or may soon be, non-existent.

Because there are only nuances between the pro and con, the results of polls, e.g., Gallup, measuring the percentage of public opinion on Asian entry are highly suspect. Asian entry is no longer a relevant question. The large preponderance of Gallup respondents, seventy-eight per cent in 1964 and seventy-seven per cent in 1965, favor some non-European migration. The question is how much? Even this question is subject to further refinement. In 1967, fifty-seven per cent of the Gallup respondents were in favor of more than 500 permanent Asian residents annually, twenty per cent had no idea, and eighteen per cent said admit none.[99] Of those that favored permanent Asian residents almost eighty per cent were for between 500 and 1,000 of them. With such general agreement indicated, the categories cease to have significant meaning. Both advocates and adversaries of immigration reform are probably included in the eighty per cent figure. The response to the same question with more narrowly defined categories of Asian entry and by a population apprised of non-Europeans already granted permanent residence annually, would probably reflect more accurately the distribution of opinion and the extent of immigration reform zeal in Australia.

Immigration policy statements seem to be obscured by respondents' impressions of what they believe their opponents are proposing. Many reformers seem convinced that most defenders of a status quo wish to invoke a rigid color bar. This kind of analysis presents fewer dilemmas for the less sophisticated reformer who is better prepared to argue with someone he believes to be a racist than with a proponent of controlled migration. In much the same way policy defenders often label reformers as "irresponsible rabble that will 'open the door' to any migrant." There is almost no evidence to support this view, but it persists as an extreme fear of over-exuberant and misguided liberalization. In both cases a mythical opponent has been fabricated to reassure some members of both groups of their purposes, but that obscures the real question—the objective policy-makers should adopt in regard to non-European migrants.

In short, it appears that public opinion polls on the immigration issue and many of the statements associated with the policy are unreliable. Occasional secretive administration of immigration policy has contributed to an information gap. Lacking information public opinion has to rely predominantly on emotional shibboleths such as "national welfare," "humanitarian spirit" and other value-loaded phrases. An uninformed public, including prominent Australians, has conducted a discussion of an issue essential to the nation's future by exchanging what have at times been ignorant opinions and by relying on historical or humanitarian explanations which are anachronistic when applied to the contemporary Australian context. The elimination of the information gap on the matter of immigration is definitely in order if public opinion on immigration is to have any validity.

7

World Opinion of the "White Australia" Policy

For several years protagonists and antagonists of the White Australia policy have used "Asian opinion" in defense of their own positions. Government officials, with few exceptions, assume there is very little antagonism. Former Minister for Immigration Opperman stated "no resentment in Asia [exists] towards Australia's immigration policy." [1] Mr. Stewart (M.P., Lang) said: "I have travelled in several Asian countries within the last couple of years and in not one have I found the degree of hostility to our established immigration policy that a lot of people would have us believe exists." [2] But policy opponents suggest "Non-whites throughout the world regard the whole notion of a 'White Australia' as deeply insulting." [3] These contradictory statements are probably a reflection of individual experiences and as such are not incompatible. But if immigration policy is to be sensitive to Asian opinion, policy-makers must accurately gauge its direction.

The influence of recent trade and strategic considerations make Australian officials much more aware of Asian attitudes, a hitherto unknown and relatively unconsidered variable in the determination of policy.

K. G. Tregonning, formerly Raffles Professor of History at the University of Malaya and a supporter of immigration reform, has indicated that Asians see Australia's immigration policy as becoming more tolerant. Expulsion of Chinese from Indonesia and racial barriers in Malaysia and Singapore have made it increasingly difficult for Asian countries to criticize Australian policy, he claims.

> Many political leaders, faced with the problems of a plural society and a multi-racial community, now find it difficult to dispute the right of another country to decide who shall settle inside its territory; many, no doubt, envy Australia its homogeneous stock, and its lack of a "Chinese Problem." On all these counts the Australian immigration policy has come to be generally accepted, even though the almost total exclusion of Asians remains for many a bitter pill to swallow.[4]

Despite Tregonning's assurances many experts agree that the policy is offensive to many Asians. One oriental observer has described the policy as an example of racial discrimination at government level.[5] For him the policy is an indication of Australia's complacency and lack of concern for Asian nations. "If Australia were concerned about the plight of Asians she would realize the value in admitting even one Asian if it thereby saved him from a life of degrading poverty."[6]

This observer is undoubtedly unaware of those Asians admitted to Australia for permanent residence. However, this is not unusual since Australia's immigration policy has been widely abused in influential Asian groups, despite the fact that very few Asians are aware of the number of non-Europeans allowed admission and offered naturalization, or of the entry requirements. Apathy is not entirely the reason for ignorance of Australia's migrant schemes; it is partially a concomitant of Australia's historic insularity and indifference to Asian affairs. Only after World War II did Australia—for a variety of reasons—become concerned with Asian opinion. A shift in immigration policy and greater concern for Asian opinion has pushed policy-makers to issue a clear and inoffensive statement of policy for Asian distribution.

This raises several complex problems. Should Australian policy-makers be concerned with official Asian government views, unofficial diplomatic exchanges, views of the press or public opinion surveys, when one or a number of these differ? Even when opinions concur, how can Australia's policy-makers judge whether the consensus is an actual reflection of opinion or obscured by ideological, national or international considerations? The government of a nation concerned with asserting its independence, for example, might be more vocal in its opposition to the migration policy than a government which, though equally opposed, depends on Australian trade and military assistance. Because it is difficult to determine which segment is the most accurate reflection of public opinion it is more important for Australia to deal effectively with its opposition than complacently accept its supporters.

Malaysia is one nation that has cautiously avoided governmental condemnation of Australia's immigration laws. In fact statements of Tunku Abdul Rahman are often employed by policy defenders as an indication of Asian views. Mr. Luchetti (M.P., Macquarie) said:

> the Tunku Abdul Rahman, a realist and a real friend of Australia, has declared his faith and belief in it [Australia's immigration policy] because he knows that it is firmly based, that it is not racial, that it is not petty and that it is not offensive. He knows that it is based on the security and well-being of the people in this land. Just as we in this country have supported that one central policy, we ought to continue with decency.[7]

If the Tunku's endorsement is a reflection of problems arising from his own pluralist society none of those using the Prime Minister's statements for their own defense choose to mention it. Many Malays feel that the large Chinese and Indian population constitutes a threat to their political dominance. This has led to friction and separate ethnic enclaves. In such an environment there is little wonder that several distinguished Malays have expressed envy of Australia's policies.

> The great wisdom and foresight of the White Australia policy are unquestionable.
>
> I do not see any sense in people particularly Asians criticising the immigration policy of Australia as long as they do not see things from the Australian angle and point of view. It is true that there are vast areas of uninhabited land which can accommodate foreign settlers but then with increasing scientific and technological advances in industry and agriculture these areas can be exploited for the benefit of the Australian nation.
>
> What many people clamouring for colored immigration do not realize is that Australia has through the Colombo Plan and other institutions brought benefit to many Asian countries, and thousands of individuals particularly in the educational and technical fields of learning. Many millions of Australian pounds have been and are being spent altruistically for the benefit of non-Australians.
>
> The White Australia Policy is the finest stroke of Australian statesmanship.[8]

Obviously not all Malays share the same opinion. Complaints against Calwell's "brutal and high-handed" deportation of Malayan seamen in 1947 were widespread.[9] Resentment has also been directed against Australia because her immigration policy is seemingly an expression of a white European sense of superiority. Malayan Chinese, due in part to the racial tensions in their homeland, are unquestionably opposed to the "White Australia bar." So too are many Malayan Eurasians who think of themselves as European and are eager to migrate. The influential English language *Malay Mail*, representing a segment of opinion critical of the policy, asked somewhat rhetorically: "How can Australia win friends and influence Asians when it continues with this discrimination against Asians?" Furthermore it noted:

> Keeping out immigrants on economic ground is understood and appreciated by Asians.
> But Australia should not practice one policy for one people and another for another people.
> Opening its doors to Italian, Greek, Hungarian and other white immigrants, and keeping out Commonwealth citizens of Asian origin is puzzling.[10]

Editorials in the *Malay Mail* have on occasion argued that Australia's "rationalization" for its immigration policy is the presumed inability of Asians to adapt themselves to "Australia's way of life." But the hypocrisy of this position, it has been maintained, is made obvious by the adaptability of 6,000 Malaysian students temporarily resident in Australia.

It would be wrong to assume that the underlying bitterness in these newspaper accounts is representative of Malaysian opinion, but it would be equally wrong to assume that Tunku Abdul Rahman's moderation is a reflection of public opinion. On the whole "White Australia" is not a major issue principally because Malaysians are grateful for Australia's aid in opposing Communist infiltration and providing support during the Indonesian confrontation. Since the country's political future depends on the protection of Western powers against potential Chinese Communist encroachments, it is in no position to chastize the policies of an ally.[11] Because most of the population is ignorant about migration and solicitous about its own racial tensions, Australia's immigration policy is not likely to provoke public anger. When Malaysians do think about "White Australia," which is not too often, or do react to an occasional unfavorable newspaper account, their sensibilities can be aroused. But it is already noticeable that this reaction is confined almost exclusively to the more educated Malaysians, whose sensitivity to the policy implications increases with exposure to Australians.

In an attempt to uncover knowledge and attitudes about Australia's policy among the better educated young people of Malaysia, Gavin and Margaret Jones, Australians who studied at the University of Malaya on an Australian government scholarship, conducted a questionnaire using high school seniors and graduate students as respondents.[12] Widespread knowledge of Australia's restrictive policy was made clear by 84.9 per cent of the high school seniors and 92.1 per cent of the graduate students who were aware that a few hundred Asians or less were allowed into the country annually. About two-thirds of the seniors associated the terms "white" or "color bar" with the policy, as did over 85.0 per cent of the graduate students. And an overwhelming majority of all students thought the policy unfair and in need of change.

A most important finding showed that graduate students were generally more opposed to the policy than were the sixth formers, and additionally, graduate students who had studied in Australia were even more opposed than their Malaysian university counterparts. The high school students were somewhat naive in their views of Australia as a "fertile country" capable of solving Asia's population problems, and for the most part, they were unaware of Australia's efforts to recruit European migrants. Interestingly, whereas 52.3 per cent of the seniors thought the policy should be changed for economic reasons and 19.0 per cent because the current policy discriminated along racial lines, only 10.6 per cent of the graduate students gave economic factors and 39.4 per cent cited racial discrimination as the basis for change.

For a variety of reasons (not all of which are clear) Malaysian students are strongly opposed to an immigration policy which seems to discriminate on racial grounds. Since the students interviewed represent the highly educated segment of Malaysian society, their future influence should not be underestimated.

The widespread knowledge of the term "White Australia Policy" almost certainly contributes to the belief that the policy is based on colour prejudice, and despite official government disclaimers of this in Australia, it is idle to expect that the term will lose its currency in Malaysia unless the administration of the policy is considerably modified.[13]

Even though they are probably better informed than the majority of Malaysians, the Indonesian population does not seem to be resentful of Australia's immigration laws. Tension can be generated in Indonesia by "half-hearted" efforts to win friendly feelings through the Colombo Plan or by Australian "sabre rattling" on the West New Guinea boundary line, but not over immigration policy. Most Indonesians, unlike Indians or Chinese, never wanted to migrate to Australia and are unlikely to change now. For the farmers of Indonesia arid Australia has few of the opportunities of their own lush fertile soil and if migration is considered, the transmigration program of their own land—albeit inadequate in scope—is considered first.[14]

Racism is not the issue in Indonesia that it is in Malaysia. This was probably true even in the days when it was the Dutch East Indies. Indonesians, therefore, regard Australia's "white" immigration policy as a relatively insignificant issue. In some quarters the policy might arouse indignation if it were described as a vestige of European colonialism. But this is the exception rather than the rule. Even when an Indonesian, Mrs. O'Keefe, was directly involved in a major controversy with former Minister for Immigration Calwell, Indonesian officials, with few exceptions, had little to say on the matter. The Indonesian Government has generally viewed Australia's policy with detachment and, in accordance with the Asian Relations Conference at New Delhi in 1947, recognizes the right of every country to determine its own demographic composition.

Indonesian attitudes toward White Australia may be characteristic of general Asian opinion. But the Philippines is an example of one nation that has taken active retaliatory measures against the abuses in Australia's immigration policy. After the Sergeant Gamboa case (see Chapter 1) the Philippine Government decided to freeze Australian passports. On April 7, 1949, the Philippines House of Representatives unanimously passed a bill prohibiting the admission of aliens whose countries categorically excluded Filipinos. A surprise adjournment of Congress "killed this legislation" and a ruling which would have terminated further appropriations for the Philippines' Sydney Consulate.[15] But the fact that the bills were passed unanimously indicated the fervor of Filipino opinion and the forces arrayed against Australia's immigration policy. Filipino newspaper editorials were uniformly opposed to the Gamboa decision as this excerpt from the *Evening Chronicle* indicates:

> If the Australians are being sadistic in the case of Sergeant Gamboa, we cannot entirely blame them. It is the natural sadism that springs from their penal origins. Had they acted otherwise, they would be untrue to the classic tradition of beachcombers newly arisen from the gutter.[16]

The widely read *Manila Times* was equally vindictive in its denunciation of Australia's laws.

> This is no longer a question of citizenship or race or anything but common decency—a quality in which the Australian immigration policy or its current interpretation seems somewhat deficient. The Philippines Government must consider a policy of exclusion so vigorously affirmed and so violently enforced if a proposal for a regional pact is proposed. Must the Philippines agree to stand guard around an iron curtain, Canberra style?[17]

In the United Nations Filipino representatives criticized Australian action and at one stage proposed a resolution which would bind all members to a "system of reciprocal immigration laws" as a means of combating "violations of the charter."[18] Filipino opinion was also reflected in Australian newspapers. A letter from an indignant Manila resident noted that Hitler's "non-Aryan policy is little different from Calwell's 'White Australia' policy." [19] The Gamboa case very quickly became a news story in almost every nation of the globe. And in very few was the Australian action treated sympathetically. Symptomatic of the widespread international support for the Philippines during this period was Mr. Malik, Soviet delegate to the U.N., who compared the trials of Hungary's Cardinal Mindszenty and the Protestant clergy in Bulgaria with Australia's policies.

> Suppose that, tomorrow, the question arose here of Australia's treatment of her aborigines, or of her discrimination against Asiatic peoples, or the White Australia Policy generally, what would be the attitude of the Australian Government? Would the Australian Government consent to listen if it was slandered in a similar manner to the Hungarian Government? [20]

When the Liberal Party replaced the A.L.P. as majority party and Calwell was deposed as Minister for Immigration, Holt, his successor, allowed Gamboa to enter Australia for permanent residence. The scars caused by the incident were not healed by this gesture, but relations between the Philippines and Australia did improve. There was still suspicion in the Philippines Government that the alleged liberalization of the 1950's and early 1960's was "a fraud." But as long as the policy did not exclude Filipino migrants unjustly there were no recriminations against it.

This verbal armistice did not last long. When Aurelio Locsin, a university-educated Filipino, was barred from permanent residence in 1965, the old wounds were opened (see Chapter 1). Sensational stories circulated in the Philippines press and anger against Australia in some sectors of the population was unrestrained. According to one report a Phillipines government official punched an Australian businessman at a party in Malacanag Palace, home of the country's president, because, he claimed, "the Australian cast aspersions on Filipino women." [21] Another Phillipines government official threatened to file expulsion proceedings against the wife of an Australian diplomat who allegedly made insulting remarks about Filipinos. And the Philippines Foreign Secretary, Mr. N. Ramos, said of Australia's policy:

> Officially our view is that Australia should review its immigration policy in accordance with the U.N. declaration of human rights.
> Otherwise we cannot have the fullest cooperation on trade matters.[22]

Maximo Soliven, the fiery Filipino journalist who is the most vociferous of Australia's critics, said:

> I will keep hammering away at Australia until it changes its policy and admits Asians. I can see little difference between South Africa's and Rhodesia's policies and Canberra's White Australia policy, which is a form of anticipatory apartheid.[23]

The Locsin incident was mainly responsible for Soliven's refusal to accept Australia as an "Asian power" at the Manila Conference of 1966.

> How can Australia be a leader in bridging many Asian difficulties when she cannot even bridge her most important difficulty with Asians—that of getting along with them?
> We welcome Australia as a friend to this "Asian peace summit"—whatever that ambitious term implies—but we wish that she would first strive to make peace with her neighbours before moralising about a "peace effort" in Vietnam.[24]

The majority leader in the Philippines House of Representatives and a delegate to the Inter-Parliamentary Conference, Mr. Justiniano Mantano, equated Australia's immigration laws with medieval practices and South Africa's apartheid policy. Filipinos were not interested in migrating to Australia, he noted, but they resented discriminatory immigration policies.[25]

The most distressing aspects of the Locsin case involved Philippines suggestions for "a black ban on Australian-made goods," a denunciation of Australia's reputedly racial policies at the United Nations and a color bar on Australian migrants. One of these suggestions was publicly acclaimed when the Philippines pushed an anti-racial discrimination resolution through the U.N. Commission on Human Rights. Mr. Lopez said his delegation adopted this measure "against the background of growing criticism and resentment in the Philippines against the so-called 'White Australia' policy." [26] Australian public relations were severely handicapped because there was no press attaché at its Manila post and little publicity about aid distribution through the Colombo Plan and SEATO. This explained, in some measure, why Filipinos were so bitterly critical of immigration policy. Soliven and his colleagues were read by hundreds of thousands of Filipinos, yet Australia did very little to counter criticism. Even well-educated and affluent Filipinos assumed Australia's policy was a complete color bar. When a handsome aristocratic Filipino matron asked an Australian columnist: "Do you think I'm white enough to come to your country?" she portrayed the sarcasm and damaged pride felt by many Filipinos. "Your Government seems to think we're all coolies," [27] a Manila surgeon noted to the same Australian reporter. Interestingly, it may not be Australia's apparent prejudices against colored races to which Filipinos object, but rather to the fact that *they* are included among the darker races. Their legend of Creation Day is testimony of this attitude.

> God began to make man in the shape of clay pots. . . . He baked the first batch too lightly, and they came out white. So he threw them away. The second batch he kept too long in the oven. They went black. The third time the pots came out brown, and man was created beautiful.[28]

From the leading agronomist to the peasant in the field there are feelings of resentment to Australia's "racial policies." Most responsible leaders express concern over any extreme action which might cut off the Philippines' only source of fresh meat, impair lucrative future trade and interfere with strategic defense arrangements. They have for these reasons remained publicly uncommitted. When questioned, President Marcos, for example, has refused to comment on Australia's immigration laws. But he has noted: "I see the need for better contact, better communications and better understanding between Australia and the Philippines." [29] Former President Diosdado Macapagal said the average Filipino thinks he is inferior to no man. "With this outlook we believe the White Australia Policy does not exist." [30] It is his contention that regional nations should break down obstacles toward goodwill. Australia, he has argued, has a growing realization of the need to woo her Asian neighbors and therefore to avoid discrimination.

The seeds of resentment have been sown in the Philippines as in no other Asian nation. It is possible that future anti-Communist defense arrangements including Australian-Philippines ties may bring the two states closer. But it will be extremely difficult to undo the impression created by Gamboa and Locsin, and to ease the resentment built up through years of discriminatory practices.

Although many Australians still harbor a residue of anti-Japanese war sentiment, Australian courage and magnanimity during the war left a favorable impression on many Japanese. Kempei Shiba, editor of *Asahi,* said he "found the Australians to be the most even-tempered people on earth, and the most undemonstrative, except when the horses come down the stretch. . . ." His personal contacts led him to the conclusion that Australians are "the kindest, friendliest, most helpful and hospitable people you could hope to meet." [31] School children in Japan, most of whom have not had Mr. Shiba's personal associations with Australians, learn about the phrase "White Australia policy" quite early in their compulsory study of Australia. Despite some rather frequent early bitterness, the average Japanese grows up regarding the policy as Australia's own business. Mr. Shiba probably characterized most of Japanese opinion when he said:

Australians got where they are the hard way. They built their country up by rolling up their own sleeves rather than taking it easy importing cheap Oriental labor. The time may come when they will change their minds about this labor, especially skilled varieties. So far as Japan is concerned, it will be too late. The difference in wage rates between Japan and Australia is no greater, all things considered, than the difference between Australia and America. Japan has turned the corner from a have-not to a have nation. Its birth-rate has dropped by 50 per cent in thirteen years, from one of the world's highest to one of the world's lowest. Japan's need to send emigrants is far, far less than Australia's need to accept them.[32]

Japanese businessmen, however, may have different opinions. Dr. Shigeo Horie, an immigration advisor to the Prime Minister, President of the Bank of Tokyo and executive director of Japan's Federation of Employers' Association, said Australia's immigration policy is "unpleasant and a reflection on Japan's national pride and prestige." If the goal of Australia's program is assimilation, he argued, the Japanese should be considered desirable migrants because they "assimilated easily, took advantage of educational and citizenship facilities and often married with the local people." [33] He also stressed their adaptability and avoidance of national enclaves outside of Japan.

For these reasons many Japanese cannot understand why Australia's laws restrict non-Europeans. Western culture is deeply ingrained in the Japanese civilization: sport cars, transistor radios, telephones, computers, rock-n-roll music and other manifestations of the occidental world circulate on a parity with most Western states, including Australia. There were sixteen million television sets in Japan's twenty million homes in 1964. If the exclusionist laws were truly based on economic grounds, argue many Japanese, Australia would have to consider Maltese, Greeks, Italians, Spaniards—in fact all the races of southern Europe with a lower standard of living than the Japanese—a greater threat to Australian trade union standards than the average Japanese worker.[34] In addition, the Japanese have a surplus of skilled technicians desperately needed in Australian industries. Yet Australia accepts unskilled immigrants from Southern Europe while Japanese are excluded. No matter how Australians explain their priorities these facts appear to some Japanese as blatant illustrations of racialism.

Increased export trade and investment in Australia have to some extent been responsible for recent liberalization since it is imperative, in some cases, that Japanese investors, merchants and technicians be domiciled in Australia. But it is still not easy for the Japanese to get there. One Japanese observer sees a need for the Australian to feel more secure about himself and his country.

> Once you get inside the Australian he's o.k., but it is hard work. Why is this occidental so inscrutable? I think it is because he is only emerging internationally. Up to the war Australia was virtually in the position of Japan under the Shogunate—a hermit kingdom. Suddenly exposed to the world, the Australian is a little on the defense. Gradually he will gain confidence, get rid of his inferiority complex and be philosophical about criticisms.[35]

Even though most Japanese are not concerned with Australia's policies, the business segment of the population, engaged in bilateral trade and investment, finds immigration legislation an interference; and an affluent westernized segment of the population, interested in travel, sometimes finds "White Australia" an affront to its dignity. With a standard of living quickly approaching Australia's, most Japanese are not interested in migrating and often maintain a relatively neutral attitude toward Australia's immigration policies. But as long as there are influential Japanese who find Australia's policies offensive, significantly closer ties between the states may be impaired. If closer ties remain a goal, the dissident part of Japanese public opinion will have to be convinced that Australia is willing to accept Japanese migrants on the same or a similar basis as Europeans.

India's Government is outspoken in its opposition to Australia's immigration policies. Even before obtaining independence in 1947, Indians were very sensitive on questions relating to color. If the Indian Government has acquiesced in the "White Australia" policy at all, it has done so, argues one editorial, "in the hope that the large number of Indians already there would receive better treatment." [36] Former Indian High Commissioner General Cariappa said Australian immigration policy is:

> driving 440 million from India and Pakistan away from the British Commonwealth and into the arms of Communism. You have a welfare state, yet 1,000 million people throughout the world cannot get a square meal a day. I have seen vast expanses of fertile country and great wealth of every description, but I have also seen your lack of people to develop this country. Australians have told me: "But General, it is only a matter of time until the White Australia policy is eased." My experience is that this is not so.[37]

Many Indians, in spite of overpopulation and poor economic conditions (perhaps because of them),[38] do not show any keenness to go abroad and settle in foreign countries. Because they are not directly concerned with migrating, they cannot object too strenuously to laws not affecting them, but they can and do object to the policy on moral grounds. Differentiation of people on the basis of skin color is what generally causes resentment. And this resentment, albeit limited in scope, has been considered a disruptive force in India's regional relations and harmonious Commonwealth ties.[39] Professor G. Greenwood wrote:

> there is little room for doubt that the policy itself has been a tremendous obstacle to the creation of goodwill between Australia and India. That this is so can be demonstrated despite assurances from Pakistan, Ceylon and India that wholesale migration is no solution to their problems and that Australia's migration restriction policy is her own affair.[40]

The *Eastern Economist,* representing an Indian intellectual group, is militantly opposed to Australia's immigration policy. It has argued that the evanescence of colonialism and Australia's apparent desire to contract herself into Asia have radically altered Asian opinion. The journal sees Asian association and an exclusive White Australia policy as incompatible.

> The wisdom of a revision of Asian restrictions was urged because although "the Australian people are still isolationist born and bred," twentieth century isolation for Australia is impossible because of the increasing strength of Communism in the East. That realization in government circles has come in part already but government circles do not yet see the White Australia policy as a bar to South-East Asian cooperation.[41]

One Indian writer claims that Australia's entry into Asia which is predicated on an understanding of racial harmony between states, is impossible as long as her immigration policy is a "war" on that potential agreement. He claims that with the popular demand for change of policy and Australia's reliance on Asia, "it is certain that in time South East Asia will call it into question." [42]

Some Indians philosophically accept Australia's policy because they feel it is "doomed by the workings of history." However, more pragmatic politicians such as Mr. Seth Govind Das argue: "in view of our [Indian] relations with the Commonwealth countries, our population should be allowed to move to those places in the Commonwealth where more and more population is needed." [43] The reference is obviously directed at Australia. Australian officials have attempted to answer this criticism by citing the racial tension in multi-racial communities and the impossibility of alleviating India's population problems by allowing several thousand or even a million migrants into Australia. Nehru, possibly for diplomatic reasons, supported Australia's stand on the matter:

it would be completely wrong and improper for us to say that because Australia or other countries happened to be sparsely populated we could raise this question and try to send our people there. It would be improper from a variety of ways and it is raising a hornet's nest without achieving anything in the near future.[44]

He believed the only way modification could make a significant difference was "to think in terms of millions, scores of millions" [45] of migrants—a suggestion, he realized, that could not be taken seriously by Australian officials.

That "scores of millions" would have to emigrate from India in order to alleviate her overcrowded conditions sufficiently is palpably clear to most Indians, but "White Australia" is still resented by many on racial grounds. Few Indians are specifically aware of administrative flexibility, but that does not stop some from claiming the policy is predicated solely on racial discrimination. Undoubtedly the phrase used to describe the policy has something to do with that. "White Australia" is legion in India's educated circles. At a news desk in India an Australian correspondent put up the heading "Floods in W. Australia"—referring to Western Australia. Glimpsing this on the galley a while later the chief sub, a Madrassi, said, "We do not use that abbreviation here. You will have to write it in full: Floods in White Australia." [46]

Dr. M. K. Vagholkar, lecturer in Mathematics at the University of New South Wales, was first introduced to Australia's immigration policy at the age of nine or ten, when most educated Indian children first learn that Australia is and plans to remain "white." An Indian geography textbook states: "Australia is inhabited by white people, and colored people are strictly forbidden to enter." [47] Dr. Vagholkar describes the policy as "very insulting to me as an Asian and as an Indian. . . . Not only that," he adds, "but if I were an Australian, it would be insulting to me." He finds the Australian claim that there is no racial prejudice in the country hypocritical. How can there be no racial prejudice, and at the same time support for "the retention of the White Australia Policy on the ground that the assimilation of non-Europeans is difficult"? He says Australians "still really think the white race is superior" and associate the black or colored man with underdeveloped countries.[48] He believes if the barriers to limited Asian migration are reduced, the difficulties of assimilation can be overcome by the younger generation and Australia can develop herself distinctively, instead of being a "secondhand British model." [49]

Antagonistic reaction to "White Australia" is sometimes based on mistaken impressions. For example, many Indians assume that Australia's color bar is completely rigid; a Nancy Prasad incident (see Chapter 9) is likely to reinforce this Indian impression. But very few Indians are aware of the relatively large number of nationals accepted for permanent residence who have successfully assimilated into the Australian community since 1957. The lack of publicity about such matters and the notoriety accorded certain deportation cases, contributes to much of the Indian misunderstanding of Australia's immigration policy.

In general, most of the people of South East Asia, with the singular exception of the Filipinos, do not know about the White Australia policy. Businessmen and others wanting to travel are very much aware of it, because they have experienced difficulty obtaining Australian visas. But most entrepreneurs can be pacified by favorable financial arrangements. More idealistic Asian students find Australia's restrictive policy very hard to understand and even more difficult to rationalize on purely economic grounds.[50]

There are, however, in every Asian country and stratum of society, some people who, if they do not wholly support the policy, can, at least, either understand or excuse it. A Chinese Australian who has resided in Hong Kong and several other Asian cities sees Australia's immigration policy as less irksome to intellectuals and skilled workers than the discriminatory employment practices in South East Asia favoring European employees with higher wages, allocations for travel and better treatment. "This attitude," he suggests, "causes more ill-feeling in Asia than the White Australia policy." [51] A Thai newspaperman said, "I have found that such an immigration law is necessary if the high standard of living is to be maintained." [52] But at the same time he noted that Thai people hold the policy against Australia. Educated South East Asians who understand or can interpret the immigration policy do not, however, represent a majority view in their respective states and are not often in a position to influence public opinion.

African opinion, while it is extremely antagonistic to the alleged principles in Australia's policy, is far less militant than Asian opinion. This is primarily a function of geographic distance, underpopulation in many areas of the continent, unfamiliarity with Australia's immigration provisions and, in some countries, racial policies that categorically exclude whites, browns and Asians.

With the evolution of independent African states and the development of an increasingly important role for Africa in the United Nations, there has been a growing consciousness of "discriminatory policies" around the globe. On several occasions Australia has been censured at the United Nations by African states for its immigration and territorial policies. African states have also taken notice of Australia's endorsement of apartheid prior to 1962 and South Africa's approbation of Australia's immigration policy. Although it was gratuitously offered, the Australian Government found South African approval a great embarrassment. Australian officials have gone to great lengths to illustrate the differences between apartheid and their own immigration policy, but on several occasions South Africans resident in Australia have congratulated their hosts on the manner in which they have handled racial problems,[53] often neutralizing the effect of government explanations.

Olabisi Ajala, a Nigerian writer on a world tour, said: "Because of the so-called 'White Australia' policy about which

I had heard so many disturbing comments . . . I had originally planned to make my visit to Australia a very short and casual one." When he arrived in Australia his impression was dispelled by what he described as Australian "acceptance and hospitality." [54] However, few Africans have an opportunity to visit Australia and their impressions remain the essence of their opinions. In some areas of black Africa it is therefore not surprising to hear Australia referred to as "the South Africa of Asia." Mr. Ajala said, "In my view the Australian Government is making very little or no effort to enlighten the Asians and Africans about its tolerant policy based on equality." [55] Ajala does not take into account that the reputation of "White Australia" would make that kind of publicity seem a sham. Likewise, the "outcast and untouchable" status of Aboriginals—"the shame and misery of Australia"—is well known by many Africans. The late Tom Mboya, Kenya's Minister of Justice, said Australia has the reputation in Africa of "a land of white people with an immigration policy based on 'White Australia' " and a domestic policy that systematically denies the Aboriginal equal rights and treatment in his own land. He added:

> Australia must face the fact that the White Australia policy is out of date and unrealistic. It conveys not only a bad image, but even a wrong impression of the country and its people.
> Every country has a right to protect the economic interests of its citizens and to rid itself of undesirable immigrants, but it is wrong to think that the whites are always desirable and the non-whites always undesirable.
> We in Africa have strong feelings on this matter because we are determined to create racial harmony and to restrain our people from victimizing those who only a few months ago were our colonial masters, and some of whom were responsible for discrimination against us.
> The White Australia policy does not help us in this very important and human effort.[56]

Non-whites in the Western Hemisphere are also agitated by Australia's immigration policy. When Jamaicans compare the United Kingdom's easy entry policies (until 1963) with Australia's "rigid color bar" they often conclude Australia is a land of "bigots in the Commonwealth." The very respected *West Indian Economist* printed several articles that attempted to expose "Australian racialism." In one, an Australian correspondent quoted Robert Menzies' belief that "The policy is actually based primarily on broad considerations of race—not of racial superiority which is an absurd and ignorant notion, but of assimilability of race," and Calwell's assertion that:

> The only claim ever made or implied in our policy is that there are different varieties of the human species distinguished from one another not by skin pigmentation but by languages, religions, standards of living, cultures and historical backgrounds, and that it is wise to avoid internecine strife, and the problems of miscegenation which such differences have caused in all countries throughout history where races of irreconcilable characteristics have lived in the same community.[57]

Not many West Indians read these statements, but for those that did the importance of race as a criterion of acceptability was quite apparent. It was also inferred that the assimilation argument was a "red herring," designed to perpetuate in Australia Kipling's fatuous dictum "that East is East and West is West and never the twain shall meet." [58]

For many West Indians, Jamaica and Grenada belie the argument that race riots are an inevitable accompaniment of multi-racialism. Felicitous multi-racial communities have convinced many that racial conflict can best be interpreted as a result of racial prejudice. Australian preoccupation with racial tension is in fact a consequence of prejudice, this line of argument concludes. Many West Indians might have understood a factor such as geographic isolation contributing to Australia's immigration policy, but they find this anachronistic and contrary to their own experiences.

Australian immigration policy classifies American Negroes as any other non-whites. Era Bell Thompson, a Negro journalist who visited Australia, said, "the Negro is likely to remain officially unwelcome in Australia for many years." She quoted a Queensland politician who argued, "Why bring U.S. Negroes here when we cannot assimilate our own colored people?" [59] Few American Negroes have been in a position or had the inclination to migrate. The Negro, as is the case with most Americans, knows little about the land Down-Under. When he does learn about it, one of the first things he usually hears is that Australia has a "racially" restrictive policy, and for him the news is bad.[60]

Internal racial problems and the better-known Rhodesian and South African policies evoke more of the American Negro's bitterness than "White Australia," about which so little is known. Nonetheless, the rare case of a Negro whose entry application is rejected causes some hostility. When the actress Leslie Uggams married Australian Graham Pratt the question of non-European admission was revived. Miss Uggams had no intention of seeking permanent residence in Australia, but many American Negroes were given the impression that even if she had applied for residence her request would have been denied.

News of Australia's policy has also been widely circulated in the United States when several segregationists, in an effort to avoid federally "imposed" integration, migrated to Australia. Selma segregationist Wiley Fancher interpreted "Australia's preference for white immigrants to mean racist attitudes." [61] To many Americans Australia is a country that enjoys all the advantages of American standards without being plagued by peculiar American problems. One Australian cotton official announced that the American southerners "have come here mainly to get away from the Negro problem. They do not say it, but that is the bloody truth. . . ." One resident, an American expatriate living in Australia, had on his car number plate a comical Confederate soldier lunging forward beside the inscription: "Hell, no, I ain't fergettin." He commented to a reporter, "Do not put down a lot about our prejudices. The north and the south and so on. We got 'em all right—but leave 'em." [62] Recently an American school teacher decided to migrate to Australia because, he said, "I disagree with forced integration" in schools.[63] When former Minister for Immigration Opperman was asked if his department investigates the racial views of prospective migrants, he replied: "I would not imagine that personal views such as those . . . would be canvassed." [64]

Since migrants are not asked questions relating to race it is impossible to estimate how many of the 50,000 American inquiries to the Department of Immigration in 1965 came from American racists or how many Americans already resident in Australia have racist views. But from random opinions expressed by Americans in Australia the number of racists is not inconsiderable. This impression of American migrants and the harsh criticism in major American publications contributes to the reactionary image many Americans have of Australia's immigration policy. A *Time* magazine reporter wrote that Australia "clings to some of the world's most restrictive immigration laws, [and] has traditionally discriminated against Asian and other non-white immigrants in order to preserve what Immigration Minister Alexander Downer has described as 'an Anglo-European community embodying all that is best of the Old World and the New.'" He called the policy "immigration apartheid." [65]

Even opinion in Australia's traditional allies, New Zealand and Great Britain, does not always respond favorably to Australia's immigration policies. In the late 1940's the New Zealand Government and a large part of the population protested that Maori were excluded as "non-Europeans" under Australia's immigration policy. To avoid any unnecessary embarrassment the Department of Immigration hastily withdrew their exclusion.

This occurred in spite of New Zealand's less publicized but still very restrictive "White New Zealand" policy.

The United Kingdom's criticism of the policy is often more severe. Before World War II the British, through Commonwealth defense arrangements, protected Australia's prerogative to the White Australia policy. Since the war, however, several British governments have viewed the policy as an embarrassment to the Commonwealth, only slightly less than apartheid. Because Australia no longer relies on its protection or influence, the United Kingdom has no power to exert any pressure whatsoever for a policy change. But one should not underestimate British dissatisfaction with what is considered at the very least an "anachronistic law." A considerable portion of public opinion, despite a number of Britishers who favor "White Australia" because of their own disenchantment with West Indian immigration, is probably against Australia's immigration policy—presuming it to be a total color bar. The *Guardian* described the White Australia policy as "the notable defect in the Australian immigration program."[66] It did not propose a migrant scheme that would give equal status to non-Europeans ("Nothing would be more likely to produce the tensions now existing in South Africa"), but it did suggest a more liberal application of the immigration policy. Likewise, *The Times* of London, although probably not an accurate indicator of public attitudes, gave its endorsement to the Student Action Movement's demand for a more liberal administration of immigration policy during the 1961 election campaign (see Chapter 5).

Since the Commonwealth has been fragmented by the controversies in South Africa and Rhodesia, it is unlikely that the British Government will accelerate the Commonwealth's inevitable demise by publicly criticizing an immigration policy less objectionable than social policies pursued elsewhere. But British liberal opinion has been notably critical of Australia's laws and many Members of the House of Commons have serious reservations about their administration.

Australia's immigration policy is not inflaming the minds of Asians or even liberal whites. It is not causing men to lift up arms in retribution or causing nations to unite in censuring Australia's legislation. Immigration, even if one concludes that Australia's law is based primarily on racial factors, is not a cause of open hostilities. But it is a factor in foreign affairs and it is one thing most foreigners know about the land Down-Under. Most non-Europeans do not have the economic viability to migrate or the education necessary to have a world view. But this condition is only temporary; economic advancement, however stalled it may be, will one day eliminate insularity. The forces that protect White Australia are in flux or disappearing entirely.

Most of the government officials canvassed in this chapter have refrained from overtly condemning Australia's immigration policy because they do not want to impair diplomatic relations or because they are concerned lest their remarks be construed as having domestic relevance. Those who have denied the implicit insult in Australia's immigration policy have very often betrayed their sense of rejection and bolstered Asian pride, by indicating that fellow-countrymen would not, in any case, consider migrating there. Investors and businessmen who think of the policy as a nuisance do not want to rupture financial ties. However, young, idealistic intellectuals in most of the emerging states of Asia and Africa are much less tolerant of Australia's position and more willing to break diplomatic relations over the issue. Race in the sensitive minds of the "new radicals" and the future leaders is a factor that could upset the status quo of international relations. In spite of government attempts at liberalization between 1956 and 1966 many, indeed most, of the younger, highly educated generation are conscious of a racially generated White Australia policy. Very few are aware of the policy's manifold provisions, exceptions to general rules and efforts to liberalize it, but this too can be considered an indictment of the Government's inability to present a credible case for its stand on immigration and a lack of concern for Asian opinion.

In many states sensitive about racial questions one egregious blunder can be the beginning of a national impression. The negative publicity in the Philippines that stemmed from the Gamboa and Locsin incidents testifies to this. In one South East Asian capital a diplomat having dinner with the country's leader was trying to explain Australia's immigration policy to his very critical host. Toward the end of the dinner the wife of one Asian representative turned to the Australian diplomat's wife and said: "Well, now we are both of us part of the Asian family. . . ." The diplomat's wife replied indignantly, "I will have you know we are British. We belong to a much superior race." [67] Despite the immediate apologies almost every newspaper in this Asian state carried the story. Needless to say it did not enhance Australia's image abroad.

Asians and Africans also resent explanations employed to justify the policy. The Japanese resent the economic argument when many of them live on a standard comparable to Australia's. The late Tom Mboya, the venerated Kenyan politician, asked, if the policy is based on economic rather than racial grounds "why should not Asian and other colored people be considered on the same economic basis as Europeans?" And if race is a criterion of assimilability, who is to be included as "white" and who colored? Standards of assimilability are also regarded with disdain by many non-Europeans who cannot understand why an Asian professional man is less assimilable than a European peasant. To many Asians these "hypocritical standards" demonstrate a sense of white superiority.

Most of the embittered critics of Australia's immigration policy will probably not go to Australia. But with egalitarianism a driving force of the age these critics will not relent in their attacks until Australia's immigration policy treats all men on relatively similar standards. An Australian's friendliness predisposes him to being a good neighbor, but the immigration policy and the widespread impression of it predisposes many Asians, Africans and "liberally-minded" whites to aloofness, rejection and hostility.

8

Foreign Affairs and Immigration Policy

Events in the twentieth century have demonstrated that immigration policy is linked to foreign relations. Even though it is not a *casus belli*, Australia's policy has characteristics, particularly racist connotations, that can cause international disequilibrium. It is also a potentially inflammatory factor that can interfere with a whole range of relations between states, including strategic defense decisions, trade, diplomacy and international agreements.

Soon after the White Australia policy became federal legislation it interfered with Australian-Asian relations. When the Japanese flexed their military muscle before and during World War I Australian diplomats responded by firmly endorsing White Australia. After Versailles Sir John Latham said "The principle of White Australia is almost a religion in Australia. . . . Any surrender of the policy is inconceivable." [1] After World War I a fear persisted that the Japanese would attempt to win a diplomatic victory they could not achieve with weapons. At Versailles the Japanese asked for a "racial equality" amendment in the

League Covenant. But this was rejected by Prime Minister Hughes as an infringement of Australia's domestic sovereignty and its right to determine its demographic composition.[2] Lord Casey, later the Governor-General, expressed the nation's abiding concern when he wrote: "Fear existed that taking tariff and immigration issues out of domestic arenas might ultimately threaten Australia's restrictive immigration policy, 'the heart of our being.' "[3]

"Yellow Hordes" and the "Yellow Peril" expressed the Australian fear of imminent Asian invasion, and in addition a possible threat to security from the non-white minority group within the country. It was argued that this minority could exert diplomatic pressure on the Australian Government or provoke tensions that would weaken the national security. "Populate or Perish" as an early national slogan was a consequence of this potential threat. In order to convince Asians that settlement was not feasible and the land was extensively utilized, Australia needed a much larger population, predominantly British and homogeneously white. This was considered the most effective way of preserving the national security.

Australian foreign policy maintained its isolation and the immigration policy its exclusiveness until World War II events shattered these assumptions and questioned a "White Australia" principle. The bombing of Darwin and the fires of Singapore were indications of Australia's vulnerability, decline of British strength and the beginning of dissolution in the Empire. In addition Asian anti-colonialism was assertive and sensitively conscious of racial separateness. Australia was faced with the task of adjusting its foreign and immigration policies to the postwar period or jeopardizing its security and economic viability. Adjustment was no simple task. Old formulas could not solve new problems, and to most experts in foreign affairs it was palpably clear that separation could not be maintained by physical barriers. A *modus vivendi* with Asia had to be found and protection had to be provided against the assumed Asian penchant for Communism. One aspect of this inchoate policy was developing "good neighborliness" with Asian states and the other was a collective security arrangement based on American strength and directed at a possible Asian Communist force. This strategy was much easier to create than to implement. The United States could provide the security, but the alliance with Americans and the escalation of military preparedness put increasing strains on Australia's alleged rapprochement with Asia. Reconciling the competing tendencies of peace and militarism was difficult. Asians suspected Australia's motives and "the neo-colonial ambitions" of the United States. Australia's association with Great Britain and the United States and its own Caucasian population caused distrust in every Asian area sensitive to the intrusions of nineteenth-century white colonialism. Some Asian states also assumed Western opposition to indigenous left-wing political movements was a reflection of neo-colonial predilections. When Australians associated their fear of the "Yellow Peril" with the Communist menace, many Asians assumed it was an effort to constrain political factions unacceptable to Western interests. This probably was not inherent in the policy itself, but Australia's historic restriction of Asian migrants and fear of Communist aggression made her appear notably unsympathetic to some Asian political movements.

Internal political ideologies of the left and right offered different solutions to Asian policy problems. The left was willing to compromise the security aspects if the "good neighbor" policy was encouraged; the right was more inclined to sacrifice good-neighborliness if it could solidify its collective security pacts. But on one issue there was a fundamental agreement: immigration policy had to be liberalized or at least purged of its racial stigma so that it did not curtail Asian faith in Australia's friendliness and interfere with military pacts that could unite the free people of Asia and Australia against the Communist threat.[4] It was quite clear that the White Australia policy hampered relations with

Asian countries. As Professor Tregonning contended, "This racial policy is repugnant to Asians and stands as a very strong barrier to Australian acceptance in Asia." [5]

But the Government failed to consider the population's emotional tie with the White Australia policy and resistance to change. It was not until 1959 that the Gallup poll indicated a majority of Australians were in favor of allowing even a small number of Asians into the country. This opposition to reform was referred to by the former Minister for Immigration Downer when he said:

> I do not believe that Australians, certainly not at this stage of their development, either desire or are ready for, an East-West potpourri. Indeed, on the basis of other nations' experience and from my knowledge of the temperament of our own people, there is a strong possibility that an inflow of Asians would defeat the very object of our foreign policy toward our Asian friends. Instead of relieving misunderstanding it would provoke tensions. It would create internal social problems which fortunately we have hitherto escaped. These in time would engender animosities which would ripple sensationally throughout every country from Arabia to Japan.[6]

Faced with this internal resistance and the alleged foreign policy requisites the Government chose to: liberalize the immigration policy moderately while it retained a rhetorical approval of the traditional principles; convince the populace of the need to change attitudes to Asia, i.e., "bridges to Asia"; explain in Asia the rationale for the policy and attempts to eliminate racial stipulations; and stress diplomatically the value of closer relations between the two continents. This strategy, reputedly for cooperation and closer ties, was designed, at least in part, to prevent threats to Australia's domestic sovereignty. Mass media and politicians perpetuated the notion that Australia was an "Asian state," but the cultural orientation of the nation remained distinctively British and Western. And even if one suggested that the British tie was weakening there was little evidence of Australia as an Asian state. Mr. Downer once again put it well when he noted:

> Today it is fashionable to say that Australia is part of Asia. Geographically, millions of years ago the two continents may have been joined, but there the nexus ends. Our population, with the exception of a fractional percentage is European. Our social origins are European, our religion and ideas are European. In a more particular sense, of course, this is still a British country with many of the virtues and faults of our northern ancestors. One of the merits of the infusion of three-quarters of a million settlers from the European Continent, as distinct from the United Kingdom, in the last fourteen years, is the possible eradication of some of our inherited, and locally acquired, defects which we exhibit in good measure. But those who would classify Australia with Asia confuse a state of being with an object of policy.[7]

Australia in the postwar years was thus faced with what amounted to a serious public relations problem: how to project an image of friendliness and mutual concern to countries whose citizens were not acceptable as permanent residents. The Government developed a series of programs ostensibly to dissociate Australia from the racial overtones of immigration policy without making any substantial changes in the policy itself. After 1950 attempts were made at regional cooperation in order to demonstrate Australia's goodwill. Participation in the Colombo Plan, ECAFE, ASPAC, Regional Banking Programs and other regional organizations attested to Australia's Asian interest. But in spite of these gestures, Australia's position as a white, prosperous, westernized society with an exclusive immigration policy made its preoccupation with "closer relations" appear transparently self-conscious.

The Government, to avoid offending its Asian neighbors, has often been put in the position of defending a policy it claims does not really exist, and embarrassing circumstances often result. At the San Francisco Convention in 1945 Dr. Evatt as Deputy

Prime Minister vigorously argued for a Charter resolution which prohibited United Nations authority from interfering in the domestic policy of member states. His argument—a reaction to the possibility that pressure would be exerted to change the White Australia policy—unwittingly forced Australia into "the racialist camp." In October 1952 the General Committee of the United Nations considered putting apartheid on the agenda; South Africa and Australia protested claiming it was essentially within the domestic jurisdiction of the South African Government, and, therefore, by article 2(7) of the Charter, beyond United Nations' authority. Lord Casey, representing Australia in the General Assembly, then argued that if the U.N. created a "precedent" and censured South Africa or attempted to put pressure on the Government in an effort to eliminate apartheid, Australia's immigration policy would not be safe from a similar scrutiny and denunciation.[8]

This position was adopted by the Menzies Government in the U.N. and at Commonwealth meetings. Menzies insisted the principle of non-interference in domestic affairs be respected in both councils in order to preserve what he considered the essential character of international associations. This explained in part his reluctance to discuss the Sharpeville incidents at the 1960 Prime Ministers' Conference and his determination to work out a formula whereby South Africa could remain in the Commonwealth at the 1961 Conference. He argued that complete self-government was "a right which we properly insist upon for ourselves in all matters within our jurisdiction, and therefore one which we must recognise and defend for other Commonwealth countries."[9] When South Africa decided to withdraw from the Commonwealth, Menzies spoke of the portent of Commonwealth fragility.

> Even though there has been a great deal of international agitation this is still a matter of domestic policy in South Africa. South Africa does not seek to apply that policy to any other country.

Foreign Affairs and Immigration Policy 211

It is as much a matter of domestic policy as Australian immigration policy is a domestic matter for us.

And to have a member of the Commonwealth virtually excluded on a matter of domestic policy presents, in my opinion, a rather disagreeable vista of the possibilities for the future.[10]

Equating South African apartheid with Australia's immigration policy aroused bitter criticism from the Australian Labor Party. Mr. Duthie, a Labor member of the House of Representatives, said that Menzies

> cannot grasp the concept of a multi-racial society within the Commonwealth. He was born in the nineteenth century and does not seem to have got out of it. If my memory serves me rightly, he once recommended that there should be an inner cabinet of Commonwealth Prime Ministers, consisting, I assume, entirely of white men. Today, the colored races are arising from the colonialism of the past and claiming a rightful place and voice in the affairs of nations. The Prime Minister does not seem to grasp this fact. . . .[11]

None of the A.L.P. speakers in the debate specified that Menzies equated apartheid and the immigration policy only as domestic issues. They stressed the international repercussions of his remarks and the harmful effect they would have on Australian links with Asia. And, indeed, when this matter was reported in Asia, Menzies' name and Australia's reputation were damaged. One Asian observer wrote: "Of the Commonwealth Prime Ministers, Mr. Menzies emerged clearly as the least committed against apartheid."[12] A report from Hong Kong indicated Menzies' statements did "grievous harm to Australian interests and good will in the Far East."[13] And the usually moderate *Straits Times* noted: "Mr. Menzies . . . is no apostle of apartheid. Yet he had spoken as strongly as Dr. Verwoerd himself on the outcome of the Commonwealth Prime Ministers Conference."[14]

Perhaps the only approval came from Malaya's leader, the Tunku Abdul Rahman, who gained Australian approval by saying that the White Australia policy unlike apartheid was "for the protection of Australians," while "the other is for the repression of Africans." He added, "The White Australia policy, as it is called is not racial discrimination. It is to protect the Australian people. If Australia's doors were wide open they would be swamped. Why create problems in Australia that would be difficult to solve?" [15]

The legalistic position, taken as an expedient to prevent intervention in domestic affairs, had severe ramifications, such as limiting Australia's influence with newly emerging Asian states. It seemingly put Australia on the side of reactionary and colonial forces and drew attention to the immigration policy, which Menzies was admittedly trying to protect.

Until 1960 Australia consistently voted with South Africa every time the issue of apartheid was raised in the United Nations General Assembly. In 1961, however, the Government indicated a shift in policy by voting for resolutions condemning apartheid. But this "shift in policy" was a calculated move. At the first draft session of the Special Political Committee, Australia refused to condemn South African treatment of Asians on the ground that it would be an infringement of domestic jurisdiction.[16] When Australia's representative, James Plimsoll, learned "that the Charter expressly set a limit to intervention by the United Nations in matters essentially of domestic jurisdiction, and that it also set limits to the General Assembly's powers" [17] he voted for the resolution. In this way it appeared as if Australia were joining with the anti-colonial states without at the same time in any way threatening her own domestic sovereignty. Menzies explained the vote as an effort to avoid being "misrepresented all over Asia about our attitude." [18] This was only part of the explanation.

Until the end of World War II, foreign affairs, particularly Japanese expansion, reinforced the principles of "White Australia." Since the war, however, if episodes in the United Nations are representative examples, a desire to secure Australia as a Western, European, and predominately white democracy, which keeps Asia at a friendly distance, has been the guiding, and continually challenged, principle of contemporary foreign policy. Former Minister for Immigration Downer, cognizant of this aim, has suggested that "national growth and our international relations will best be serviced by continuing our present policies"—orientated toward Europe, the United Kingdom and the United States. He claims these "well-tried" policies preserve "homogeneity, readiness of absorption, familiarity of religion, the same fundamental attitudes to living." [19]

The manifestation of immigration aims in foreign policy also has implications for Australia's administration of Papua-New Guinea. When Australia received the territory of New Guinea under a League of Nations mandate, Prime Minister Hughes negotiated terms which permitted Australia to administer the territory in accordance with its own policies. The primary objective of this negotiation was to obtain the authority to regulate immigration to New Guinea, since as Hughes argued, "those islands which lay like ramparts along our coast should not be in the hands of an actual or potential enemy." [20] The vital point was the prohibition of Japanese immigration; Hughes won this victory at Versailles when the League rejected the Japanese amendment for racial equality in migration policies. New Guinea as a first line of defense is still accepted by many Australians who believe "an attack on New Guinea is an attack on Australia." This opinion was reinforced to an extent by the West Irian dispute and the contemplated Indonesian invasion of Papua-New Guinea in 1961. It also had some relevance during World War II when a Japanese invasion of New Guinea preluded an invasion of Australia. Military factors have, therefore, played an important role in the maintenance of Australia's New Guinea immigration program.

When the Government decided to allow naturalization eligibility for Asians already in Australia (1957–1958) Asian residents in New Guinea were offered the same privilege. By the end of 1962 approximately 1,623 Asians had been granted territorial citizenship.[21] Mr. Hasluck, then Minister for Territories, stated:

> Those who will be affected by the decision are people living wholly in the European manner alongside, or integrated with the European community. They have no home except the Territory, and in all the implications of the term they can be regarded as good citizens. They have English education, are of Christian religion, and in every way are fitted by cultural and general social background to live on equal terms with other Australian citizens.[22]

He added on another occasion that "all possible measures would be taken to prevent the build up of a multi-racial community in the Territories." [23] This, he claimed, was compatible with the aspirations of the indigenous people.

Plausible though these statements may be as a defense of the present restrictions on immigration to New Guinea, they pose serious questions concerning the policy adopted in regard to migration *from* Papua-New Guinea *to* Australia. Persons born in Papua, an external territory, are Australian citizens by birth. Persons born in New Guinea, a Trust Territory, are "Australian protected persons." But for the purposes of migration neither Papua nor New Guinea is part of Australia. As a matter of policy "natives of Papua and New Guinea are not normally eligible to enter Australia for residence (unless immediate family relationship with a resident of Australia is involved)." [24] For purposes of immigration Papuans and New Guineans are regarded as Melanesians and admitted to Australia "under conditions similar to those applying to non-European people generally." [25]

Another policy advocate claims there is more than just a military justification for a restrictive migrant program to New Guinea. Sir A. Grenfell Price contends that the application of "White Australia" in Papua-New Guinea saved the indigenous population "from the sufferings and corruption which the inflow of Asiatics had inflicted upon the natives of Tahiti and other islands of the Pacific." [26] It was this line of defense that the Department of Territories used in the General Assembly. Several Asian states argued that Australia's migration program in Papua-New Guinea was interfering with the expansion of such key industries as tea growing, copra and pearl diving in which non-Europeans had greater expertise.[27] The Department justified its policies by referring to the unrestricted entry of Indians into Fiji in the nineteenth century and the consequent racial problems once Indians outnumbered native Fijians. It also noted that an extended stay for these non-Europeans would ultimately lead to intermarriage. If this occurred, a representative argued, it would make it almost impossible to deport non-European workers when the local population no longer needed their services.[28]

Since 1960 several member states in the United Nations have criticized Australian administration in the Territories. Liberia accused Australia of "inadequately" administering New Guinea. Mr. M. Eastman, the Liberian delegate, alleged that segregation existed in the colonies. "We all know how Australia feels about races," he asserted; "just because Australia adhered to a 'white policy' gave it no rights to impose it in New Guinea."[29] The United Arab Republic and Togo called for "immediate free elections" in the Territories. Tanzania warned that the Australian Government would not incorporate the Territories as a seventh state "simply because of racial considerations."[30] The Tanzanian representative also accused Australia of exploiting the resources of Papua-New Guinea and "using the Territories as a military staging area to support the war in Vietnam."[31] Mr. Seydon Diallo of Guinea told the Trusteeship Council that "Australia was guilty of criminal colonialism in its two Pacific Territories." He added that Australia "was the most backward nation when it came to meeting the dictates of the conscience of the world."[32] Consistent with these denunciations, the Afro-Asian bloc led a campaign for a series of resolutions which said Australia should grant independence to Papua-New Guinea "as soon as possible."[33] The resolutions also called upon Australia to remove "all discriminatory electoral qualifications" in the Territories and to "hold elections on the basis of universal adult suffrage."[34]

When Australia escalated her commitment to Vietnam in 1965 and 1966 several Communist states, particularly the Soviet Union, accused Australia of moving lethargically to terminate her colonial situation in order to use the areas as staging zones in her "struggle against the national liberation movements in South East Asia, and in particular against the people of Vietnam."[35] In a 1967 statement the Liberian representative joined the Soviet Union in expressing his disapproval of the slow pace with which Papua and New Guinea were being prepared for independence.[36] A special committee report submitted in late 1967 noted "some political, economic, and social advances" in the Trust Territories but it stressed the point that these advances were considered "inadequate for a consistent and rapid implementation" of independence.[37] Similar expressions of dissatisfaction with the speed at which Australia was pursuing independence in Papua-New Guinea and alleged racialism in the Trust Territories, were made in 1968 by representatives from several African states.[38]

It has been argued that partially to silence its detractors in the United Nations the Federal Cabinet decided to relax the immigration restrictions in Papua-New Guinea for Africans and Asians with specialized skills and to accelerate its program of economic modernization.[39] According to the new regulations specialists would be allowed to work in the Territories for periods up to two years. In conjunction with changes in economic policy a Japanese company was permitted a lease for a ship-building industry in Rabaul. It was reported that twelve Japanese technicians began their two-year contracts in May, 1967.[40] By 1968 the Japanese community in Papua-New Guinea had grown substantially and the prospects for further expansion of Japanese investments and concomitant migration were good, despite the fact that many Australians were worried by the growing Japanese economic role in the Trust Territories.[41]

These moves by the Holt and Gorton Governments have been a radical about-face from Menzies' policies. When Mr. Barnes, Minister for Territories, allegedly approved of moderate

Japanese migration to New Guinea in 1965, Menzies told the Minister to repudiate the suggestion. According to the newspaper accounts, he said "There is to be no migration of Japanese—you had better make that clear." [42]

It is difficult to determine Australia's future administrative policy in Papua-New Guinea. Australia must reckon with the eventuality of New Guinea's independence, at which time the island will cease to be an Australian base and will become a potential military ally. But the possibility that New Guinea will want independence in 1970 raises serious defense questions. As an independent state and the master of its foreign and defense policies New Guinea will have to decide between neutrality, a bilateral alliance with Australia and participation in a multilateral defense agreement in the South Pacific. If New Guinea chooses to be allied with Australia or a South Pacific defense community it would probably do so as an "equal member." In that case it might become embarrassing for the Australian Government to maintain restriction of territorial migrants to Australia, while it bases its "first line of defence" on an association with New Guinea.

It has become apparent since World War II that Trust Territory policies and strategic considerations, while not directly influencing immigration policy, do make rigid restriction an increasing source of tension and interference in the formulation of Australian-Asian agreements. As a member of SEATO and a participant at the Honolulu and Manila Conferences Australia has been united with Asian states in several strategic agreements. However, these arrangements do not assure Australia's role in area defense pacts. One American correspondent sees racial animosities in the South Pacific as making a "New Asia" concept "farcical." "Just how trustworthy, loyal alliance could be fashioned out of a group of nations who are divided by such racial feelings, defies imagination," [43] he added. Several Australian columnists have also noted that Australian participation in the Malaysian and Vietnam struggles in order "to protect the democratic instinct of the people" is unrealistic when one considers Australia's restriction on Malaysian and Vietnamese migrants.⁴⁴ Not only has Australia's immigration policy made its military stand in South East Asia appear indefensible, it has also acted as an ideological tool for Communists. O. O. Trullinger summarized the problem the following way:

> One of the outstanding examples of the Red appeal to Asian humanity outside the sphere of economic well-being is that of the color question. . . . While the present restrictions on immigration by Asiatics into Western territories are maintained so long will the undeniable basic hostility between Asia and the West endure.⁴⁵

Australia's Asian policy has been based on assumptions which have been attacked at one time or another by government critics: China is an immediate threat to the stability of Asia and ultimately to the stability of Australia; and Communist insurgency can best be controlled by uniting with the "free nations" of South East Asia and the United States as a countervailing force. The long-range fear of Chinese Communist infiltration in the South Pacific and the immediate fear of instability in South East Asia have prescribed Australia's alliance with the United States and her attempt to "build bridges of mutual interest" in Asia. These prescriptions are based upon the need to fill the European power vacuum in South East Asia left as a result of post World War II ferment and upon the Australian realization that independence cannot be protected by Britain's rapidly dissipating strength.

Just as the United States is committed to maintain the status quo in South East Asia, Australia is formally committed through her SEATO and ANZUS obligations and emotionally committed by what is considered "a threat to self-preservation." Arthur Burns, Professor of Politics at the Australian National University, examining this relationship said: "Australia's strategic involvement in South East Asia was very largely consequent upon her major alliances—with the United States and with the United

Kingdom. They were our 'bridges with Asia.' " [46] The Government has accepted these alliances as the prerequisite for peace in the area. As Britain began to disengage herself from military obligations east of Suez, Australia, supported by the United States, has opted to fill this vacuum and aid in the creation of viable states that can protect themselves against anticipated Communist encroachments throughout the region. Abandonment of traditional British interests has ineluctably involved Australia in Asian affairs. However, an immigration policy specially designed to exclude Asians together with the maladroit handling of deportations under its jurisdiction has created a legacy of suspicion in many of the Asian states with whom Australia desires military pacts. Further suspicion is aroused by Australia's high standard of living in an area conspicuously typified by poverty. Even Australia's aid to Asia has very often been construed as a rationalization for "White Australia." By granting aid, it has been argued, Australia demonstrates its concern for Asians if they remain in Asia.

Australian statesmen realize, in spite of statements such as the late Harold Holt's "All the way with L. B. J.," that alliances with any state are not immutable. Australia cannot change its geographic position no matter how hard it wishes, but the United States can change its position in the Pacific. There are no guarantees the United States will indefinitely opt to remain an Asian power. In fact it appears quite likely, if Henry Kissinger's recent comments are any guide, that U.S. forces in Asia will continue to recede. Recognizing this prospect as early as 1968 (after the Tet offensive), Mr. Gorton, Holt's successor as Prime Minister, visited President Johnson in an effort to determine the earnestness of America's commitment to Asia and the Pacific area generally. By his own admission he was trying to extract assurances that the United States: will retain some troops in the region as a manifestation of its "special" association with Australia; will encourage firm multi-lateral area pacts through economic and military assistance to South East Asia; and will continue to supply sophisticated "military hardware" to Australia under ANZUS agreements.[47] As a consequence of the last proposal Australia has been able to purchase several American F-111's (known popularly in Australia as the "flying Edsels"). However, the increased cost of the planes over their initial estimate and their purported malfunctioning have caused the Gorton Government considerable political discomfort.[48] In addition, the non-proliferation treaty has introduced further complications into Australia's defense strategy. Since Mainland China with a nuclear arsenal and potential for a sophisticated delivery system will not be a signatory to the treaty, Australia may be chary to sign without American guarantees to protect her from possible nuclear blackmail. At this juncture these strategic considerations are dictating a more flexible Australian stance. On the one hand, it is likely the Gorton Government will continue to encourage its special relationship with the United States in order to employ American power as a counterweight against widespread insurgency and possible Chinese sabre-rattling; on the other hand, the imminent reduction of American forces and consequent strains in the Australian-American axis warrant less reliance on the United States and greater cooperation with South East Asian states. If geographic propinquity is any guide to foreign policy decisions, cooperation with South East Asia may ultimately serve Australia better than any alliance with a Western power.

The Philippines is one nation extremely sensitive to slights by the Australian Immigration Department. Notable cases of Filipino exclusion have caused widespread antagonism. It has been suggested that a whole generation of Filipinos know the name of Gamboa as well as any of their national heroes. And, in retaliation for the rejection of Aurelio Locsin by the Department of Immigration in 1966, the Filipino Government administered a "Brown Filipino" policy in respect to Australian migrants and merchants travelling to the Philippines. But as long as the expediencies of defense are given priority over national antagonisms there will probably be no interference in regional defense pacts between the two nations. Nonetheless, many Filipinos regard Australian-Asian solidarity as a myth illustrated by the perceived contradictions in the administration of immigration policy. A loyal alliance, it has been noted, cannot be constructed out of nations so divided by racial animosities. Filipinos may have exaggerated the so-called exclusiveness of the White Australia policy but as long as it remains a galling affront to them nothing but synthetic solidarity is possible.

If Australia is to form strong Asian alliances, interferences with Australian strategic considerations will have to be scrapped or modified to suit Asian opinion. Presumably this will include the "offensive" immigration policy. The late Mr. Holt and his successor Mr. Gorton have hinted at a change by stating that "the [immigration] policy would not remain static." They have maintained a commitment to redefine it as Australia grows and the world changes. Prime Minister Gorton, in his relatively short tenure as government leader, has been particularly sensitive to the apparent contradictions of a White Australia policy excluding Asians and a defense policy relying on Asian goodwill.

Since it still may be politically undesirable to liberalize the policy dramatically (on this point there is widespread disagreement), Australia has been trying to meet some of her Asian responsibilities by stressing regional trade, investment and diplomacy, techniques that are conspicuously designed to encourage interdependence and to avoid aspersions such as "neo-colonialism" and "white paternalism."

In his first year as Prime Minister, Mr. Holt visited Malaysia, Singapore, South Vietnam and the Philippines. The following year he met with the leaders of Taiwan, Cambodia, Burma, Japan and Indonesia. He was intent on making the geographic fact of Australia's location a political reality. The late Mr. Holt remarked after his last tour to South East Asia:

> It became clear that Australia has been accepted as a member of the Asian and Pacific community.

We are not on the outside looking in, but we are regarded as one of the countries of the area, involved in its problems. . . .[49]

Complementing Holt's diplomatic overtures, Mr. Gorton has taken systematic steps toward developing Australian-Japanese ties. Growing Japanese interest in international affairs is believed to be the impetus for some form of regular diplomatic consultation between the two countries. It has been contended that Australia would consider more consultations, even if they were not held regularly, in order to discuss regional problems of mutual concern.[50] Joint Japanese-Australian ventures can do much toward raising the standard of living in the region and consequently improving Australia's Asian image. Increased diplomatic contacts with Asian states may also mean more Asians coming to Australia. If other factors do not illuminate the need for liberalization of the immigration policy, Mr. Gorton has noted, the exchange of ideas at the diplomatic level might.

In September, 1966, Senator Raul Manglapus of the Philippines was invited to Australia to deliver the Dyason lecture, a biennial address on international problems. The theme of his lecture was Australia's potential role as a bridge between East and West and her role in building "a truly multi-racial society."[51] The concept of Australia as a bridge between two worlds was not a new one. What made his presentation different was its boldness and reliance on "Australia's historic duty" rather than her self-preservation. This point has been dismissed as misguided idealism and "adolescent" optimism by some, but it has also provided a new dimension in the discussion of immigration policy. Since this speech, certainly not because of it, there are signs of a very moderate change toward multi-racialism. As already noted, in 1968 an estimated 1,500 non-Europeans were to be accepted for permanent residence in Australia.[52] (In 1966 approximately 400 non-Europeans were granted a similar status.)

As the concern for Asia has increased so too has the discussion of aid programs. A pamphlet distributed by the Department of External Affairs noted, "Australian aid abroad was not only given for humanitarian reasons but also because the countries of South East Asia are our very near neighbors, that what happens in Asia directly affects Australia and that Australia's own interests are best served by politically stable and economically prosperous neighbors." [53] Obviously the Government intends to use foreign aid as an instrument of foreign policy. With a growing involvement in South East Asia, increased aid seems the logical extension of policy. Former Prime Minister Holt announced, "As we grow nationally so our contribution in both of these directions (military and civil aid) can be expected to grow." [54] Thus far, however, this rhetoric has been an exaggeration of Australia's aid allowance. Total foreign aid expenditure, including Papua-New Guinea, has been the equivalent of a little more than 0.6 per cent of the nation's gross national product. When the appropriation for Papua-New Guinea is excluded, the Australian total is approximately 0.2 per cent of the gross national product. And this figure has remained fairly stable for the last six years.

Australia wants to use this aid to balance her interests *vis-à-vis* Asia. But even though it wants to be in Asia in one sense, it does not want to be saddled with huge aid contributions which might neutralize trade advantages. This is one reason why Australia has been much more generous with technical assistance programs and student exchanges than direct financial aid. Nevertheless, as long as money remains the most important influence in aid programs the Government will have to consider a more flexible approach to appropriations. If regional stability is considered to be the *sine qua non* of foreign policy, then the amount of aid will have to be considered in respect to the challenges to Australian self-interest. Mr. Whitlam, Leader of the Labor Party, put this point well when he said: "We will have no secure future until the people in our region are confident that we will help them to achieve the same objectives that we insist on having for ourselves." [55]

Stability was obviously one of the main considerations in extending aid to Indonesia after the defeat of the attempted Communist coup in 1964. Government officials decided that almost $700,000 in aid was not too high a price to pay for an Indonesian entente. Since Australia's security and the security of Papua-New Guinea could be promoted by extending aid, officials in the Department of External Affairs were willing to pay. Similar logic was applied to Australian aid for India. Since India is the largest non-Communist state in Asia and a presumed counterweight to Chinese Communist influence, it is in Australia's security interest to be on friendly terms with her. This, despite government disclaimers, partially accounts for the allocation of one quarter of Colombo Plan aid to India.[56]

It is ironic that aid, which can be one of the most effective aims of foreign policy, can be used by the Government as an explanation for the retention of its immigration policy. Too often the Department of External Affairs has been willing to contribute financial aid in order to fortify an Asian economy and reduce the possibility of Asians wanting to migrate to Australia. A danger exists that the Government will begin to rely upon the positive effects of aid programs as a substitute for significant immigration changes. However, this tendency will probably be moderated by the influences of diplomatic relations and trade.

European experiments in economic cooperation have brought Australian attention since 1960 to the question of intra-regional trade. Australia expected Britain's likely acceptance into the Common Market and the concomitant loss of preferential access to the British Market. In preparation for the consequences of this possibility, Australia has begun to rethink and reorder her trade and financial policies.

Indirectly, British entry into the European Economic Community (EEC) might also affect Australia's immigration policy. If British economic growth is accelerated as a result of participation in the Common Market, the English will be less inclined to migrate. With migrant sources declining in the United Kingdom and thriving economies of Southern Europe, Australia might be forced to reconsider the luxury of a restricted policy. Rapid economic growth throughout the Australian continent is not possible without a rapidly increasing work force, and a population of only twelve and a quarter million growing at the rate of 1.9 per cent a year is not sufficient to meet the needs of economic development.

The "booming Pacific" is probably a phrase adopted by advertising agents in order to extol the virtues of trade in the ocean bloc. But since the escalation of the Vietnam war, investment expansion has dramatically changed the financial opportunities in the region. The Australian Government prefers to leave businessmen to their own investment devices, but trade policies, particularly between Australia and Japan, have been negotiated in order to make up for the diminution of British trade and increase possibilities for expanded regional trade. Although most of the countries in ECAFE (Economic Commission for Asia and Far East) continue to focus their trade on the "developed world," the Commission itself attests to greater mutual cooperation in and concern for the area.

In time, economic solidarity elsewhere in the world could intensify Asia's export-import price squeeze, making her dependent on a few commodities whose export prices decline while prices of necessary capital imports regularly increase. This inclination, already evident throughout Asia, is forcing countries, Australia included, to rely more heavily on intra-regional trade. The development of Western trading blocs may either back Australia into an Asian trade community or force it to supplicate for associate membership in the European Common Market. (The latter is of course contingent on British acceptance into the EEC.)

The Department of Trade is now adjusting to the shrinking Western market by concentrating its energies on Asian trade. Since a trade agreement was signed in 1957—the same year non-European naturalization was permitted for the first time—Australian exports to Japan have almost tripled. (In 1956, Australian exports to Japan were worth $172.9 million; less than twelve years later they were approximately $642 million.[57]) Australia displaced the United States as the largest supplier of coal to Japan by 1966 when ninety-three per cent of Australia's coal exports went there.[58] With increasing sales of iron ore and other products to Japan, and with Britain's austerity measures, it was no surprise that in 1967 Japan replaced Great Britain as Australia's best customer. By the end of 1968 nearly one fifth of all Australian exports—principally primary materials—went to Japan.[59] And if Japanese ambition is any guide this trade will be expanded in 1969. (A touring team of government financial advisers recently announced that Japan is prepared to buy or trade for all of Australia's surplus cotton "from now on." That surplus is expected to reach 280,000 bales by 1970.)

Similarly, Australia's exports to Formosa from 1964–1965 to 1967–1968 increased by over 50 per cent and exports to the Philippines, despite a threatened trade boycott because of the 1966 Locsin case, increased by more than $20 million during the same period. At the same time, however, Australian export-import trade with Europe declined. The trend is obvious; but exports only partially indicate the drift in Australia's financial fortunes.

Since 1960 Japan has invested 100 million dollars in Australia. Japan has become the financial giant in the South Pacific that has not only invested considerably in Papua-New Guinea, but has already developed three automobile assembly plants on Australian soil and been enthusiastically encouraged by the Australian Department of Supply to invest in the Woomera communications satellite project. Moreover, the Japanese have placed their imprint on the entire range of Australian industries. According to official sources, there are 48 Japanese companies directly represented and approximately 22 more indirectly involved in Australia in fields as varied as textiles, shipping, mining and chemicals, to name just a few.[60] By 1968, Japanese automobiles, after less than ten years in the Australian market, accounted for eleven per cent of Australia's total automobile sales, including home produced and imported vehicles.[61]

Yet for all the trade and investment with Asians, Australians are incredibly ignorant of their new financial partners. Exchange visits, study groups, communication and migration schemes still have the obstacle of Australia's immigration policy to contend with. Mr. R. W. C. Anderson of the Associated Chamber of Manufacturers suggested the Government make a full-scale examination of this problem. He added: "Broadly the issue is this: the tides of Australian trade are running less strongly to Western Europe and more strongly to Asia. Should not therefore the direction of our national energies of all types, political, business and cultural be changing correspondingly?"[62]

A common market of Australian-Asian states, a frequently discussed goal of participants in regional trade, necessitates the free movement of men and materials. But many Japanese industrialists have long considered Australia's immigration policy a major barrier to full development of a two-nation cooperation in capital investment projects and regional financial schemes. The discussion leader at the 1964 meeting of the Australia-Japan Business Cooperation Committee, Mr. F. Doko, cited the Port Hedland Copper Mining Project as an example of Japanese capital loss due to prejudicial hiring practices. The venture, which was terminated because of technical difficulties, was plagued in the beginning by "Article 291 of West Australia's mining laws," which hampered Japanese operations by ruling against the employment of Asians and Africans in the area. Revision of the law in 1963 permitted hiring of Asians and Africans subject to ministerial approval. "But," as Mr. Doko indicated, "the situation is still unstable since the Minister is empowered to revoke the approval at any time."[63] Since 1966, however, a small trickle of Japanese migrants, primarily businessmen, have been able to settle in Australia without incidents. A few hundred were naturalized between 1966 and 1968 and it was estimated in 1968 that Sydney had a Japanese community of about 850 residents.[64]

The formulation of foreign policy, strategic considerations and trade agreements are usually not intentionally designed to vitiate the "White Australia" principles. Neither are the events of recent Asian history and the European migration program consciously intended to prepare public opinion for a radical change in immigration policy. But all of these factors have made "White Australia" an embarrassment and more importantly a deterrent to the smooth functioning of foreign affairs. At present the immigration policy is not enough of an embarrassment or a sufficient interference in foreign affairs to warrant its complete abandonment. Only recently have foreign considerations reached parity with the historic dedication to White Australia. Thus far, their effect on the content of the policy, albeit open to disputation, has been, in this author's opinion, only marginal. But relations with Asia in commerce, diplomacy and strategic arrangements are only beginning to have important implications for the national interest.

If the recent past is any guide to future policy decisions, foreign affairs will soon surpass immigration policy as a government priority. When this occurs immigration policy, which was initially a safeguard for the defense and the economy of the body-politic, will be an indulgence endangering the very safety and prosperity it was designed to protect. Former Minister for Immigration Downer once said: "If Australia is to survive in the form which most of us would like, it can only do so, paradoxically, by undergoing alterations in outlook and customs which our European migrants will bring."[65] In the not too distant future statements such as this may have to be revised to include many non-European as well as European migrants. If Australia sees its future role as a leader of regional development, it may have to reconsider the desirability of an ethnically homogeneous population.

9

The Prasad Deportation: A Test Case

The case of Nancy Prasad has become a fable in its own time. Some have given Nancy Prasad credit for Mr. Opperman's March, 1966, statement "liberalizing the 'White Australia' policy." Others claim this incident amplified the role color plays in the administration of the policy, while still others allege that Opperman endorsed discrimination on the basis of skin color. Only one factor about the incident is singularly apparent: the lack of a dispassionate discussion of the issues in much newspaper reportage and by many spokesmen representing both sides of the argument. Emotional harangues and press notoriety compounded the already awkward position of the Immigration Department.

Mr. Shiri Prasad first came to Australia at the age of forty-nine in September, 1961, on a three-month holiday sponsored by the Fijian Government as a reward for two decades of service to the Public Works Department. When he arrived in Australia Mr. Prasad arranged to live with his married sons resident there.

After three days Mr. Prasad accepted the offer of a job by the company which was employing his eldest son, Roy. The foreman in charge of Mr. Prasad's section, Mr. John Schenk, was pleased with his new employee's work and accompanied him to immigration authorities in Sydney in order to discuss the possibility of a visa extension. Mr. Schenk described a meeting in which an immigration officer said that Prasad " 'had no right to work here' and trod on me properly for engaging him." Furthermore the officer said, " 'Shiri's time was up and could not be extended.' "[1]

Mr. Prasad's version of this encounter is quite different:

> . . . he [John Schenk] took me to Immigration Dept. and approch [sic] the authorties [sic] in Sydney and *was told* that when I'll be at the age of 50 years then I could stay with my children. . . .[2]

Confident he could return to Australia as an aged dependent and permanent resident, Mr. Prasad returned to Fiji once his visitor's visa expired. After several weeks in Fiji he retired from his job and received £2,000 superannuation pay. With this money he planned to transport his entire family to Australia. But when he applied for admission as a permanent resident, an Australian immigration official in Fiji allegedly said, "Not a chance in the world, mate, for you blacks."[3] Despite this refusal for permanent entry Mr. Prasad applied for and received another visitor's permit. He reasoned that in three months, the extent of his visitor's stay, he would reach his fiftieth birthday and would be eligible for permanent residence "as promised."[4]

In April, 1962, Mr. Prasad brought his wife, four children, including Nalnie or Nancy, and his mother-in-law to Sydney as tourist visitors. Their entry was approved in "good faith" since it had been declared that the family would spend a few months sightseeing and visiting with Mr. Prasad's two eldest sons, who had married Australians,[5] and would then return to their homeland. When Mr. Prasad reached his fiftieth birthday he returned to the Department of Immigration offices in Sydney and was reputedly told that "no promise" of permanent residence had been made. Mr. Prasad also noted that "new faces" were in the office; "the men who made the promise were not there." [6] After a series of deputations, immigration authorities granted the Prasads an extension of time in order to "enjoy a longer holiday." [7] In the period between April, 1962, and April, 1963, when the visa extension expired, Mr. Prasad, "although fully aware that he had been admitted to Australia as a holiday visitor for a limited period only, . . . bought two houses in a Sydney suburb." [8] On subsequent occasions he advanced the argument that this investment entitled him to remain in Australia. Mr. Daly (M.H.R. for Grayndler), acting as Mr. Prasad's representative, requested a permanent visa for the family on the grounds that "all Mr. Prasad's interests are now in Australia and he has no ties whatever in Fiji. In fact his youngest child was born in Australia. I am also advised that he owns certain property in this country. In view of the circumstances, Mr. Prasad is anxious to settle here with his family." [9]

Mr. Downer, former Minister for Immigration, responded to this request by emphasizing the conditions for permanent residence in Australia. The birth of a child in this country, he maintained, does not automatically entitle the family to naturalization nor does "the fact that two of Mr. Prasad's sons have acquired Australian citizenship . . . confer any right of residence upon the remainder of the group." [10] In spite of the policy demands limiting his prerogatives, the Minister granted Mr. Prasad a three-month extension (till September) in which to settle all of his commitments, and noted that he would "press upon them [the Prasad family] the need to conclude their departure arrangements within that time." [11] In September, the month of supposed departure, Prasad claimed that definite arrangements had been consummated for his permanent employment with a Sydney company—a factor, he felt, that would assure him a permanent visa. Downer, while recognizing the firm's commitment, wrote to Daly: "as you will appreciate,

[Prasad's employment] is not a factor which has any bearing on the application of our established immigration policy."[12] Disappointed and forlorn over his inability to remain, Mr. Prasad said: "Our family is going to be split down the middle and it will kill my wife. I'm sure Mr. Downer could treat our case sympathetically if he wanted to."[13] Despite refusals from the Minister's office, Mr. Prasad persisted in his efforts to remain in Australia. It was not until a deportation order was issued that the family made preparations to depart.[14] Just before departure Mr. Downer sent a telegram to Mr. Prasad in which he reputedly wrote, "permission to live in Australia will only be considered" when the family returned to Fiji and reapplied.[15]

The day before the Prasads were supposed to leave Australia Mr. Prasad revealed the news that his twenty-year-old daughter Sandra, in Australia on a visitor's permit since 1961, had married an Australian and intended to remain in the country. The Immigration Department spokesman pointed out, however, that Sandra had remained in the country by virtue of departmental sufferance since 1961 and that marriage did not automatically secure permanent entry since that decision was entirely within the Minister's purview. Nonetheless, Sandra remained in Australia while the rest of the family—Mr. Prasad, his wife Marie, his daughters Sushil, ten, Carol, three, Doreen, thirteen months (born in Australia), his son Peter, six, and his mother-in-law, Mrs. Bachi Gela, boarded the liner Orsova bound for Fiji.[16] Another daughter, Nancy, five, was in Prince Alfred Hospital with a throat infection and was "refused a doctor's certificate to travel with her parents."[17] Other members of the Prasad family remaining in Australia, in addition to Nancy and Sandra, were two sons—Roy, twenty-four, and Sam, twenty-two, both of whom were married to Australian girls. Before leaving the country Mr. Prasad said, "I will continue to fight to return to Australia." He noted on November 5, 1963, that "the family had until November 12 to leave but were going voluntarily because he thought it would assist his chances to return."[18] Mr. Prasad

The Prasad Deportation: A Test Case   233

made a last appeal to the Immigration Department in the hope the Minister would allow him to remain until Nancy recovered. Fearing a repetition of earlier procrastination Mr. Opperman, then recently appointed Minister for Immigration, refused it and stated that one of Prasad's married children could care for Nancy until her recovery was complete.[19]

Once back in Fiji Mr. Prasad again found employment and applied for reentry as an aged dependent, but his application was refused. With his father out of the country Roy assumed responsibility for the family's readmission. He wrote to the Members of Parliament pleading "for help to overcome this injustice," which was his description of the deportation order, and listed the following reasons for readmission:

> Three of the children are settled in Australia.
> The youngest, my sister, was born here.
> My family are British subjects.
> My father is a property owner here.
> My father is an ex-serviceman who fought in the last World War.
> There were nearly one thousand people who signed petitions in the last minute bid to stop the Immigration Department from forcing my parents out of this country.
> My parents dearly wish to stay close [sic] the children and grandchildren as any human being can understand.[20]

Mr. Heydon, Secretary of Immigration, answered Roy Prasad's letter by writing:

> The situation is that your parents do not come within the categories of persons eligible to settle permanently in Australia. I am instructed to inform you that, in the circumstances, your request is therefore not one to which favourable consideration may be given.[21]

Another reason for reentry, although not included in Roy Prasad's letter, was Nancy's presence in Australia. But when

Mr. Shiri Prasad cited this as a reason for his return Opperman replied:

> Mr. Prasad Senior saw the child's presence here as an opportunity to press for re-entry to Australia of himself and the rest of his family. He has repeatedly stated this as his goal. It is, of course, quite well known that in administering immigration requirements generally, we try to avoid situations where parents are kept apart from their young children.[22]

Because of the notoriety of the case and the questionable condition of Nancy's health, the Immigration Department, notwithstanding considerable resistance by some officials, agreed to the request that Nancy's stay be extended another two months. Roy, charged with the care of Nancy during this period, "made repeated representations and efforts . . . to have Nancy allowed to stay . . ."[23] permanently. But once Nancy recovered Mr. Opperman ordered the girl's return to her parents in accordance with "earlier assurances" given by Roy. When Roy contended that "personal commitments" prevented him from doing this, the deportation order was signed.[24] The Federal Government paid the air fare for Nancy and also paid for the child's brother to escort her to Fiji and to return to his home in Australia.[25]

On April 3, 1964, Roy issued a statement to the press in which he claimed that "police were searching for the child, so that she had to go into hiding."[26] Mr. Opperman flatly denied the charge and described it as "a figment of the imagination."[27] Whether or not she was in hiding became an irrelevant question, however, when Roy Prasad sought an injunction restraining Mr. Opperman from deporting Nancy. In the affidavit Roy said his sister, Mrs. Powditch, "wanted to adopt Nancy legally and bring her up in Australia."[28] Adoption papers had already been prepared with this in mind. His parents, so it was alleged at the time, agreed to these proceedings. Roy said, "my father appealed to me to keep Nancy in Sydney so that she would have a better life."[29] Mr. Leary, the barrister representing Nancy, sought the injunction under a section of the Migration Act of 1958 which forbade deportation of a child if legal proceedings to obtain guardianship had commenced.[30] It was recognized by Leary that Mr. Opperman retained legal custody of the child and that she remained in Australia "by virtue of his discretion."[31] When the High Court ruled on the application, the judges took note of the Department's attempts to have Roy cooperate with an undertaking to return Nancy to Fiji and said "it seems clear that it is only in the hope that pressure might be brought to bear upon the Minister to alter his earlier decision that the proceedings have been brought."[32] The circumstances, the judges maintained, made it clear that the injunction could not be issued. Roy Prasad responded to the decision by declaring "I shall fight this order with all legal means at my disposal."[33]

Notice of the Court's decision led to an attempt by Immigration Department officials to serve a deportation order on Nancy. Their search for the girl was unsuccessful. It was reported that she was "being held in a secret hideaway" while government officials pursued her in vain.[34] Mr. Opperman issued a statement to the effect that Nancy be on the evening flight to Suva or her sister and brothers would be subject to jail sentences for detaining her illegally.[35] On April 7, 1964, the Immigration Department announced it would defer Nancy's deportation in accordance with the solicitor's notification that an appeal would be lodged against the Court's earlier decision.[36]

In August, 1964, Justice Myers of the New South Wales Equity Court heard the petition for Nancy's adoption by her sister and brother-in-law, Mr. and Mrs. Powditch, as well as a statement by Mr. Prasad Senior, in which he asked the Court to consider Nancy's adoption due to his "unemployment in Fiji." After hearing the evidence for both sides the judge refused the application. He said the earlier decision was equitable and there was "no doubt" that the application was submitted "in the hope that it would prevent deportation of the child to Fiji." [37] Another ground for his refusal "was that the child's adopting mother would be her own sister." [38]

Mr. Powditch and his wife almost immediately appealed the decision to the Full Supreme Court. A deportation order against the child was once again stayed pending a decision of the Court. The three judges hearing the case, Justice Sugarman (presiding), Justice Walsh and Justice Collins, unanimously dismissed the appeal. In a joint judgment they said:

> The adoption of a young girl by her older sister, the parents of both still living, could be justified only in exceptional circumstances, if at all. The considerations which argue against such an adoption are at least as strong, and perhaps even stronger, than those against adoption by grandparents.
>
> It is said that the applicants are willing and well able to care for, maintain and educate the child, whereas her parents in Fiji are unable to do these things adequately because of poverty. Granted all this, it should not require the making of an adoption order to secure to Nalnie such advantages as these may be in being cared for by an older sister rather than her mother and father.
>
> In all ordinary experience such arrangements when they are brought about, are the results of a sense of family duty and sisterly affection, and do not require an adoption order.
>
> It would seem strangely remote from human nature that a sister, otherwise willing to care for a younger sister, should insist upon becoming, in law, her mother to the exclusion of the natural mother of both of them.
>
> This case will not be found to be one in which a sister is insisting upon adoption as a condition of taking care of her younger sister.
>
> The truth lies in another direction.
>
> The applicant, Shashi Powditch, is a prohibited migrant, having outstayed her entry permit.
>
> Perhaps, having married and had a child here, she has some expectation of being allowed to remain.

That is not in any way a matter for our consideration, being entirely within the direction of the Minister.

What is of much more significance, by way of its relevance to the true reason for the making of the present application, is that the child, Nalnie, is also a prohibited immigrant against whom a deportation order has been made.

The history of the case is one of continued manoeuvre to avoid the child's return to Fiji and there was "no doubt" the application was made in the hope that it would prevent the child being deported.[39]

During these Court proceedings the Immigration Department temporarily suspended its requirements for deportation, albeit they could have been legally enforced.[40] The Department's cooperation was matched by Mr. and Mrs. Powditch's agreement to take the child back to Fiji once the Court action had been exhausted. According to immigration officials Mr. Powditch cooperated with the Department up to the intended hour of departure and allegedly reproved the planned demonstrations at the time of departure.[41]

On August 6, 1965, the planned day of embarcation, *The Australian* condemned Nancy's deportation as an insensitive reaction to a legal "technicality" and a perfect example of "the knotty moral problems involved in administering our immigration policy. . . ."[42] Mr. Baltinos, spokesman for the New Settlers' Federation of Australia, claimed the government assertion that it did not have a White Australia policy was "hypocritical." "This is particularly evident in Immigration Department's action of deporting six-year-old Fijian girl, Nancy Prassod [*sic*]—a British subject," he said. The Federation agreed to assist the Prasad family even though "foiled by the Minister's ruthless opposition" and it promised to join student demonstrations at Mascot Airport to expose the inequities in the immigration policy.[43]

At Sydney Airport, half an hour before a Qantas jet was to leave for Fiji, Nancy Prasad was abducted by sympathizers of the Prasad cause amid cheers of 100 university students, many of whom displayed placards bearing slogans such as "Let Nancy Stay"; "Nancy's Crime? Colour"; "11th Commandment, Thou Shalt Be White." [44] The demonstrators cheered in earnest when Charles Perkins snatched Nancy from the arms of Mrs. Powditch, hurried her off to a waiting car and drove away leaving the police thoroughly confused.[45] Mr. Powditch, responding to press questions after the spellbinding scene, "denied any prior knowledge of the seizure." [46] However, later, he added that "it did have my consent. It was done with split second timing. The signal for Nancy to be taken was for me to let go of her hand and look at my watch. . . ." [47] Mr. and Mrs. Powditch maintained that the kidnapping was due to: "The colour question. . . . Nancy is a coloured person and is merely being deported on one criterion—the colour of her skin. This is immoral and ludicrous." [48] As a matter of fact Mr. Powditch even denied "any deportation order had been served upon Nancy by the Immigration Department." "Nancy was a free passenger and not a deportee," he said. It was readily admitted, however, that the Department paid for his ticket as well as those for Mrs. Powditch and her young son who were to accompany Nancy to Fiji.[49]

At approximately 8:15 p.m. Nancy was returned to her brother Roy and Mrs. Powditch inside the Sydney University grounds by her abductor Charles Perkins. Mr. Perkins, a student leader who is part Aborigine, said Nancy was abducted as a protest against the White Australia policy.

> We did it in the hope that she might be allowed to stay. It was not done as a publicity stunt but more with the idea that what we had done would give some people second thoughts. We felt that it was wrong for the little girl to be thrown out of the country because of her color. And it was because of this that we decided to take her. Repercussions of what we may have done are yet to be found out but we hope there will be some slight reaction to this archaic policy of the government. We hope it will achieve that Nancy will be allowed to stay here and live as any other Australian.[50]

Mr. Opperman claimed:

> It has been my concern, that, in accordance with the undertakings given by the family, the child, Nalnie Prasad, should be returned peacefully to her mother and father in Fiji.
>
> It never has been the intention that the child should be deported forcibly.
>
> I have been anxious that the child should be spared the ordeal of being the innocent centre of an organized demonstration and emotional disturbance that could only be harmful to her and beyond her comprehension. . . .
>
> Accordingly, arrangements were made with the child's brother-in-law, Mr. R. A. Powditch, for him to escort the child in the plane to Fiji, and for a quiet departure that would be in the best interests of the child.
>
> My Department offered to provide transport and, in accordance with my own and Mr. Powditch's expressed wishes, made arrangements for the privacy and comfort of the child at the airport before flight departure.
>
> Unfortunately the relatives chose not to abide by these arrangements and insisted on taking the child to the front entrance of the airport where the demonstration had been organized.
>
> The action of lawless people in abducting the little girl in complete disregard of her welfare and peace of mind will be condemned by all decent Australians. . . .[51]

He also noted on a later occasion the "irresponsibility" of Mr. Charles Perkins in abducting Nancy. "It's a laugh," he said, "that Perkins screams his head off about the condition of the coloured people in Australia, but he tried to keep Nancy here." [52]

Opperman responded to charges of racism in the case by calling them "gravely misrepresented." He argued "this is a case of a child being returned to her lawful mother who is living under good circumstances." [53] Court action, he noted, decided that the adoption should not be permitted and "that the question of whether she should be deported is for my decision as Minister for Immigration." [54] Mr. Opperman further cited as other alleged misrepresentations reports that Mr. Prasad could not afford to keep Nancy.

> He is the man who brought several members of his family to Australia on an expensive extended holiday trip and took them home at his own expense. He also is the man who purchased two houses while he was in Sydney. He also owns houses in Fiji.
>
> It has been stated in the Press that he is unemployed, but in fact he is in employment at a relatively high wage.[55]

Mr. Heydon, Secretary of Immigration, asserted that Prasad belongs to the same social club as the Australian Commissioner in Fiji. While the standards of the club do not compare with those in Australia, he continued, it likewise does not reflect the destitute and unemployed portion of Fiji's population.[56]

Reg Powditch answered these charges with the statement:

> It must be understood that the Prasad family in Suva are not living in good circumstances. They are in fact very poor. . . .
>
> It was also said that Mr. Prasad bought two houses in Australia and here in Suva.
>
> Mr. Prasad left a Government job in Suva and on retirement was paid superannuation money of £1,800. £1,000 of this was spent on return fares to Australia, as we all know that one cannot leave here for Australia or New Zealand before one has paid for return fares.
>
> The rest of this money was also spent. He gave his two sons £350 deposit for a house for themselves and also paid £350 deposit on a house for his wife and children. This house has not been paid for and has now been repossessed.
>
> He owns one house in Fiji, which the family live in and the other is owned by a finance company, being paid off by the occupants.[57]

On August 8, 1965, Nancy was returned to her parents in Fiji. No sooner had she landed than the press commenced a series of accusations directed at immigration officials. Notwithstanding the substantial evidence produced by Mr. Opperman's office, many publications attacked what was often termed "another illustration of 'White Australia.'" The *Daily Mirror*

The Prasad Deportation: A Test Case 241

described the case as a blatant illustration of racism. "The Prasads, who are Indians born in Fiji, are not acceptable to our holy Immigration Department presumably because of the color of their skins. . . ." [58] The *Canberra Times* called this case just another example of "the White Australia policy in action." It substantiated this view with the claim that "The Government has nothing against this girl or her family except the colour of the skin. It is as simple as that and as unjust." [59] A *Bulletin* editorial on this matter, while avoiding any broad denunciation of non-European immigration policies, bemoaned the lack of "imagination and flexibility on the Department's part. . . ." [60] And the *Nation* suggested, "that the colour question plays some part is an inescapable inference" in the analysis of the case.[61]

Compounding the Immigration Department's difficulties in this case was a press release by Mrs. Prasad in Suva in which she said, "I am not at all happy about it [Nancy's return]. I am very upset and I would like Nancy to stay in Australia. I have got a lot of children here, not including Nancy. These children here are not even being fed properly." [62] According to one immigration official these remarks represented a dramatic *volte-face* from Mrs. Prasad's earlier desire to be reunited with her child.[63] On August 7, 1965, it had been reported in a headline story in the *Sun* that Nancy's aunt in Suva after talking to Mrs. Prasad was assured that the mother "wants her [Nancy] to come home." [64]

A spate of public pronouncements condemning Mr. Opperman's action was released by pressure groups for immigration reform. In Sydney, the superintendent of the Central Methodist Mission and an ardent opponent of White Australia, Reverend Alan Walker, compared Australia's actions in the Prasad case to those in a totalitarian state. He said Mr. Opperman "should be protected from having to treat every case in a special and arbitrary manner." [65] A Geelong Democratic Labor Party (D.L.P.) member called on his party to defeat the Minister for Immigration at the next election because of his "inhuman behaviour" in the

Prasad case.[66] The D.L.P. State Conference in Victoria "pointed out that the boom had been effectively lowered on the adults. There was no real need to penalise the child." [67] And the Association for the Defence of the Family wrote:

> I challenge you, Mr. Minister, to put the question of her residence in Australia to a real test. Please allow Nancy to return to Australia with Mr. and Mrs. Powditch, forget the White Australia Policy, and don't just deny its existence as a policy, especially as it is well known in Australia and abroad that restrictions are applied for colour or racial reasons.[68]

In reply to his antagonists Mr. Opperman held to the view that he was primarily interested in the child's welfare. He contended that the Prasad home in Suva was located in one of the better suburbs and Nancy was not living in conditions of abject poverty. "Careful enquiries I have caused to be made and reliable reports in the press and on television show this." [69] The evidence Mr. Opperman referred to was supported in no small part by a *Sun-Herald* television program, August 15, 1965, filmed in the Prasad home.

In the program the narrator said:

> The Prasads live in a neat weatherboard house in the fashionable Suva suburb of Samabula. It's surrounded by a well-kept green lawn, fringed by palm trees. Though by Australian standards it's not a big house for a family the size of the Prasads—parents and six children—it's must [*sic*] better than the average Indian home in Fiji. Many much bigger families live in much smaller houses. Although some of the Prasad children slept three to a bed, I understand this was a temporary arrangement, as there seemed to be enough bedding for the usual number of occupants.[70]

The narrator gratuitously suggested that the "real reason" why Mr. Prasad wants Nancy to return to Australia is because "once she is here there would be no legitimate excuse for the Immigration Department to refuse entry to the rest of the family." [71]

The Prasad Deportation: A Test Case   243

Despite this alleged plotting by Mr. Prasad, the program ended with the question, "If Nancy had been white, would the Immigration Department still have deported her?" [72]

When the Australian Broadcasting Commission made a program about Nancy which disagreed with the *Sun-Herald* program and the Immigration Department judgments about the Prasad's living conditions and Nancy's adjustment to her new home, "Mr. Opperman in effect accused the television station of showing a fake film of Nancy Prasad in Fiji." But this is a film, it was alleged, he "refuses to see." [73] Opperman replied to this allegation with his own version of the film:

> I have no confidence at all that this film will give a fair picture of the situation.
>
> I shall give one example of the sort of thing to be expected. It is said the film shows Nalnie being refused admission to the local school. In actual fact consent to the child's enrolment was given before Mr. Powditch left Fiji.
>
> It may well be significant that Mr. Powditch called at the school with a cameraman and asked the headmaster whether the child would be admitted if she were under six years of age. The headmaster shook his head and this was filmed. The headmaster was then told the child was six years of age and was asked whether, in view of this, she would be admitted; and he at once agreed to her admittance. I shall have nothing to do with a film which is obviously unlikely to give a balanced account of the situation.[74]

It was also pointed out on a later occasion that, contrary to family claims, English was spoken by Nancy's schoolmates and was "the only medium of instruction at the school in question." [75] That Nancy would be unable to speak English in Fiji, a claim made in support of her retention in Australia, was deemed invalid by the immigration office. The manager and class teachers at the school Nancy attended also noted, "She would not need to know Hindustani in order to commence her studies here. We have children of other races in the School who do not know a word of Hindi." [76]

Mr. Opperman's objective, held rather consistently throughout the matter, was to have Nancy "returned to her rightful place with her mother and father and to avoid any unnecessary disquiet to her in the process." [77] The charge that flexible administration would have alleviated the tensions arising from the case was dismissed by Mr. Opperman as a sanction for "attempts to circumvent normal requirements" and an encouragement for "many others to do likewise." [78] It was recalled at this juncture what Mr. Prasad said on August 9, 1965, in Fiji: "Tell them back in Australia that we all want to come back to be a family again, to be with my grandchildren again." [79]

There are a number of factors in this case bearing on the Immigration Department's attitude that did not receive widespread publicity. Although it was recognized by the Supreme Court, few newspapers revealed the fact that Shashi Prasad remained in Australia by the sufferance of the Immigration Department. In 1963 she was granted an extension on her visa to take a nurses' entrance examination. Before the exam was to be given she married an Australian, R. A. Powditch, which she assumed would entitle her to immediate citizenship. This, in fact, was not the case. The Department did not exercise its legal authority to deport her because it probably did not want to exacerbate tensions arising from the Nancy Prasad matter. In any case she remained an illegal migrant in Australia. Opperman also claimed that Roy Prasad came to Australia under a student visa and obtained employment even though this was specifically prohibited by his entry requirements. [80]

Another source of evidence not revealed by the Immigration Department was a letter written by an Australian resident in Fiji, and a neighbor of the Prasads, to the Minister for Immigration and Mr. Calwell, Leader of the Opposition Labor Party. [81] Notably prejudiced against Fijian Indians but seemingly well informed about life in Fiji, this source sent an account of the

The Prasad Deportation: A Test Case   245

Prasad family to the Minister in order to "elucidate inaccurate Press reports," of the case.[82]

According to immigration officials color was not a factor in decisions made by the Minister. But to allow the Prasads admission under the circumstances in this case, would have been to sanction the flaunting of the immigration procedures and laws. Nancy Prasad was no challenge to the immigration policy, so it was suggested, but her father might have used her acceptance as pressure for the subsequent entry of himself and his family. "This is the kind of dangerous precedent we try to avoid." [83] Mr. Opperman added another dimension to the problem when he said: "If I'd have said allright [let Nancy stay] because of the newspaper publicity, it's a precedent I would later regret. There are Prasads all over Hong Kong. We were sending Nancy to her parents not away from them." [84] The major consideration in the case, said Department spokesmen—although apparently not the only one in Mr. Opperman's mind—was the welfare of the child.

Whether Mr. Opperman's actions were in the best interests of the child is a contentious point. When she was forced to leave Australia, Nancy reportedly said, "I don't want to go. . . . I don't want to lose my friends." [85] After her return to Fiji Nancy was reportedly quite content to be back with her parents. Mr. Prasad labelled this news erroneous. "Nancy is not happy here at all," he said. Furthermore he was quite upset when press releases suggested she was happy in Fiji. "Reports like that will spoil our fight to get Nancy and ourselves back to Australia," [86] he commented. John Dynon, the spokesman defending the family, argued that since Nancy was resident in Australia more than half her life, there could be no valid objection to her remaining. If the Minister were truly concerned about her welfare, the argument continued, he would have considered the emotional impact of sundered friendships on this six-year-old child.[87] Mr. Powditch asserted that even though the Department was allegedly returning Nancy to Fiji for her own welfare, a psychiatrist said in an affidavit "that taking her back . . . could have some mental effect on her."[88] Mr. Opperman thought it was in the best interests of the child to be with "her rightful parents in Fiji" and no other arrangements could satisfactorily meet Nancy's needs. Furthermore he noted that "photographs in the Press show the little girl as happily reunited with her family."[89]

Press and journal reports attempted to challenge arguments used by Mr. Opperman in defense of his position. The editors of the *Nation* contended that the financial condition of the Prasad family "is completely irrelevant to a question of justice." What they considered relevant was the avoidance of exacerbating relations between Australians and Fijians who covet their positions in the Fijian economy.[90] This editorial dismissed Mr. Opperman's assertion that Fijians did not resent the treatment of Nancy Prasad. The *Fijian Times,* the supposed source of Opperman's claim, "happens to be Australian owned and controlled and every intelligent person in Fiji knows this."[91] To cap the argument the editorial asked somewhat rhetorically, "If Nancy Prasad is not accepted as a migrant, who is? At her age, she would take nobody's job. She has no political convictions, which is always something for a Minister to fall back on if he refuses admission."[92] Some newspapers were equally blunt in their denunciation of Mr. Opperman's action. The *Daily Mirror* characterized the case as ". . . one of the most depressing examples yet of Australian bureaucracy at its lumbering, insensitive, boorish, overbearing, pig-headed, undiplomatic, pompous, bureaucratic worst."[93]

The *Canberra Times* also opposed Mr. Opperman's protestations:

> White Australia remains as a practical political policy of discrimination against prospective migrants on the basis of skin colour. It is hypocrisy to claim otherwise. The limited extent of the "exceptions" is amply demonstrated by this latest case. One would not have thought that Nancy Prasad's integration would prove difficult.[94]

The Prasad Deportation: A Test Case 247

On another occasion the *Mirror* claimed the "facts [in the case] are simple."

> If Nancy were a six-year old white foreign child her relatives would decide where she would live and with whom.
> But as Nancy is a six-year old colored foreign child the Minister for Immigration, Mr. Hubert Opperman, decides.
> And he has decided to apply the color bar.
> Make no mistake about it. It is the color of Nancy's skin that has got her booted out of Australia. It is because of the color of her skin that the Immigration Department evicted her from a home where she was happy and cared for back to parents who don't want her.
> And this in the same week that Mr. Opperman made the outstandingly fatuous remark: "My Government does not have a White Australia policy." [95]

The Adelaide *News* described Mr. Opperman's action as one that "would be funny were it not so sad, so offensive to ordinary kindness and common sense, and so damaging to Australia's image in Asia." [96] This interpretation of the case was widely accepted in some press circles and Mr. Opperman was often vilified for his "injudicious administration of an odious policy," but he did receive some support. The *Advertiser* applauded the effort of the Minister for Immigration "to temper the impact of inflexible laws. He certainly showed concern for the child's welfare by trying to ensure that her departure would be free of the emotional stress of publicity and clamor." [97] Distorted propaganda abroad due to irresponsible attacks on departmental actions was what the *Mercury* deplored in its appraisal of the aftermath of the Prasad case. "The Immigration Department," it noted with pride, "has acted, in this case, with a tolerance and restraint which few other countries would have shown." [98] Brisbane's *Courier-Mail* described the case as "a cunning and deliberate attempt to break our laws and at the same time appeal to Australians' spirit of humanity in order to have the break condoned. . . ." The editorial commended the decisions of the Department: ". . . the Immigration Department has acted neither harshly nor unfairly." [99]

Individual opinion varied too. One officeholder of an international organization claimed that all visas are issued for a specified period and if after the expiration date one has not left the country deportation proceedings follow.

> This would not be because I am Australian and white but because I was breaking the law and failing to keep an undertaking implicit in the granting of a tourist visa.
> The situation in which the Prasad family find themselves is precisely this, and the action taken by the immigration authorities is in accordance with international practice.[100]

On the other hand one observer termed the Department's decision "another example of the Government's increasingly bureaucratic and dogmatic behaviour. For a Government claiming to be Liberal, its attitude has become increasingly illiberal, intolerant and inflexible." [101] The President of the University Branch of the Queensland Association for Immigration Reform implied that sides were taken in the Prasad case on the basis of two conflicting "sets of facts." One set claimed Nancy's father was destitute; the Prasads wanted Nancy to remain in Australia; and the Fijian population was vexed by the color bar directed at a six-year-old girl. The other claimed Nancy's father was able to support her; both parents wanted the girl to return to Fiji; the Fiji press was favorable to the decision; and "Roy Prasad also favoured Nancy's return." [102]

Another opinion labeled "facts" as irrelevant. "This whole affair of trumped up racialism is designed to breed disrespect for the laws of the land. . . . This little girl was a visitor here—and the time came, the visit being over, for her to return home." [103] Others just as pleased with the Department's action thought easing the policy could cause the kind of racial disturbances seen in almost every part of the globe. "We have been spared these tribulations by our immigration policy," [104] said one government sympathizer.

One professor wrote:

> My knowledge of the facts satisfies me that both the Minister and the Department of Immigration have handled the matter with the greatest consideration and humanity. If you wish to alter the law to permit unrestricted immigration from all countries you are free to advocate this. But why should we admit Nancy Prasad rather than all the millions of little girls who might have a more promising future here? [105]

Another professor at the University of Sydney was mortified at the "inhumanity and insensitivity" in the decision. He maintained: "There is a tradition in British law, the prerogative of mercy. I would have thought that this would be a case for using such a power of compassion." [106]

In an even less favorable account of the incident one irate graduate student castigated Mr. Opperman's administration of policy.

> Scarcely had he disowned the white-Australia policy (last Thursday), when on the stage stepped the menacing six-year-old figure of Nancy Prasad, instantly recognizable as a threat to Australia's racial homogeneity.
>
> The Minister is not slow to act. She is chased through the streets of Sydney by Commonwealth police with a warrant for her arrest, seized, and interrogated for several hours and deported in dramatic circumstances with the world's press in attendance.
>
> The author of this farce does not seem to know what he is doing, and treats public opinion and elementary decencies with impartial contempt.[107]

Olabisi Ajala, the well-known African journalist, made a direct appeal on Nancy's behalf to Mr. Opperman's political judgment. He importuned the Department to reconsider its decision since "Political wisdom . . . calls for second thoughts."

Nancy's deportation would do more harm to Australia in Asia and Africa than a thousand goodwill missions could rectify.

For Nancy's only misfortune is the color of her skin, and Asians and Africans will see her as yet another victim of the White Australia policy. . . .

In most of these countries, Australia has been violently condemned for her immigration policy towards colored people. Asians and Africans cannot understand it in this era of "winds of change."

I travelled through Lebanon, India, Korea, Malaya, the Philippines and many other such countries. Everywhere I heard the same story: Australia was following in the footsteps of racially intolerant South Africa.

For a black person like myself, enjoying Australian hospitality, understanding and racial equality, it is painful to see Australia misrepresented abroad. The ugly image must be killed now, and you have the power to do it.

A compassionate gesture to Nancy Prasad will help to wipe away the stain of White Australia. Please let her stay.[108]

This kind of dramatic plea was countered with a claim that the dramatics associated with Nancy Prasad led one to overlook the facts. "But for the child's state of health at the time of her parents' departure she would have accompanied them as a member of the family and the incident would have been closed." [109]

Emotional, at times overzealous, responses were shown by public letters and the active support civil rights workers received in their petition demanding Nancy's return. One man collected five hundred signatures in less than two hours by standing on a street corner in Balmain, a Sydney suburb. Another petitioner, according to reports, collected two hundred signatures in a few minutes in a Sydney hotel.[110] Despite this evidence to the contrary, Senator Henty claimed that displeasure with the Immigration Department's decision had been exaggerated and "the Fiji Government was satisfied with the Australian Government's handling of the case." [111] The *Mirror,* in retort, rejected these remarks as "irrelevant." An editorial argued that it "is the opinion

The Prasad Deportation: A Test Case 251

of Asian governments which really matter . . . like those of India, the Philippines, Indonesia and Malaysia." These are the states most likely to censure Australia's decision, it claimed. With the same caustic adjectives used on other occasions the *Mirror* editorial proceeded to denounce the Government as "inhuman, unimaginative, insensitive, undiplomatic, mulish, overbearing, tactless, pompous, and more incredibly stupid than any government has the right to be." [112] The *Mirror's* Hong Kong correspondent reported that Asian enthusiasm over the A.L.P. decision to delete the term "White Australia" from its policy had dissipated with reports of the Prasad case. He wrote "there was a violently adverse reaction in the Press at the news that the long fight to keep Nancy . . . in Australia had failed and she had been deported." [113] Foreign bitterness was expressed by several Manila columnists, particularly the vociferous Maximo Soliven, who excoriated the "real motives" behind Opperman's decision as blatant racism.[114] Although it is difficult to assess Fijian opinion from the notably British *Fijian Times,* several letters sent to the newspaper give some impression of the local mood on this issue. One local resident wrote:

> I believe that the White Australia policy is only a scapegoat in this affair. Nancy's relatives want her in Australia. The Australian Immigration Authority wants her back in Fiji with her parents for a simple reason—that the permit that allowed Nancy and her parents into Australia must be honoured.[115]

Another letter to the editor stated that the latest development in the story is "a sad commentary on the state of the Australian public's attitude." [116] A correspondent who signed his name "Bags" wrote, "The total lack of a sense of proportion is astonishing," [117] and another pointed out a fear many Fijians shared because of the Prasad incident when he referred to "many in Fiji who are astonished at the seeming subterfuge practised, and who are concerned lest in some places the reputation of the Colony's citizens should suffer as a result." [118] Still another Fijian, who felt that the reputation of the small group of islands would be damaged by Nancy's notoriety, wrote:

> The basic fact about the Prasad case is that these people [Prasads] have broken the law in Australia and deserve the consequences. They deserve no sympathy.
>
> Do the Powditches care that by their actions they have made things difficult for all Fiji-Indians in the eyes of Immigration authorities? [119]

A Fijian Indian who "jumped ship" and married an Australian girl claimed that he was being "terrorised" by Department officials who were tightening up migrant controls as a result of the Prasad case.[120]

The reaction of several liberal Australian parliamentarians was not as favorable as some of the opinions expressed in the *Fijian Times*. Senator McManus, D.L.P., characterized the Department's administration of the case as the "type . . . we had in the days of the Sergeant Gamboa and Mrs. O'Keefe cases."[121] Senator Fitzgerald (A.L.P.), unwilling to take sides on the issue, said, "It will create a very bad image abroad."[122] And Mr. Allan D. Fraser, M.P. (A.L.P.), described Nancy Prasad as having "all the qualifications of the migrants on whom we spend £1,000 to bring to Australia, so urgent is our need." He continued his appraisal with a political innuendo to the effect that "Mr. Opperman, while declaring that the Liberal Party has no White Australia policy, has given a harsh demonstration of it."[123] But these views did not represent the majority of parliamentary opinion. In fact the case was conspicuously absent from debate; only once was it mentioned from 1962 to 1965. When the issue did arise Allan Fraser spoke for many of his colleagues when he said:

> The action taken by the Department of Immigration to require the little girl to return to her parents was simply in the normal course of the administration of the existing policy, but the fact that is now apparent is that a case of this nature, into which an

element of pathos enters, is very widely publicized in Australia but far more widely and sensationally publicized in Asian and African newspapers to the very great detriment of Australia. . . .[124]

With Nancy back at home, Mr. Opperman assured the press that Fiji was "the only place where this little girl really belongs,"[125] but that statement did not satisfy those seeking the girl's return to Australia. On August 23, 1965, Mr. Opperman reported that the family, seeking the girl's readmission, had developed a "nuisance campaign." He noted that "any further approaches to him would be useless."[126] Furthermore, Mr. Opperman once again refuted allegations that Nancy was living in substandard conditions in Fiji. Information he had received from Mr. Hamilton, the Australian Commissioner in Fiji, and other sources indicated Nancy was living in "a good house in congenial surroundings."[127] These factors as well as legal considerations led him to the conclusion that the decision concerning Nancy "had been in the best interests of the girl and the claim made for keeping the girl in Australia on compassionate grounds, has been disproved."[128] It was made quite clear that as far as the Immigration Department was concerned the case was closed. One editorial suggested that the decision to close the case was "not before time."[129] The irony of the incident, it was reported, was that the Minister's desire to be patient, sympathetic and flexible was used to repudiate the obligations legally undertaken by the Prasad family. This was clearly understood by newspapers in Fiji; the editorial claimed "even . . . the Hindi press was almost wholly favourable to Australia." In a concluding statement "the dubious methods used in the Prasad affair" were condemned as those that "discourage Governments from administering the law flexibly."[130]

Dismayed but not discouraged with Mr. Opperman's "intransigence" Powditch and his wife applied to the British Foreign Office for permission to take Nancy to England. The Powditches planned to remain there until such time as Nancy could be adopted. Prior to their departure for London Powditch, at Nandi Airport in Fiji, said that Nancy wanted to return to Australia with him immediately. "She was crying and wanted me to bring her back with me," [131] he related.

With the case almost concluded, Charles Perkins, the student reformer who was Nancy's abductor, wrote a public letter explaining his position. He attempted to point out "the only really important things" in regard to Nancy Prasad and Australia's immigration policy. For one thing, he wrote, the policy "whether it be called White Australia or not—is based on one criterion alone and that is the color of one's skin—or, more specifically, race." "Further," he reasoned, "it is immaterial whether Nancy Prasad was returned to a pig sty, or a palace, in Fiji. . . . The principle being contested surely is the fact that we have operating effectively here in Australia an immigration policy based on race. . . ." As an alternative to the present or an open door policy it was suggested that a selective system of immigration be implemented. "This," it was argued, "would enable any person, regardless of race, to enter the country, providing he meets requirements. . . ." Finally Perkins described his adventurous kidnapping as an event that "educated the general public . . . to Australia's racialist, and archaic immigration policy. It brought the whole issue out into the open to be discussed and analysed." [132]

Perkins' arguments were used by Nancy's sister and brother-in-law in their accusation that Nancy's case was misrepresented by Opperman. Mrs. Powditch, Nancy's sister, distributed pamphlets accusing the Minister of deporting Nancy "because the colour of her skin was not white" to delegates at the Australian Citizenship Convention outside the Canberra Theater. "It is inconceivable that any other consideration could be relevant in the case of a six-year-old child," she wrote in this open letter. Because of this consideration she accused "the Minister of being a regimentor of people whose skin pigmentation does not match his own. This is one of the worst aspects of racialism." [133]

Once in England to commence adoption proceedings, Powditch expressed his gratitude to those, including Perkins, who supported his cause, and at the same interview revealed his plans for Nancy's future. "We had planned to go back to Australia once we made Nancy our legal daughter . . . ," he said. "We simply left to beat the ban. But we have changed our minds. We are staying in England. . . ." He noted that his family had no resentment toward Australians, only gratitude. "The trade unionists who helped pay for our flights home, the Sydney students who did what they could for Nancy by kidnapping her when she was being thrown out . . . everyone." But the Australian Immigration Department was caustically reproved for "their heartless law" and "their cruelty in forcing Nancy to leave the only home she had known." [134] It was admitted by Shashi Powditch that the purpose of taking Nancy to London was "to beat the White Australia policy through adoption." [135] However, it was recently noted by Roy Prasad that "the adoption case has been adjourned a few times now and the indication I got from Mr. Powditch was that the way things stand now there is very little chance [of adoption]." [136]

The March, 1966, ministerial statement liberalizing established immigration policy provided, among other things, that permanent residence might be available to: "persons who, by former residence in Australia or by association with us have demonstrated an interest or identification with Australia that should make their residence here feasible." [137] When one columnist asked if Nancy was eligible for reentry under this provision she received the "unusually unequivocal answer" of "No." [138]

Ultimate authority in such cases remains within the Minister's purview regardless of the entry categories. This, in spite of the announced liberalization, is the most notable feature in the administration of the policy. As far as some critics are concerned absolute ministerial discretion is one of the most egregious examples of arbitrary power. In a printed attack on ministerial discretion Mr. Hayden (M.H.R., Oxley) denounced the "discrimination" in the Department and the lack of explanations for departmental action.

> We had the case of a six year old Fijian girl deported from this country. Why was she deported? There are questions here to which we would like answers. . . . Would she have had a better future in Australia? I wish the Minister and his Department had answered some of these questions in their deliberations.[139]

"The case is officially closed," commented Mr. Opperman.[140] Its repercussions have only just begun, said some critics of the Department. Both views have some validity. While the Minister retains absolute discretion in all cases, he is, nonetheless, affected by public pressures. It was reported during the period of Mr. Opperman's liberalization proposals that "the new Prime Minister [Mr. Holt] was determined to avoid a repetition of the Nancy Prasad case. . . ."[141] This report attributed "Holt's rethinking of the migration policy" to the pressures resulting from the Prasad incident.[142] In a review in the *Australian Quarterly* one political analyst wrote: "it seems likely that the timing of the changes had a lot to do with the unfavorable publicity Australia was receiving overseas as a result of the Nancy Prasad and Aurelio Locsin cases."[143] In view of the timing, a link between the announced immigration reforms and the Prasad case was an irresistible conclusion for the press and even more astute analysts. An Immigration Department official, however, argued "there is no relationship at all between recent liberalization of the policy and the Nancy Prasad Case."[144] He noted that since the same proposals were made in 1964 and rejected by Robert Menzies[145] the text of the Department's program was not affected by Nancy Prasad's notoriety. This does not imply that the Government has not been affected by being in the spotlight of considerable negative press opinion. In the exchange of international views, Nancy Prasad probably did Australia more damage than any other single deportation decision involving "White Australia,"[146] suggested one newspaper correspondent. The same reporter

The Prasad Deportation: A Test Case   257

suggested that when the Prasad family appeals were rejected, "the whole world looked on in a mixture of horror and astonishment while this bewildered child was at last loaded onto a plane to take her away." [147]

Immigration officials may have tried to forget the Prasad issue but as late as March, 1966, the Department was still beseiged by petitions demanding Nancy's reentry. The New Settlers' Federation, civil rights organizations, and some immigration reform groups still use Nancy as a symbol of Australia's color bar.

Most of the evidence accumulated indicates that Mr. Opperman was legally correct in deporting the child; but this does not answer some objections raised against his decision. The Immigration Department assumed, not without precedent, that Mr. Prasad would use the child as a lever to gain entry into Australia for himself and his family. Likewise, the Department was justifiably fearful that others in a similar situation would try the same tactics in order to remain permanently. While these arguments are quite logical and consistent with departmental experience, they do not take into consideration the absolute discretion with which the Minister is empowered. There would probably have been no great public objection to the Minister permitting Nancy to remain while admonishing the remainder of the family that his decision did not sanction their reentry. There have been illustrations in Australia's recent past when an exception was made in the interpretation of policy.

Some immigration reformers have asked what possible harm could have come to Australia or her immigration policy if a six-year-old girl were permitted permanent residence. They argue that the Minister's decision was a manifestation of the abuses inherent in White Australia. The argument could be made, with some justification, that Mr. Prasad had no other recourse for permanent entry but the use of misrepresentation. In 1965 only one distinguished Fijian and two dependents, and eight Fijians of mixed descent were accepted for permanent residence.[148] If Mr. Prasad had employed the ordinary legal channels for admission it would have been quite unlikely he would be considered for permanent entry. His application would not come under "the distinguished and highly qualified category" in the policy, thereby prohibiting, for all practical purposes, his qualification for permanent residence. Opperman was probably slandered when the Prasads called him a racist; but as the defender of a seemingly discriminatory policy he perpetuated for many the sense of racial restriction.

That Australia has the right to decide which people will populate its land is entirely reasonable. That race should be a basis for administering this decision is increasingly unreasonable. The Prasad case represented the attempted justification of the reasonable by the unreasonable, thereby casting doubt and confusion on the whole affair.

10

Conclusions

Most of Australia's immigration laws reflect her position as a white, wealthy, sparsely populated continent in the midst of non-white, poor, overcrowded nations. The desire to maintain a Christian, democratic, industrial, egalitarian, peaceful, wealthy and literate population is the rationale for non-European restriction. But in the post World War II period both the fact and the rationale have been called into question by external and internal spokesmen of immigration reform as well as the "forces of history." Notwithstanding determined opposition to reform and the association of White Australia with the national ethos, the last decade has been punctuated by at least some liberalization of the non-European immigration policy.

Since World War II pressure groups have been actively campaigning for immigration reform but limited resources and significant opposition have interfered with their success. Despite the fact that reformers are becoming more acceptable, government policy-makers mainly oppose them. Immigration officials fear an excess of zeal and irresponsibility in reform proposals even though there has been little evidence to substantiate this fear.

Large segments of the population have a vested interest in maintaining the status quo and opposing immigration reform. It is significant indeed that, with this opposition, reform has occurred at all.

An unwitting ally of immigration reform has been the fragmentation of an international status quo. The once permissive and silent colonial states are now vocally assertive, independent states. In the colonial setting racism could be manifested with impunity, but in non-white liberated states, fiercely nationalistic and racially conscious, any policy tainted by non-white racialism is condemned in the United Nations Assembly by the Afro-Asian bloc, which constitutes a majority of the members. In diplomatic circles the trend toward egalitarianism cannot be discounted by politicians administering immigration policy. The changing world scene has forced Australia to be predisposed to treat all men by roughly equal standards. Not to do so, is to opt out of the one institutional arena that permits the exchange of national views and negotiations for the settlement of international disputes.

Australian politicians realize the indefensibility of racial notions in a world increasingly sensitive to such issues, but most believe the principles on which White Australia was adopted should be retained. To satisfy these competing and seemingly contradictory tendencies, politicians have often relied on rhetorical rather than real policy revisions. And when the rhetoric could not conceal an underlying racial position only those changes needed to mollify opinion were enacted, while the basic ingredients of immigration legislation remained unaltered. Thus liberalization for most politicians has been a way of concealing the "real" policy and at the same time promoting Australia's position as a "progressive, anti-colonial state."

Some liberalization has also occurred because of fortuitous events in foreign states. After the Chinese revolution of 1948 Australia considered retaining Chinese war refugees rather than deporting them to a state where they would have been prosecuted. Once in Australia by the Government's sufferance, policy adjustments had to be made to account for the *de facto* residence status of these Chinese. Similarly, British economic problems in the postwar era have led to an increasing disengagement of military forces east of Suez and a growing desire for Common Market membership. These trends have encouraged Australia to rely on American and SEATO alliances as an alternative to British protection and to turn to Asia as a source of trade and investment. In both cases, an exclusive immigration policy stands as a possible source of interference in strategic and economic decisions deemed essential to national welfare. Although there is no direct causal relationship between regional concerns and liberalization of immigration policy, indirectly more regional contact makes a restrictive immigration policy more indefensible. As long as the immigration policy retains the widespread image of being "racial" many Asians (and others) will resist Australian entry into the economic and strategic community of the Asian region. It is not too farfetched to conceive of non-whites excluding "White Australia" as a member of any regional pacts with the rationalization that its "differentness" excludes it from the community of Asian interests. The possibility of an inverted "white policy" imposed against Australia has already been explored by the Philippines after the Gamboa and Locsin incidents. With these considerations in mind, it is apparent that a White Australia policy jeopardizes the national welfare and, as a policy that excludes most non-Europeans, cannot be maintained.

Australians generally have become more attuned to their contemporary problems in the postwar period. With few exceptions, Australian Gallup polls have continually indicated a moderation of public opinion on the immigration issue. This change in the public's view of the policy is due to several factors. In addition to a more sophisticated attitude toward foreign affairs and Australia's regional role, Colombo Plan and other non-European students, despite some disenchantment with Australia, have also helped to change the Australian stereotype of their Asian neighbors. Furthermore, non-Europeans resident in Australia, particularly in the Melbourne community, are examples of the smooth adjustment of the "allegedly unassimilable." By observation many Australians now regard the once "sacred cow" of the "White Australia principle" as expendable. Newspaper editorials note the public's changes of opinion and have reflected it in their own opposition to rigid administration of the immigration laws. Their publicity for immigration reform and the notoriety accorded several *causes célèbres* have contributed to the pressures for liberalization. Lastly, the Nancy Prasad case and other incidents which have been predominantly displayed in newspaper headlines have often "tugged at the heart strings" of the general public and illustrated, whether wrongly or rightly, "the harshness, inhumanity and arbitrary" manner in which the policy is administered.

It is impossible to estimate accurately which of these factors is most responsible for policy reform. In fact, all of the factors mentioned are complementary. Political decisions and newspaper reportage are affected by public opinion but they, in turn, shape public opinion. Likewise, pressure groups exert reform influence in public circles but they are influenced by what they perceive to be unrepresented opinion in the public. The combination of factors, each interacting with the other, has created a unique climate for liberalization in the 1960's.

Nonetheless, liberalization to date has been, and probably will continue to be, modest. The limited extent of the change indicates a persistent Australian faith in a predominantly homogeneous society and an implicit belief that non-Europeans are unassimilable. Government leadership is not likely to change this situation. Australian political leaders still maintain the belief that "a free country has the absolute right to determine its demographic composition." They maintain the view that Australia's "freedom from intolerance and discrimination" should be retained. But at what price? One could argue that administering a discriminatory policy intolerantly in order to retain a land allegedly free from intolerance is the utilization of an immoral mean for a moral end.

The fear of conflict in a multi-racial community has combined with Australian nationalism to produce a fear of any migrants who will not "fit in." These forces are responsible for a resistance to further liberalization and for the lack of a meaningful dialogue about possible Asian contributions to Australia.

Presumably population is one of Australia's major problems. It was this issue that influenced the migrant recruitment program and it is this issue which is at the core of strategic considerations and the paranoid expression of "populate or perish." H. L. Harris concluded that Australian population problems can be solved in one or more of three ways: increase the birthrate; induce people to come to Australia from Great Britain and Europe; "discard prejudices so that Australia can learn how to attract and assimilate types less like Australians." [1] The first of these proposals has had almost no impact on Australia. Despite a rising birthrate, Australians have been unable to appreciably increase the population, and with widespread use of "the pill" the prospect for a higher birthrate in the future is not promising. The second proposal has been the focus of migration programs since 1947. When the Government surmised British migrants could not be attracted to Australia in numbers that would serve the nation's population needs, bilateral agreements were signed with several European states to supply additional migrants. The United Kingdom, Greece, Italy and Malta now supply almost seventy-five per cent of Australia's migrants and, according to immigration officials, migrant recruitment will remain predominantly confined to these and other European countries. However, persuading Europeans to come to Australia is an increasingly difficult task. As social comforts, higher standards of living, and job security increase, Europeans are becoming more reluctant to leave their homelands for promises of affluence in the glamorized land Down-Under. An inability to lure Europeans from their new prosperity has provoked some, often self-conscious, discussion of Mr. Harris's third proposal: the acceptance and "assimilation" of types less like Australians. This would involve not only further liberalization of the immigration policy but a reevaluation of migration goals and perhaps the addition of another dimension to the national character. If population continues to be a primary concern for Australians, large-scale Asian immigration may be inevitable in spite of the national predilections against this possibility. Furthermore, Australian notions of homogeneity may have to change to accommodate the diversity of culture imposed by Asian migration.

The Department of Immigration, as well as most Australians, stresses homogeneity or assimilation as a goal of migrant adjustment, even though the words themselves are not used very often. But a conciliatory attitude to nothing but conformity induces the migrant to cling to Old World traditions and cultural patterns he knows best, and interferes with the very result immigration officials desire. Homogeneity is sometimes thought of as the indispensable basis of Australian society. But this is a viewpoint obscured by complacency, an inflated view of the "national character" and a Panglossian attitude that "this is the best of all possible worlds." In an atmosphere where homogeneity is the goal of the host culture, any semblance of nonconformity or national identity is a potential source of conflict.

Australia's future may be predicated not only on a burial of the White Australia policy, but acceptance of cultural differentiation which recognizes the right of groups to retain differences as long as they also maintain some loyalty to their adopted land. By forthrightly denying a rigidly restrictive immigration policy and stating the expected level of Asian intake, the Government could begin to prepare the nation for what has been occurring without fanfare for a decade. Public announcements of this shift in attitude will enable the Government to initiate a more comprehensive education program in secondary schools designed to develop an understanding of Asian culture, traditions and religion. To avoid social tension sociological projects can be instituted to obtain data on the community's level of tolerance.[2] If, as the late Prime Minister Holt suggested, Australia's geographic location is taken into consideration, programs on a community basis should develop appreciation for Asian culture. The racial prejudices Australians sometimes develop, usually occur at lower socio-economic levels. But this condition is not inexorable. By allowing only sponsored and relatively skilled immigrants into the country most discrimination can be avoided.

Australia's immigration program is unique; by attempting to raise the population by one per cent each year it has embarked on an unparalleled migration course. But with the traditional sources of migrants disappearing and with Australia facing competition for migrants from Canada and other states, she should take the lead in encouraging the emigration of her skilled neighbors to the north. If passage is paid for certain European migrants, there is no reason why this practice cannot be applied to some non-European migrants. Only by treating non-Europeans as Europeans are today can Australia erase the stigma of racialism and meet the problems demanded by her own demographic needs. Just as good sense and reasonableness demand an Australian tolerance for distinctive European traditions, so too, should this tolerance apply to non-European distinctiveness. In the last analysis immigration policy will require from Australians not less love of their own, but more tolerance of others.

Appendix: Australian Newspapers

Australian newspapers, like any which comprise a national press free of government censorship, must appeal to differing tastes and interests in their readers. But perhaps because Australia's population is so homogeneous and overwhelmingly middle class, one is more struck by the similarities between publications than by their extreme differences. Almost without exception, for example, the Australian press, although quite free in its criticism of government policy, endorses the side of the Liberal-Country Party coalition at election time. Because there is little support even from trade union members for an exclusively Labor-oriented newspaper, there are, at present, no Labor Party dailies of widespread circulation in the major cities.[1]

In addition to a homogeneous readership, similar viewpoints may also reflect the fact that influential metropolitan newspapers are gradually coming under the control of a very few owners. The fifteen capital city newspapers are controlled by only five companies:

Herald and Weekly Ltd. owns: *The Sun-News Pictorial* (Melbourne); *The Herald* (Melbourne); controls: *The Courier-Mail* (Brisbane); *Telegraph* (Brisbane); *The Advertiser* (Adelaide); has an interest in: *The Mercury* (Hobart).

John Fairfax, Ltd. owns: *The Sydney Morning Herald; The Sun* (Sydney); *The Sun-Herald* (Sydney); controls: *The Canberra Times;* has an interest in: *The Age* (Melbourne).

Australian Consolidated Press Ltd. owns: *The Daily Telegraph* (Sydney); *The Sunday Telegraph* (Sydney).

Considered as an owner, News Ltd., Mirror Newspapers Ltd., and Nationwide News Pty. Ltd. and their subsidiaries, own: *The News* (Adelaide); *The Daily Mirror* (Sydney); *The Sunday Mirror* (Sydney); *The Sunday Times* (Perth); *The Australian* (national); one-half of *The Sunday Mail* (Adelaide).[2]

To stress certain similarities between publications, however, is not to deny the existence of basic differences in quality, approach and objectives. In the capital city newspapers these differences fall into two categories: the objective and sober reporting of news exhibited by the morning "broadsheets"; and the more sensationalized and entertaining approach of the afternoon and Sunday "tabloids."[3]

The following newspapers quoted in the text fall into the first category: [4]

Newspaper	*Circulation*
The Sydney Morning Herald	294,000
The Age (Melbourne)	186,268
The Courier-Mail (Brisbane)	249,069
The Advertiser (Adelaide)	209,116
The Canberra Times	26,613
The Australian (printed simultaneously in Sydney, Melbourne, Brisbane)	100,240

Of these, perhaps the two most prestigious are the *Sydney Morning Herald* and *The Age,* the latter being also somewhat

Appendix: Australian Newspapers

more conservative. Both *The Advertiser* and *The Courier-Mail* tend to be reserved in their criticism and prefer the role of guardian of the status quo to that of social reformer. *The Canberra Times* and *The Australian* are first-rate newspapers which are more national in scope than the other capital city dailies, although *The Canberra Times* circulates almost exclusively in the Australian Capital Territory.

Other morning newspapers cited which are not broadsheets are: *The West Australian* (Perth), circulation 190,651, *The Daily Telegraph* (Sydney), circulation 342,000, and *The Mercury* (Hobart), circulation 50,858, all of which are quite serious tabloids; the best of these is *The Daily Telegraph* and the most conservative is *The Mercury*.

Afternoon and Sunday newspapers which fall into the second category mentioned are:

Newspaper	Circulation
The Sunday Telegraph (Sydney)	685,000
The Daily Mirror (Sydney)	365,872
Sunday Mirror (Sydney)	543,763
The Daily News (Perth)	100,171
The Sun (Sydney)	342,812
The Sun-Herald (Sydney)	748,092

There are two exceptional afternoon newspapers: *The News* of Adelaide (circulation 135,428), a socially conscious newspaper which has begun to lose some of its reputation as a crusader but is still concerned with exposing injustices in the country; and *The Herald* of Melbourne (circulation 498,133), a "serious" broadsheet comparable to morning publications.[5]

The only newspaper cited which is no longer in existence is *The Argus* of Melbourne. For most of its history an ultraconservative daily, *The Argus* was purchased by a London-based firm in 1948 and changed its format radically. For the next nine years, until its demise in 1957, it was a highly sensationalized paper which resembled a tabloid much more than a broadsheet.

Notes

Chapter 1

1. *Commonwealth Parliamentary Debates (C.P.D.)*, L (1966), 584.
2. *The Sydney Morning Herald*, October 9, 1961; *The West Australian* (Perth), October 9, 1961. Statement attributed to Sir Alexander Downer.
3. *C.P.D.*, L (1966), 69 (Mr. Hubert Opperman).
4. *Ibid.*, XXVII (1960), 1564.
5. Mr. Arthur Calwell was Minister for Immigration before 1960 but his statement was made in the March, 1966, debate on this issue.
6. Charles Price, "White Restrictions on Colored Immigration," *Race*, VII, No. 3 (1966), 219–20.
7. *Ibid.*, p. 221.
8. *Ibid.*, p. 223.
9. *Ibid.*
10. Myra Willard, *History of the White Australia Policy* (Melbourne: Melbourne University Press, 1923), p. 189.
11. *Ibid.*, p. 193.
12. *Ibid.*, pp. 192, 194; W. K. Hancock, *Australia* (London: Ernest Benn Ltd., 1930), p. 80.
13. A. Yarwood, *Asian Migration to Australia: The Background to Exclusion 1896–1913* (Melbourne: Melbourne University Press, 1964), pp. 24–25.
14. Willard, *op. cit.*, p. 202.
15. See Etienne Dennery, *Asia's Teeming Millions: Its Problems for the West* (London: Jonathan Cape, 1931); W. D. Forsyth, *Myth of Open Spaces* (Melbourne: Melbourne University Press, 1942); H. L. Wilkinson, *The World's Population Problems and a White Australia* (London: P. S. King, 1930).
16. Gordon Greenwood, *Australia: A Social and Political History*

(Sydney: Angus & Robertson, 1955), p. 205.
17. David Johanson, "History of the White Australia Policy," K. Rivett (ed.), *Immigration: Control or Colour Bar?* (Melbourne: Melbourne University Press, 1962), pp. 2–3.
18. Willard, *op. cit.*, p. 28.
19. A. P. Elkin, "A White Australia," in W. D. Borrie (ed.), *A White Australia: Australia's Population Problem* (Sydney: Australasian Publishing Co., 1947), p. 177.
20. G. Greenwood, *op. cit.*, p. 22.
21. Robin Williams, "The Reduction of Intergroup Tensions," Social Science Research Council, *Bulletin 57* (1947), p. 54.
22. Johanson, *op. cit.*, p. 4.
23. Willard, *op. cit.*, p. 21.
24. Elkin, *op. cit.*, p. 177.
25. Johanson, *op. cit.* (quoting *The Argus* [Melbourne], April 10, 1855), p. 4.
26. Willard, *op. cit.*, p. 21.
27. Johanson, *op. cit.*, pp. 5–6.
28. Willard, *op. cit.*, pp. 40–42; Greenwood, *op. cit.*, p. 177.
29. Johanson, *op. cit.*, p. 7.
30. *Ibid.*, p. 8; Greenwood, *op. cit.*, p. 123.
31. Greenwood, *op. cit.*, pp. 123–24.
32. Johanson, *op. cit.*, p. 10.
33. *Ibid.*, p. 14.
34. Clive Turnbull, "White Australia," in R. J. Gilmore and D. Warner (eds.), *Near North* (Sydney: Angus & Robertson, 1948), p. 76; Johanson, *op. cit.*, p. 15.
35. Greenwood, *op. cit.*, p. 127; Turnbull, *op. cit.*, p. 77.
36. Yarwood, *op. cit.*, p. 5.
37. *Ibid.*, p. 13.
38. Johanson, *op. cit.*, p. 16.
39. Yarwood, *op. cit.*, p. 8.
40. Willard, *op. cit.*, p. 188.
41. Yarwood, *op. cit.*, pp. 24–25.
42. *Ibid.*, p. 19.
43. *Ibid.*, p. 2.
44. Johanson, *op. cit.*, p. 14.
45. K. E. Beazley in *C.P.D.*, L (1966), 607.
46. Yarwood, *op. cit.*, p. 26.
47. Beazley, *op. cit.*, p. 608.
48. Greenwood, *op. cit.*, p. 204.
49. Yarwood, *op. cit.*, p. 83.
50. Beazley, *op. cit.*, p. 607; Yarwood, *op. cit.*, pp. 24–25; Johanson, *op. cit.*, p. 14.
51. Johanson, *op. cit.*, p. 18.
52. *Ibid.*; quoted from W. F. Whyte, *William Morris Hughes* (Sydney: Angus & Robertson, 1957), p. 144.
53. Yarwood, *op. cit.*, pp. 139–40.
54. *Ibid.*, p. 89.
55. Johanson, *op. cit.*, p. 18.
56. *Ibid.*, p. 25.
57. C. Dodd, *Changing Attitudes To The White Australia Policy 1945–56,* honors thesis (University of Queensland, 1964), p. 9.
58. *Ibid.*, pp. 11–12.
59. During the war the Minister of Immigration allowed many war refugees into the country, exempting them from the dictation test (the usual method of screening non-European immigrants), but they were considered "prohibited immigrants" if they applied for permanent residence. A. C. Palfreeman, *The Administration of The White Australia Policy* (Mel-

bourne: Melbourne University Press, 1967), p. 86.
60. *Ibid.*, pp. 87–88.
61. Dodd, *op. cit.*, pp. 15–16; Palfreeman, *op. cit.*, pp. 102–103.
62. Dodd, *op. cit.*, p. 17.
63. Palfreeman, *op. cit.*, p. 51; Geoffrey Paul, *The White Australia Policy and South East Asia*, unpublished masters thesis (Harvard University, 1952), p. 67.
64. Dodd, *op. cit.*, p. 17.
65. Quoted in Palfreeman, *op. cit.*, p. 23.
66. N. Harper and G. Greenwood, *Australia in World Affairs 1950–55* (Melbourne: Cheshire Publishers, 1957), p. 6.
67. Anthony Clunies Ross, "Student Life: The Fifties," *Mum* (Spring, 1961), p. 30.
68. W. D. Borrie, *Immigration* (Sydney: Angus & Robertson, 1949), p. 67.
69. Werner Levi, *Australia's Outlook On Asia* (Sydney: Angus & Robertson, 1958), p. 158.
70. Hancock, *op. cit.*, p. 80.
71. See Minister for Immigration Hubert Opperman's statement in *C.P.D.*, L (1966), 69.
72. Donald Horne, *The Lucky Country* (Adelaide: Penguin Books, 1964), p. 128.
73. O. A. Oeser and S. B. Hammond, *Social Structure and Personality in a City* (London: Routledge & Kegan Paul, 1954), p. 52.
74. Yarwood, *op. cit.*, p. 142.
75. Horne, *op. cit.*, p. 129.
76. Oeser and Hammond, *op. cit.*, pp. 52–53.
77. J. Lyng, *Non-Britishers In Australia* (Melbourne: Macmillan & Co., 1927), pp. 169–70, 179.

Chapter 2

1. H. Opperman, *Australia's Immigration Policy* (Canberra: Government Printers, 1966), p. 8.
2. *Ibid.*
3. *C.P.D.*, L (1966), 68.
4. *Ibid.*, pp. 575–76.
5. Opperman, *op. cit.*, p. 8. Since 1945 approximately 21,500 persons of mixed descent have emigrated to Australia. (Information provided by the Department of Immigration, September 1, 1968.)
6. *C.P.D.*, L (1966), 68.
7. *Ibid.*
8. *Ibid.*, p. 69.
9. *Ibid.*, pp. 574–75.
10. *Ibid.*, p. 576.
11. *Ibid.*, p. 585.
12. *Ibid.*, p. 586.
13. *Ibid.*, p. 588.

14. *Ibid.*, p. 681.
15. *Ibid.*, p. 589.
16. *Ibid.*, p. 599.
17. *Ibid.*, pp. 601, 602.
18. *Ibid.*, p. 602.
19. *Ibid.*, p. 603.
20. *Ibid.*, p. 607.
21. *Ibid.*, p. 585.
22. Unpublished statement issued by Labor Party Immigration Committee.
23. Fred Daly, *Recommendations: For A.L.P. Immigration Committee*, unpublished (August, 1965), p. 3.
24. Interview, September 14, 1966.
25. Interview, September 29, 1966.
26. Interview, September 15, 1966.
27. Interview, September 29, 1966.
28. *The Australian*, February 22, 1966; *The Age* (Melbourne), February 22, 1966.
29. Interview, September 13, 1966.
30. Interview, March 2, 1967.
31. *The Mercury* (Hobart), January 19, 1966; *The Sydney Morning Herald*, January 19, 1966.
32. Don Aitkin, "Political Review," *Australian Quarterly* (June, 1966), p. 100.
33. Information supplied by Department of Immigration, February 4, 1966.
34. Robert Cooksey, "Foreign Policy Review," *Australian Quarterly* (June, 1966), p. 117.
35. *Ibid.*
36. Interview with Mr. Peter Heydon, September 13, 1966.
37. R. Cooksey, *op. cit.*
38. Interview, October 5, 1966.
39. Interview with member of the Victoria Association for Immigration Reform (V.A.I.R.), November 5, 1966.
40. *The Canberra Times*, January 28, 1966.
41. *The Australian*, January 24, 1966.
42. *The Canberra Times*, February 5, 1966.
43. *The Sydney Morning Herald*, February 11, 1966.
44. *The Australian*, February 22, 1966.
45. *The West Australian* (Perth), January 24, 1966.
46. *The Courier-Mail* (Brisbane), March 11, 1966.
47. *The Canberra Times*, March 11, 1966.
48. *The Mercury* (Hobart), March 10, 1966.
49. *The Age* (Melbourne), March 10, 1966.
50. *The Sunday Telegraph* (Sydney), March 13, 1966.
51. *The Sydney Morning Herald*, March 10, 1966.
52. *The Advertiser* (Adelaide), March 10, 1966.
53. *The Daily Telegraph* (Sydney), March 11, 1966.
54. *The Straits Times* (Singapore), quoted in *The Daily Telegraph* (Sydney), March 11, 1966.
55. *The Kuala Lumpur Daily*, quoted in *The Daily Telegraph* (Sydney), March 11, 1966.
56. *The Star* (Hong Kong), quoted in *The Daily Telegraph* (Sydney), March 11, 1966.
57. Quoted in *The Daily Telegraph* (Sydney), March 11, 1966.

58. Quoted in *The Canberra Times,* March 10, 1966.
59. *The Hindu,* quoted in *The Daily Telegraph* (Sydney), March 14, 1966.
60. *The Times of India,* quoted in *The Daily Telegraph* (Sydney), March 14, 1966.
61. *The Straits Times* (Singapore), quoted in *The Canberra Times,* February 24, 1966.
62. Quoted in *The Age* (Melbourne), March 23, 1966.
63. Quoted in *The Canberra Times,* March 11, 1966.
64. *Ibid.*
65. Quoted in *The Courier-Mail* (Brisbane), March 12, 1966.
66. Department of Immigration, "Brief Notes on Australia's Established Immigration Policy," December, 1963.
67. Department of Immigration, "Summary of Rules Generally Applying to Entry of Non-Europeans," August 25, 1966.
68. *The Courier-Mail* (Brisbane), March 12, 1966.
69. "The Missing Migrants—Is It Discrimination?" *The Australian,* March 14, 1966.
70. Interview, October 16, 1966.
71. *The Australian,* March 11, 1966.
72. Information provided by Department of Immigration, February 3, 1966; private letter, May 1, 1967.
73. Information provided by the Department of Immigration, October 29, 1966.
74. *The Age* (Melbourne), March 10, 1966, estimated "more than 2,000 non-Europeans eligible for residence status and citizenship"; *The Canberra Times,* March 10, 1966, had 5,000 "Asians in Australia . . . eligible immediately for citizenship"; the Department of Immigration estimated approximately 4,000, May 2, 1967.
75. Information provided by Department of Immigration, May 2, 1967.
76. Private letter, May 1, 1967.
77. Department of Immigration, October 29, 1966.
78. *C.P.D.,* LII (March 7, 1967), 398.
79. *The Australian,* March 21, 1967.
80. Interview with Mr. Opperman, March 2, 1967.
81. *C.P.D.,* LII, 397–98.
82. Department of Immigration, October 29, 1966.
83. Interview with Mr. Opperman, March 2, 1967.
84. *The Sydney Morning Herald,* February 21, 1966.
85. *The New York Times,* January 7, 1968; *C.P.D.* (26th Parliament, June 13, 1968), p. 2307.

Chapter 3

1. Information provided by the Department of Immigration, September 1, 1968.
2. Assimilation presupposes the rejection of old values and the adoption of new ones. The nature of social contacts is decisive in the process. When contacts are intimate and intense, fusion of a migrant group into the host community is promoted. The substitution of one nationality pattern for another is the culmination of the process. Integration, on the other hand, implies interaction between the migrant community and the host society with a resultant change in the cultural amalgam, but without the migrant's loss of cultural identity. This concept rests upon a belief in cultural differentiation within a framework of social unity. It recognizes the right of groups to retain their differences so long as the differences do not cause disruption or disunity. Plural societies stress the retention of distinctive cultural heritage in the host society. According to this notion each group maintains its separateness in a mosaic of distinct cultural entities within the framework of a national pattern. Each group, anxious to preserve its traditional ways, endeavors to create a subculture of its own. William S. Bernard, "The Integration of Immigrants" (Unesco, 1956), p. 2; M. G. Smith, *Stratification in Grenada* (California: University of California Press, 1965); H. P. Fairchild (ed.), *Dictionary of Sociology* (New York: Philosophical Library, 1944), pp. 276–77; R. E. Park, "Assimilation Social," in E. Seligman, A. Johnson (eds.), *Encyclopedia of the Social Sciences*, II (New York: The Macmillan Company, 1930), 281; R. E. Park and E. Burgess, *Introduction To The Sciences of Sociology* (Chicago: University of Chicago Press, 1921), pp. 736–37.
3. C. F. Yong, *The Chinese in New South Wales and Victoria 1901–1921*, Ph.D. thesis (Australian National University, 1966), p. 372.
4. *Ibid.*, pp. 377–78.
5. *Ibid.*, p. 379.
6. *Ibid.*, p. 381.
7. J. Lyng, *Non-Britishers in Australia* (Melbourne, Macmillan & Co. Ltd., 1927), p. 169.
8. Quoted in *ibid.*, p. 179.
9. Quoted in *The Australian*, May 31, 1966.
10. Oeser and Hammond, *Social Structure and Personality in a City*, p. 56.

11. Lyng, *op. cit.*, p. 170.
12. Conversation with President, 1966.
13. P. Tennison, "The Assimilation of a Race," *The Australian*, January 23, 1967.
14. Quoted in *ibid.*
15. *Ibid.;* although it was reported "intermarriage occurs twice as often as marriage with a Chinese partner," there is no authoritative evidence to justify the claim.
16. *Ibid.*
17. P. Tennison, "Chinatown's Own Cultural Evolution," *The Australian*, January 21, 1967.
18. *Ibid.*
19. Private letter, May 21, 1962.
20. Private letter, March 12, 1962.
21. Interview, November 26, 1966.
22. Quoted by Alan Trengove in "Mr. Wu Waits," *The Sun* (Sydney), April 16, 1966.
23. Quoted by A. Trengove in "The Marriage Question," *The Sun* (Sydney), April 18, 1966.
24. *Ibid.*
25. A. Trengove, "Citizen or Expatriate," *The Sun* (Sydney), April 19, 1966.
26. *Ibid.*
27. *The Australian*, April 2, 1967.
28. *The Courier-Mail* (Brisbane), December 8, 1966.
29. Figures released by Department of Immigration. This figure has remained fairly constant over the succeeding three years.
30. Quoted by A. Trengove in "Mr. Wu Waits," *op. cit.*

31. Quoted by A. Trengove in "A Bit of An Affront," *The Sun* (Sydney), April 20, 1966.
32. N. Harper, "Asian Students and Asian Studies in Australia," *Pacific Affairs*, XXXI, No. 1 (March, 1958), 60.
33. Roy Adams, "Overseas Students in West Australia," *Hemisphere* (July, 1965), p. 35.
34. "Through the Eyes of a Foreign Student in Australia," *Australian Teacher*, XL (July, 1964), 24.
35. Edmund Young, "Asian Student Organizations in N.S.W.," *Asiana* (Spring, 1956), p. 54.
36. *Ibid.*, pp. 57–58.
37. *Ibid.*, p. 59.
38. Mary Hodgkin, *Australian Training and Asian Living* (University of Western Australia, 1966), p. 172.
39. N. Harper, *op. cit.*, p. 62.
40. Anthony Clunies Ross, "Student Life: The Fifties," *Mum* (Spring, 1961), p. 30.
41. Mary Hodgkin, "Asian Student In an Australian University," *Educand* (November, 1958), p. 172.
42. Mary Hodgkin, *Australian Training and Asian Living*, p. 172.
43. *Ibid.*, p. 108.
44. Quoted in Leonard Radic, "Problems of Asian Students," *The Age* (Melbourne), June 13, 1964.
45. *Ibid.*
46. M. Hodgkin, *Australian Training and Asian Living*, p. 115.
47. M. Hodgkin, "When Australians Marry Asians," *Quadrant* (August–September, 1964), p. 27.
48. Quoted in A. Trengove, "A Bit of An Affront," *op. cit.*
49. *Ibid.*

50. Before March, 1966, the rules governing administration of the immigration legislation stated that non-European students can reapply for admission after spending five years in their homeland; since that time, however, the ruling has been abandoned and each student's case is said to be determined by his ability to find employment in Australia and the need for his services in his homeland.
51. A. Trengove, "A Bit of An Affront," *op. cit.*
52. Quoted in *ibid.*
53. W. D. Borrie, R. Rodgers, *Australian Population Projections 1960–1975* (Australian National University, 1961), p. 21.
54. W. D. Borrie and R. Dedman, *University Enrolments in Australia, 1955–1970* (Australian National University, 1957), pp. 11–12.
55. N. Harper, "Asian Students in Australia," *Vestes,* VI (June, 1963), 96.
56. *Ibid.,* p. 97.
57. Quoted in *The Canberra Times,* May 26, 1966.
58. Quoted in *ibid.*
59. *The Straits Times* (Kuala Lumpur), September 19, 1965.
60. Milton Gordon, *Assimilation in American Life* (New York: Oxford University Press, 1964), pp. 70–71, notes that criteria of assimilation include the following: altered cultural patterns; the acceptance of large-scale primary group relationships with groups and institutions in the host society; intermarriage; a new sense of nationality; shunning discrimination or prejudicial attitudes; and avoidance of value or power struggles with the host community.

Chapter 4

1. Quoted in P. Westerway, "Pressure Groups," *Forces in Australian Politics,* J. Wilkes (ed.) (Sydney: Angus & Robertson, 1963), p. 121.
2. R. Dixon, *Immigration and the White Australia Policy* (Sydney: Communist Party, 1945), p. 14.
3. *Ibid.*
4. *Ibid.,* p. 4.
5. *Ibid.,* p. 15.
6. *Australia's Way Forward,* Program of the Communist Party

of Australia, 21st National Congress (June, 1967), p. 8.
7. J. Jupp, *Australian Party Politics* (Melbourne: Melbourne University Press, 1964), p. 96.
8. Senator Gair (D.L.P. spokesman), quoted in *The Australian*, November 8, 1966.
9. J. T. Kane, quoted in *The Australian*, August 22, 1966.
10. *News Weekly* (a party organ), November 3, 1966.
11. *The Canberra Times*, August 22, 1966.
12. *The Sydney Morning Herald*, March 24, 1949.
13. *Ibid.*
14. A. Calwell, *Australian Tradition In Immigration* (Government Publications, 1949), pp. 1–10.
15. *The Sydney Morning Herald*, March 24, 1949.
16. A. Calwell, *Danger For Australia* (Government Publications, 1949), p. 7.
17. Calwell, *Australian Tradition In Immigration*, p. 5.
18. *Ibid.*, p. 6.
19. *Ibid.*, p. 15.
20. Interview, September 22, 1966.
21. *C.P.D.*, CXC, 527.
22. See A. Calwell, *How Many Australians Tomorrow?* (Melbourne, 1945).
23. Australian Natives' Association *Advocate* (January–February, 1962), pp. 3–4.
24. *The Canberra Times*, November 11, 1966.
25. Westerway, *op. cit.*, p. 135.
26. K. Gott, "White Ants in the A.L.P.," *Nation* (May 5, 1962), p. 5.

27. Perth correspondent, "The Parson Bows Out Of Politics," *The Bulletin* (December 2, 1961), p. 4.
28. *Immigration Quarterly* (June, 1961), p. 1.
29. Gott, *op. cit.*, pp. 5–6.
30. *Ibid.*, p. 5.
31. *Ibid.*
32. *Labor Party Conference* (1961), p. 67.
33. *Fact* (May 24, 1962), p. 1.
34. Victorian Association for Immigration Reform letter to The Australian Labor Party (A.L.P.), September, 1964.
35. F. Daly, *Report of Immigration Review Committee of the A.L.P.* (August, 1965), p. 1.
36. F. Daly, *Recommendations For Immigration Committee*, unpublished (August, 1965), pp. 6–9.
37. *Ibid.*, pp. 9–10.
38. *Ibid.*, p. 10.
39. *Ibid.*, p. 3.
40. *Official Report of the Proceedings of the 26th Commonwealth Conference* (August 2–6, 1965), pp. 25–26.
41. *The Canberra Times*, August 3, 1965.
42. *The Australian*, January 20, 1966.
43. *The Age* (Melbourne), August 3, 1966.
44. *The Sydney Morning Herald*, August 3, 1965.
45. *Ibid.*, January 19, 1965.
46. *The Age* (Melbourne), January 19, 1966.
47. *The Canberra Times*, January 20, 1966.
48. *C.P.D.*, LII (1966), 1312.
49. *Ibid.*, p. 1321.
50. *Ibid.*, p. 1322.

51. *Ibid.*, p. 1323.
52. Conversation with an A.L.P. member, September 29, 1966.
53. J. Cairns, *Living With Asia* (Melbourne: Lansdowne Press, 1965), p. 107.
54. *C.P.D.*, IX (February 23, 1956), 54.
55. Mr. Abbott quoted in *The Daily Mirror* (Sydney), February 24, 1947.
56. *The Sydney Morning Herald*, February 18, 1950.
57. Quoted in G. Greenwood, *Australia in World Affairs 1956–60* (Vancouver: University of British Columbia, 1963), p. 98.
58. *Ibid.*
59. *Ibid.*, p. 99.
60. Quoted in *The Bulletin*, March 5, 1966.
61. *The Age* (Melbourne), May 20, 1961.
62. *The Australian*, April 28, 1965.
63. *Ibid.*, October 10, 1966.
64. *The Canberra Times*, December 8, 1966.
65. A. Downer, "Commonwealth Club Luncheon," Government Publications (December 4, 1959), p. 6.
66. H. Opperman, *Australia's Immigration Policy*, paper delivered to Youth and Student Seminar on International Affairs (Canberra: Government Printers, May 28, 1966), p. 17.
67. Quoted in K. Rivett (ed.), *Immigration: Control or Colour Bar?* (Melbourne: Melbourne University Press, 1962), p. 40.
68. *C.P.D.*, XXVI (1960), 701.
69. A. Palfreeman, *Australia's Policy on Non-European Immigrants*, M.A. thesis (Australian National University, 1962).
70. *C.P.D.*, XXXVII (1962), 1872–73.
71. *The Australian*, August 20, 1966.
72. *The Sun* (Sydney), July 29, 1964.
73. Quoted in *The Australian*, September 9, 1966.

Chapter 5

1. Peter Westerway, "Pressure Groups," in *Forces in Australian Politics*, J. Wilkes (ed.) (Sydney: Angus & Robertson, 1963), p. 121.
2. R. Joseph, quoted in *The Sydney Morning Herald*, February 18, 1950.
3. *The Daily Mirror* (Sydney), July 6, 1954.
4. *The Sydney Morning Herald*, March 28, 1949.
5. Interview, September 13, 1966.

6. Interview, September 15, 1966.
7. G. L. Kristianson, *Politics of Patriotism* (Canberra: Australian National University Press, 1966), pp. 67–68.
8. *Ibid.*, p. 100.
9. *Ibid.*, p. 219.
10. *Ibid.*, p. 220.
11. L. F. Crisp, "Review," *The Canberra Times*, June 25, 1966.
12. Kristianson, *op. cit.*, p. 221.
13. *The Courier-Mail* (Brisbane), March 17, 1952.
14. *Official Minutes,* Returned Servicemen's League (R.S.L.) Congress (1961), p. 39.
15. *Official Minutes,* R.S.L. Congress (1960), p. 5.
16. *Official Minutes,* R.S.L. Congress (1960–1965).
17. *Official Minutes,* R.S.L. Congress (1961), p. 39.
18. Westerway, *op. cit.*, p. 137.
19. *Official Minutes,* R.S.L. Congress (1960), p. 6.
20. *Official Minutes,* R.S.L. Congress (1963), p. 60.
21. Amendment to Constitution, 1962 Congress Rule 3B, *Returned Servicemen's League Constitution*.
22. Westerway, *op. cit.*, p. 136.
23. *Official Minutes,* R.S.L. Congress (1962), p. 44.
24. *Official Minutes,* R.S.L. Congress (1961), p. 39.
25. *Official Minutes,* R.S.L. Congress (1963), p. 59.
26. *Official Minutes,* R.S.L. Congress (1965), p. 51.
27. Interview, October 19, 1969.
28. *R.S.L. Standing Policy,* p. 59.
29. Private letter, October 31, 1966.
30. *The Australian,* September 1, 1965.
31. *The Daily Mirror* (Sydney), July 6, 1954.
32. *The Courier-Mail* (Brisbane), April 13, 1953.
33. Private letter, October 31, 1966.
34. *Ibid.*
35. *Ibid.*
36. *Ibid.*
37. T. N. P. Dougherty, "White Australia Policy Was Key to Our High National Standards" (Brisbane: A.W.U., 1962), p. 104.
38. *Ibid.*, p. 106.
39. James Hall, "Are The Barriers Weakening?" *The Australian,* June 28, 1965.
40. *Ibid.*
41. Gizen-No-Tek (pseud.), *Colorphobia* (Sydney: R. T. Kelly, 1903), p. 236.
42. *Methodist Church Statement of Policy on Social Issues,* p. 5.
43. *The Sydney Morning Herald,* November 26, 1947.
44. *Australian Intercollegian,* November 24, 1947.
45. *Australian Intercollegian,* May 5, 1949.
46. Private letter, November 4, 1966.
47. Private letter, November 9, 1966.
48. *Ibid.*
49. Private letter, November 4, 1966.
50. *Australian Intercollegian,* November 11, 1949.

51. Bishop Moyes in N.S.W. Association for Immigration Reform, *White Australia: Time For A Change* (Sydney: 1963), p. 10.
52. *The Australian*, September 12, 1966.
53. *The Australian*, September 30, 1966.
54. Private letter, October 25, 1966.
55. Private letter, October 26, 1966.
56. Private letter, November 8, 1966.
57. *Australian Intercollegian*, February 9, 1948.
58. *Australian Intercollegian*, June 11, 1949.
59. Mannix, quoted in *Rural Life* (June, 1959), p. 3.
60. A. Palfreeman, "Administration of White Australia Policy," *Rural Life* (June, 1959), p. 44.
61. "Social Justice Statement of 1951: Future of Australia," *Rural Life* (June, 1959), p. 61.
62. *Rural Life* (April, 1964), p. 7.
63. National Catholic Rural Movement (N.C.R.M.) Policy, *Rural Life* (April, 1964), p. 7.
64. *The Sydney Morning Herald*, November 14, 1963.
65. "Report on White Australia Debate at National Union Council of NUAUS" (National Union of Australian University Students), 1959, pp. 1–3.
66. Anthony Clunies Ross, "Student Life: The Fifties," *Mum* (Spring, 1961), p. 30.
67. Statement by a former Secretary of A.L.P. Club at Melbourne University, November 11, 1966.
68. "Student Action!" *Farrago* (student newspaper), December 6, 1961.
69. L. Chipman, "Student Action in Victoria," *Vestes*, V, No. 1 (March, 1962), 33.
70. *Ibid.*
71. *Farrago*, December 6, 1961.
72. Chipman, *op. cit.*, p. 34.
73. "Time for a Change in Migration Policy" (handbill).
74. "Facts and Arguments on White Australia" (handbill), p. 2.
75. Letter, "Student Action," Student Action Committee, undated.
76. *Farrago*, December 6, 1961.
77. "Student Action Songs" (mimeo sheet).
78. *The Sydney Morning Herald*, November 25, 1966.
79. *Honi Soit* (student newspaper), March 13, 1962.
80. *Farrago*, December 6, 1961.
81. Student Action handbill, undated.
82. Letters to the Editor, *The Age* (Melbourne), November 24, 1961.
83. Letters to the Editor, *The Bulletin*, January 6, 1962, p. 23.
84. Letters to the Editor, *The Age* (Melbourne), November 28, 1961.
85. *The Times* (London), December 8, 1961.
86. *Farrago*, December 6, 1961.
87. *The Sunday Mirror* (Sydney), April 16, 1962; *The Age* (Melbourne), April 16, 1962.
88. "Student Action Songs."

89. *Secretary of Student Action Notes* (1961–1962).
90. *Farrago,* December 6, 1961.
91. *Ibid.*
92. Circular letter from J. A. C. Mackie, May 6, 1959.
93. There were 36 signatories to the pamphlet *Control or Colour Bar?* but not all of them were active participants in the book's construction.
94. Private letter, January 11, 1967.
95. K. Rivett (ed.), *Immigration: Control or Colour Bar?* (Melbourne: Melbourne University Press, 1962), p. viii.
96. "Statement of Aims," N.S.W. Association for Immigration Reform (1962), p. 2.
97. Professor Stone in N.S.W. Association for Immigration Reform, *White Australia: Time For A Change* (Sydney, 1963), p. 29.
98. Letters to the Editor, *The Sydney Morning Herald,* July 19, 1963.
99. K. Rivett (ed.), *op. cit.,* p. 135.
100. Victorian Association for Immigration Reform, *Why Does White Australia Matter?* (Melbourne, 1960), p. 5.
101. Westerway, *op. cit.,* p. 134; K. Gott, "White Ants in The A.L.P.," *Nation* (May 5, 1962), p. 5, indicated that West Australia had approximately 270 members and was the largest of the Associations.
102. Private letter, January 11, 1967.
103. Donald Horne, *The Lucky Country* (Adelaide: Penguin Books, 1964), p. 113, quoted in "Immigration Reform: Where Do We Go From Here?" (1966).
104. *The Australian,* February 22, 1966, quoted in "Immigration Reform . . ." (1966).
105. Interview with member of the Department of Immigration, September 13, 1966.
106. K. Rivett, quoted in Westerway, *op. cit.,* p. 134.
107. Private letter, January 11, 1967.
108. *Ibid.*
109. *Ibid.*
110. *Ibid.*
111. Interview with official of the National Civic Council, November 5, 1966.
112. B. A. Santamaria in *Rural Life* (June, 1959), p. 54.
113. *News Weekly,* October 26, 1966.
114. *News Weekly,* April 27, 1966.
115. *Rural Life* (June, 1959), p. 55.
116. B. A. Santamaria, *The Sunday Magazine,* Episode No. 39 (September 30, 1962).
117. Westerway, *op. cit.,* p. 145.

Chapter 6

1. N. J. Powell, *Anatomy of Public Opinion* (Englewood Cliffs, N.J.: Prentice-Hall, Inc., 1953), p. 4. W. Albig, *Modern Public Opinion* (New York: McGraw-Hill Book Company, 1956), pp. 8–9. W. Lippman, *Public Opinion* (New York: The Macmillan Co., 1947), Ch. 1.

2. There were 47,000 non-Europeans in Australia in 1901, 21,400 in 1933, 39,000 in 1967, and almost 41,000 in 1968.

3. O. A. Oeser, S. B. Hammond, *op. cit.*, p. 64.

4. *Ibid.*, pp. 64–65.

5. *Ibid.*, p. 66.

6. *Ibid.*, p. 54.

7. Arthur Huck, "Australian Attitudes to the Chinese" (pamphlet) (Melbourne, August, 1964), p. 7.

8. *Ibid.*, p. 11.

9. *Ibid.*, p. 12.

10. *Ibid.*, p. 22.

11. K. Rivett (ed.), *Immigration: Control or Colour Bar?* p. 119.

12. *Australian Gallup Poll* reported in *The Sun*, February 16, 1967.

13. *Australian Gallup Poll*, Nos. 1698–1710, 1963.

14. *Australian Gallup Poll*, Nos. 1884–1899 (February, April, 1966).

15. A. Hughes, "Political Attitudes in a Sample of Melbourne Voters: A Survey During the Federal Elections of 1963," Australian Political Science Association Conference (August, 1964), Appendix.

16. Calculations from computer cards supplied by Mr. Morgan of the Gallup poll.

17. Scores were computed from a sample derived from NUAUS survey at twelve universities; report submitted at 28th Annual Council Meeting (1964), p. 7.

18. *The Australian*, August 3, 1966.

19. *Truth* (Melbourne), quoted in K. Rivett (ed.), *op. cit.*, p. 120.

20. *Truth* (Melbourne), August 24, 1952.

21. *The Bulletin*, July 6, 1960, p. 36.

22. Editorial, "Australia For The White Man?" *The Bulletin*, January 25, 1961, pp. 19–20.

23. *The News* (Adelaide), July 6, 1960.

24. *The Canberra Times*, July 13, 1964.

25. *The Australian*, May 14, 1965.

26. C.G.H., "Time to Change 'White Australia,' " *The Catholic*

Worker (December, 1962), p. 14.

27. "A Less White Australia," *Round Table* (June, 1963), p. 232.

28. Editors, "Open Letter," *Crux*, LXVII, No. 3 (June–July, 1964), 3.

29. Editors, "Color Blindness," *Nation* (July 2, 1960), p. 4.

30. Sir John Latham, "Australian Immigration Policy," *Quadrant*, V, No. 2 (Autumn, 1961), 4.

31. *Ibid.*, p. 8.

32. N. B. Nairn, "White Australia Justified," *The Catholic Worker* (April, 1962), p. 7.

33. Quoted in *The Sydney Morning Herald*, November 11, 1960.

34. J. T. Lang, "The Defence of White Australia," *Century* (June 3, 1966).

35. Quoted in Barry Wain, "Controversy Makers," *The Australian*, March 1, 1967.

36. Ross Gollan, "Sydney Spectator," *The Sydney Morning Herald*, September 2, 1960.

37. Australian Broadcasting Commission (A.B.C.) Debate: "That Asian Immigration into Australia Should Be Increased Substantially" (transcribed from the program), recorded on July 4, 1966.

38. *The Australian*, May 27, 1965.

39. W. D. Borrie, *Immigration* (Sydney: Angus & Robertson, 1949), p. 73.

40. Quoted in *The Sydney Morning Herald*, June 2, 1949.

41. Quoted by L. R. Johnson, M.H.R. (Hughes), *C.P.D.*, L (1966), 602, 603.

42. H. L. Harris, "Australians From Overseas," in W. D. Borrie (ed.), *White Australia* (Sydney: Australasian Pub. Co. Pty. Ltd., 1947), p. 137.

43. R. Coombe on A.B.C., *op. cit.*, p. 6.

44. Sir Alan Watt on A.B.C., *ibid.*, p. 9.

45. G. Greenwood, "The Australian Political Scene," *Pacific Affairs* (1947), p. 287.

46. W. D. Borrie, "Aspects of Australian Demography," *Foreign Affairs* (1947), p. 50.

47. Eric and Elizabeth Marshall, *Asia, The White Australia Policy and You?* (Melbourne: East-West Committee, 1949), p. 27.

48. *The Age* (Melbourne), May 20, 1965.

49. James Hall, "Are the Barriers Weakening?" *The Australian*, June 25, 1965.

50. W. Macmahon Ball, "Our Record of Double Think," *Nation* (May 7, 1960), p. 6.

51. P. Samuel, "Racial Discrimination," *The Catholic Worker* (April, 1962), p. 6.

52. J. Mackie and K. Rivett, "A Reply to Sir John Latham," *Quadrant*, V, No. 4 (Spring, 1961), 14.

53. Douglas Brass, "Looking On," *The Australian*, November 2, 1966.

54. Letters to the Editor, *The Australian*, January 27, 1967.

55. Private letter, December 22, 1962.

56. Private letter, January 6, 1962.

57. A. Calwell, quoted in *The Australian*, May 26, 1965.

58. Letters to the Editor, *The Australian*, September 9, 1964.

59. Letters to the Editor, *The Australian*, December 30, 1964.
60. "Guest Opinion," *The Daily News* (Perth), July 23, 1963.
61. Quoted in "White Australia—Yes or No?" *Peacemaker* (February, 1963), p. 3.
62. Letters to the Editor, *The Sydney Morning Herald*, September 8, 1965.
63. Letters to the Editor, *The Australian*, September 20, 1966.
64. Letters to the Editor, *The Australian*, July 30, 1964.
65. Private letter, July 11, 1961.
66. Private letter, December 19, 1961.
67. Letters to the Editor, *Honi Soit*, April 13, 1961.
68. Letters to the Editor, *The Herald* (Melbourne), December 7, 1961.
69. Quoted in Douglas Brass, "Looking On," *The Australian*, October 19, 1966.
70. Letters to the Editor, *The Sydney Morning Herald*, July 9, 1963.
71. Letters to the Editor, *The Sydney Morning Herald*, December 12, 1962.
72. Letters to the Editor, *The Canberra Times*, July 4, 1964.
73. Letters to the Editor, *The Australian*, September 29, 1966.
74. Letters to the Editor, *The Australian*, September 5, 1966.
75. Mr. Baxter, quoted in *Union Recorder* (Sydney U. newspaper), March 23, 1961. Debate on "Abolish the White Australia Policy?"
76. Letters to the Editor, *The Australian*, May 21, 1965.
77. Quoted in "The Under 25's," *The Daily Mirror* (Sydney), March 11, 1966.
78. Letters to the Editor, *The Australian*, September 29, 1966.
79. Letters to the Editor, *The Australian*, May 21, 1965.
80. Quoted in *Peacemaker* (February, 1963), p. 3.
81. Letters to the Editor, *The Sydney Morning Herald*, June 27, 1962.
82. Quoted in "The Under 25's," *op. cit.*
83. Letters to the Editor, *The Australian*, September 29, 1966.
84. A. Hughes, "Political Conversation In a Small Group," seminar paper, Australian National University (March 29, 1967), p. 6.
85. *The Advertiser* (Adelaide), July 4, 1963.
86. *The Sun* (Adelaide), July 6, 1963.
87. *The Sydney Morning Herald*, July 6, 1963.
88. *The Sun* (Sydney), August 13, 1963.
89. Private letter, July 8, 1963.
90. Private letter, July 6, 1963.
91. "So Kind of The Professor," *The Poultry Farmer* (July 20, 1963), p. 44.
92. Quoted in *On Dit* (student newspaper), July 19, 1963.
93. Letters to the Editor, *The Sydney Morning Herald*, July 9, 1963.
94. Private letter, July 29, 1963.
95. Private letter, July 31, 1963.

96. Private letter, August 30, 1963.
97. Draft of Professor Robin Winks' reply to the press.
98. *Ibid.*
99. *The Sun* (Sydney), February 16, 1967.

Chapter 7

1. *The Canberra Times,* May 19, 1965.
2. Quoted in *C.P.D.,* L (1966), 612.
3. Kenneth Rivett (ed.), *Immigration: Control or Colour Bar?* p. 88.
4. K. G. Tregonning, "Australia's Imperialist Image In Asia," *Australian Quarterly* (September, 1961), p. 45.
5. Oriental Observer, "White Policy—Anti-Asian Policy," *East Wind* (May–June, 1962), p. 5.
6. *Ibid.,* p. 6.
7. *C.P.D.,* XXX (1961), 750.
8. Letters to the Editor, *The Sydney Morning Herald,* November 3, 1959.
9. *The Courier-Mail* (Brisbane), March 26, 1949.
10. *The Malay Mail,* January 29, 1964.
11. Alice Tay Er Soon, "What Malayans Think of Us—Young Brother To Tuan Besar," *The Bulletin* (January 4, 1961), pp. 22–23.
12. G. Jones and M. Jones, "Australia's Immigration Policy: Some Malaysian Attitudes," *Australian Outlook,* XIX (December, 1965), 272–85.
13. *Ibid.,* p. 283.
14. Charles Meeking, "Little or Nothing," *The Bulletin* (January 25, 1961), p. 18.
15. *The Sydney Morning Herald,* April 18, 1949.
16. *Evening Chronicle,* printed in *The Sydney Morning Herald,* March 29, 1949.
17. *Manila Times,* printed in *The Sydney Morning Herald,* March 29, 1949.
18. *The Argus* (Melbourne), April 20, 1949.
19. Letters to the Editor, *The Sydney Morning Herald,* April 22, 1949.
20. *The Sydney Morning Herald,* April 21, 1949.
21. Wallace Crouch, "Filipinos Are Bitter At Our Immigration Laws," *The West Australian* (Perth), April 29, 1966.
22. *Ibid.*
23. *Ibid.*

24. *The Canberra Times,* October 24, 1966.
25. *The Australian,* April 18, 1966.
26. *The Canberra Times,* April 4, 1966.
27. George Farwell, "The Ugly Australian," *The Australian,* May 20, 1965.
28. *Ibid.*
29. *The West Australian* (Perth), April 29, 1966.
30. *The Age* (Melbourne), March 23, 1966.
31. Quoted in Massey Stanley, "We Are A Compulsory Subject," *The Bulletin,* January 11, 1961, p. 23.
32. *Ibid.*
33. *The Australian,* September 4, 1964.
34. J. M. Richards, "Off the Floor and into the West," *The Listener,* August 9, 1962.
35. Massey Stanley, *op. cit.,* p. 23.
36. *The Courier-Mail* (Brisbane), March 5, 1948.
37. *The Courier-Mail* (Brisbane), June 22, 1954.
38. Execrable economic conditions, it can be argued, probably give them a limited view of the world, few educational opportunities, and little money with which to travel.
39. *The Courier-Mail* (Brisbane), June 30, 1954.
40. G. Greenwood and N. Harper, *Australia in World Affairs 1950–55* (Melbourne: Cheshire, 1957), p. 265.
41. Quoted from *Eastern Economist,* August, 1950, in *ibid.,* p. 266.
42. Quoted in *ibid.*
43. Quoted in *ibid.,* p. 267.
44. G. Greenwood and N. Harper, *Australia in World Affairs 1956–60* (Institute of International Affairs, University of British Columbia, 1963), p. 33.
45. *Ibid.*
46. Neil McInnes, "To Indians: Distant, Insignificant," *The Bulletin,* December 28, 1960.
47. Dr. Vagholkar, "My Experiences in Australia," June 22, 1963 (talk delivered at conference on "Planned Immigration—Today and Tomorrow"), p. 1.
48. *Ibid.,* pp. 3–4.
49. *Ibid.,* pp. 6–7.
50. *The Courier-Mail* (Brisbane), March 9, 1966. This was presented as one of several articles on Asian views of Australia's immigration policy.
51. Interview, Mr. Channing, November 26, 1966.
52. *The West Australian* (Perth), October 1, 1964.
53. *The Daily Mirror* (Sydney), July 26, 1968.
54. Olabisi Ajala, quoted in *The Sun-Herald* (Sydney), December 9, 1962.
55. *Ibid.*
56. *The Australian,* September 11, 1964.
57. Australian Correspondent, "The White Australia Policy," *West Indian Economist,* March, 1960, p. 26.
58. *Ibid.,* pp. 26–27.
59. Quoted in *The Australian,* September 9, 1966.
60. *The Sun-Herald* (Sydney), September 11, 1966, p. 27.
61. *Ibid.,* p. 28.

62. Ian Moffitt, "The Challenge of Wee Waa," *The Australian,* December 2, 1966.

63. Jonathan Gaul, "California Rangers," *The Canberra Times* (supplement), October 21, 1966.

64. *Ibid.*

65. "Australia: Asians, Keep Out!" *Time* magazine (December 13, 1963), p. 25.

66. Quoted in *The Sydney Morning Herald,* March 16, 1963; *The Manchester Guardian,* March 4, 1962.

67. *The Australian,* May 20, 1965.

Chapter 8

1. Sir John Latham, *The Significance of the Peace Conference From an Australian Point of View* (Melbourne, 1930), p. 9.

2. A. Yarwood, *Asian Migration to Australia: The Background to Exclusion 1896–1923* (Melbourne: Melbourne University Press, 1964), pp. 96–97.

3. R. G. Casey, *Australia's Place in the World* (Melbourne: Robertson & Mullens, 1931), p. 13.

4. Werner Levi, *Australia's Outlook On Asia,* pp. 199–200.

5. John Wilkes (ed.), *Australia's Defence and Foreign Policy* (Sydney: Angus & Robertson, 1964), p. 39.

6. Sir Alexander Downer, *Influence of Migration on Australian Foreign Policy,* Roy Milne Lecture (Sydney, 1960), pp. 7–8.

7. Downer, *op. cit.,* p. 7.

8. G. Greenwood and N. Harper, *Australia in World Affairs, 1950–55* (Melbourne: Chesire, 1959), p. 264.

9. *The Sydney Morning Herald,* April 12, 1961.

10. *The Age* (Melbourne), March 22, 1961.

11. *C.P.D.,* XXX (1961), 714.

12. Bruce Grant, *The Age* (Melbourne), March 31, 1961.

13. Reported in R. Hughes, *The Courier-Mail* (Brisbane), March 25, 1961.

14. *The Straits Times* (Singapore), March 24, 1961.

15. *C.P.D.,* XXX (1961), 660–61.

16. United Nations Special Political Committee, *Official Records,* 227th Meeting (March 21, 1961), pp. 5–6.

17. United Nations Special Political Committee, *Official Records,* 227th Meeting (April 7, 1961), p. 85.
18. *The Sydney Morning Herald,* May 1, 1961.
19. Downer, *op. cit.,* p. 8.
20. Quoted in Sir A. Grenfell Price, *Australia Comes of Age* (Melbourne: Georgian House, 1945), p. 79.
21. *C.P.D.,* XXXIX (1963), 868.
22. *C.P.D.,* XVI (1957), 714.
23. *The Sydney Morning Herald,* June 19, 1957.
24. Reply to press inquiry by Jack Stanaway, *The Sydney Morning Herald,* August 6, 1965.
25. Reply to press inquiry by Stan Hutchinson, *ibid.*
26. Sir A. Grenfell Price, *op. cit.,* p. 93.
27. J. R. Hall, "Asian Labor Ban Holds Up N. G. Growth," *The Australian,* December 27, 1966.
28. Christopher Forsyth, "Firms Say Racial Ban Is Slowing New Guinea Growth," *The Australian,* December 12, 1966.
29. *The Canberra Times,* December 12, 1966.
30. Peter Hastings, "Copper and Cargo Cult," *The Australian,* December 31, 1966.
31. *The Canberra Times,* December 16, 1966.
32. *Ibid.*
33. *The Canberra Times,* December 22, 1966.
34. *Ibid.*
35. Soviet representative Shakov at "Special Committee On The Situation With Regard To The Implementation Of The Granting Of Independence To Colonial Countries And Peoples," United Nations General Assembly, *Official Records,* 486th Meeting (October 11, 1966).
36. "Report of Trusteeship Council," United Nations General Assembly, *Official Records,* Twenty-Second Session, Supplement No. 4(A/6704) (July 27, 1966–June 30, 1967), p. 11.
37. "Report Of the Special Committee On The Situation With Regard To The Implementation Of The Declaration On The Granting Of Independence To Colonial Countries And Peoples," United Nations General Assembly, *Official Records* (A/6700/Add. 13) (November 24, 1967).
38. "Report Of Trusteeship Council," United Nations General Assembly, *Official Records,* Thirty-Fifth Session (T/SR1335-1339, 1341) (July, 1967–June, 1968).

In the report filed by a visiting mission of the Trusteeship Council in 1968 it was noted that Mr. Tambi, President of a municipal council in the Western Highlands of New Guinea, "believed that the United Nations was 'pushing' Australia to give the Territory independence." "Report of United Nations Visiting Mission To The Trust Territory of New Guinea 1968," *ibid.* (T/1678) (May 22, 1968), p. 14.

39. Interviews with three officials of the Department of Immigration, two Labor Party Members of Parliament, and one Liberal Party official.

40. *The New York Times,* December 25, 1968.
41. *Ibid.*
42. *The Sydney Morning Herald,* May 19, 1965.
43. Clayton Fritchey, "Whites Only," *New York Post,* December 31, 1966.
44. Douglas Brass, for example, wrote, "it is no longer good enough to preach Asian fellowship and responsibility on the national front while maintaining strict anti-Asian exclusiveness with individuals," *The Australian,* July 19, 1967.
45. O. O. Trullinger, *Red Banners Over Asia* (Boston: Beacon Press, 1951), p. 207.
46. Arthur Burns' commentary in Wilkes, *op. cit.,* p. 59.
47. *C.P.D.,* 26th Parliament (June 4, 1968), pp. 1920–22.
48. Mr. Stewart (Labor MP) asked the Minister of Defence Mr. Fairhall whether he believed "that the F-111 aircraft is a super battle bird and the greatest thing with wings since angels?" *C.P.D.,* 26th Parliament (April 2, 1968), p. 640.
49. Christopher Forsyth, "Australia (and Mr. Holt) Turn to Asia," *The Australian,* February 2, 1967.
50. *The Australian,* January 18, 1967.
51. Julie Rigg, "Manglapus," *The Australian,* September 17, 1966.

52. *C.P.D.,* 26th Parliament (June 13, 1968), p. 2307; *The New York Times,* January 7, 1968.
53. Quoted in *The Australian,* October 11, 1966.
54. *Ibid.*
55. *The Australian,* November 17, 1966.
56. *The Canberra Times,* August 20, 1966; Statistics compiled by K. M. Archer, *Official Year Book* of The Commonwealth of Australia, Bureau of Census and Statistics (Canberra, 1967), p. 108; *Australian International Aid,* Department of External Affairs (Canberra, October, 1967), p. 7.
57. Statistics compiled by K. M. Archer, *Overseas Trade 1967–68,* Bulletin No. 65, Commonwealth Bureau of Census and Statistics (Canberra), p. 1000.
58. *Ibid.,* p. 996.
59. *The New York Times,* December 25, 1968; K. M. Archer, *Overseas Trade 1967–68,* p. 1000.
60. Department of Treasury statement in *The New York Times,* December 25, 1968; "Japan Is Aiding Australian Industry," *The Bulletin,* March 9, 1968, pp. 37–39.
61. *C.P.D.,* 26th Parliament (March 27, 1968), p. 482.
62. *The Canberra Times,* January 9, 1967.
63. *Financial Review,* September 4, 1964.
64. *The New York Times,* December 25, 1968.
65. Downer, *op. cit.,* p. 14.

Chapter 9

1. Private letter, December 19, 1966.
2. Private letter, October 11, 1966.
3. *Ibid.*
4. *Ibid.*
5. *The Canberra Times,* August 7, 1965.
6. Private letter, October 11, 1966.
7. *The Sydney Morning Herald,* August 7, 1965, "Statement by the Minister for Immigration, The Hon. Hubert Opperman, M.P.," August 6, 1965.
8. Mr. Opperman quoted in *The Sydney Morning Herald,* August 7, 1965.
9. Private letter, February 21, 1963.
10. Private letter, July 17, 1963.
11. *Ibid.*
12. *Ibid.*
13. *The Daily Mirror* (Sydney), September 24, 1963.
14. "Statement by the Minister . . . Opperman, M.P.," August 6, 1965.
15. Private letter, December 12, 1966.
16. *The Daily Mirror* (Sydney), November 5, 1963.
17. "Prasad Case," Department of Immigration, August 15, 1965.
18. *The Daily Mirror* (Sydney), November 5, 1963.
19. Interview with a Department of Immigration spokesman, September 13, 1966.
20. Public letter, R. Prasad to Members of House of Representatives, January 13, 1964.
21. Private letter, February 7, 1964.
22. "Prasad Case," Department of Immigration, August 25, 1965.
23. *Ibid.*
24. *The Daily Telegraph* (Sydney), April 2, 1964.
25. *The Age* (Melbourne), April 4, 1964.
26. *Ibid.*; "Prasad Case," *loc. cit.*
27. *The Age* (Melbourne), April 4, 1964.
28. *The Sydney Morning Herald,* April 11, 1964.
29. *The Daily Mirror* (Sydney), April 9, 1964.
30. *The Sydney Morning Herald,* April 11, 1964.
31. *Ibid.*; *The Daily Telegraph* (Sydney), August 5, 1964.

32. *The Daily Telegraph* (Sydney), June 18, 1965.
33. *The Daily Mirror* (Sydney), April 8, 1964.
34. *The Canberra Times*, August 7, 1964.
35. *Ibid.*
36. *Ibid.*
37. *The Daily Telegraph* (Sydney), August 5, 1964; *The Canberra Times*, August 7, 1964; *The Advertiser* (Adelaide), August 9, 1965.
38. *Ibid.*
39. *The Daily Telegraph* (Sydney), June 18, 1965; *The Advertiser* (Adelaide), August 9, 1965; "Re Prasad and Infants' Custody and Settlements Act (1964–65)," *New South Wales Reports* (1965), p. 331.
40. "Prasad Case," *loc. cit.*
41. *Ibid.*
42. *The Australian*, August 6, 1965.
43. *The Age* (Melbourne), August 6, 1965.
44. *The Sydney Morning Herald*, August 7, 1965; *The Advertiser* (Adelaide), August 7, 1965.
45. *The Advertiser* (Adelaide), August 7, 1965; *The Age* (Melbourne), August 7, 1965.
46. *The Age* (Melbourne), August 7, 1965.
47. *The Fiji Times*, August 9, 1965.
48. *The Age* (Melbourne), August 7, 1965.
49. *Ibid.*
50. *The Advertiser* (Adelaide), August 7, 1965.
51. (Department of Immigration) Press Statement, August 8, 1965; *The Fiji Times*, August 9, 1965.
52. Interview with Mr. Opperman, March 2, 1967.
53. *The Canberra Times*, August 7, 1965.
54. *Ibid.*
55. *Ibid.*
56. Interview with Mr. P. Heydon, September 13, 1966.
57. *The Fiji Times*, August 11, 1965.
58. *The Daily Mirror* (Sydney), November 6, 1965.
59. *The Canberra Times*, August 7, 1965.
60. *The Bulletin*, August 14, 1965, p. 13.
61. *Nation*, August 21, 1965, p. 14.
62. *The Sydney Morning Herald*, August 9, 1965.
63. Conversation with Department official, September 13, 1966.
64. *The Sun* (Sydney), August 7, 1965.
65. *The Sydney Morning Herald*, August 9, 1965.
66. *The Age* (Melbourne), August 9, 1965.
67. *News Weekly*, September 19, 1965.
68. Private letter, August 12, 1965.
69. "Prasad Case," *op. cit.*
70. Text of *Sun-Herald* television program, "Nancy Prasad Story," August 15, 1965, p. 2.
71. *Ibid.*, p. 5.
72. *Ibid.*, p. 6.
73. *Nation*, August 12, 1965, p. 4.
74. Immigration Department press release, August 13, 1965.
75. "Prasad Case," *loc. cit.*
76. Private letter, November 15, 1966.
77. "Prasad Case," *loc. cit.*

78. *Ibid.*
79. *Ibid.*
80. Interview with Mr. Opperman, March 2, 1967.
81. Private letter, August 9, 1965.
82. *Ibid.*
83. "Prasad Case," *loc. cit.*; interview with Mr. Opperman, March 2, 1967.
84. *Ibid.*
85. *The Daily Mirror* (Sydney), August 6, 1965.
86. *The Daily Mirror* (Sydney), August 17, 1965.
87. Private letter, August 12, 1965.
88. Mr. Powditch quoted in *The Fiji Times,* August 11, 1965.
89. "Prasad Case," *loc. cit.*
90. *Nation,* August 21, 1965, p. 4.
91. *Ibid.*
92. *Ibid.*
93. *The Daily Mirror* (Sydney), June 22, 1965.
94. *The Canberra Times,* August 7, 1965.
95. *The Daily Mirror* (Sydney), August 9, 1965.
96. *The News* (Adelaide), April 3, 1964.
97. *The Advertiser* (Adelaide), August 9, 1965.
98. *The Mercury* (Hobart), August 9, 1965.
99. *The Courier-Mail* (Brisbane), August 10, 1965.
100. Letters to the Editor, *The Sydney Morning Herald,* August 11, 1965.
101. *Ibid.*
102. Letters to the Editor, *The Australian,* August 12, 1965.
103. *Ibid.*
104. *Ibid.*
105. Letters to the Editor, *Nation,* September 18, 1965, p. 16.
106. Quoted in *The Daily Mirror* (Sydney), August 8, 1965.
107. Letters to the Editor, *The Age* (Melbourne), August 12, 1965.
108. *The Sunday Mirror* (Sydney), April 5, 1964, p. 24.
109. Letters to the Editor, *The Daily Mirror* (Sydney), August 17, 1965.
110. *The Canberra Times,* August 11, 1965.
111. *The Daily Mirror* (Sydney), April 8, 1964.
112. *Ibid.*
113. *Ibid.,* August 9, 1965.
114. *The West Australian* (Perth), April 29, 1966.
115. Letters to the Editor, *The Fiji Times,* August 13, 1965.
116. *Ibid.*
117. *Ibid.*
118. *Ibid.*
119. Letters to the Editor, *The Fiji Times,* August 25, 1965.
120. Letters to the Editor, *The Fiji Times,* August 13, 1965.
121. *The Daily Mirror* (Sydney), August 9, 1965.
122. *Ibid.*
123. *Ibid.*
124. *C.P.D.,* XL (1963), 1369.
125. *The Canberra Times,* August 11, 1965.
126. *The Age* (Melbourne), August 23, 1965.
127. *Ibid.*
128. *Ibid.*
129. *The Advertiser* (Adelaide), August 24, 1965.
130. *Ibid.*

131. *The Age* (Melbourne), September 27, 1965.
132. Letters to the Editor, *The Australian*, October 5, 1965.
133. *The Sydney Morning Herald*, January 19, 1966.
134. Mr. Powditch quoted in *The Daily Mirror* (Sydney), February 20, 1966.
135. *The Canberra Times*, March 21, 1966.
136. Private letter, December 12, 1966.
137. Department of Immigration, "Summary of Rules Generally Applying to Entry of Non-Europeans," August 25, 1966.
138. Quoted in Julie Rigg, *The Australian*, March 14, 1966.
139. *C.P.D.*, LII (September 27, 1966), 1313.
140. *The Advertiser* (Adelaide), August 24, 1965.
141. Paul Dougherty, *The Daily Mirror* (Sydney), February 21, 1966.
142. *Ibid.*
143. Don Aitkin, "Political Review," *Australian Quarterly*, XXXVIII, No. 2 (June, 1966), 100.
144. Interview, September 13, 1966.
145. *The Australian*, February 22, 1966; *The Canberra Times*, February 22, 1966.
146. *The Sun* (Sydney), February 22, 1966.
147. *Ibid.*
148. Information provided by the Department of Immigration, October 4, 1966.

Chapter 10

1. H. L. Harris, "Australians From Overseas," in W. H. Borrie (ed.), *White Australia* (Sydney: Australasian Publishing Co. Pty. Ltd., 1947), p. 137.
2. H. London, "Liberalizing White Australia Policy: Integration, Assimilation or Cultural Pluralism," *Australian Outlook* (December, 1967).

Appendix:
Australian Newspapers

1. W. Sprague Holden, *Australia Goes to Press* (Melbourne: Melbourne University Press, 1962), p. 251.
2. W. Sprague Holden, "Metropolitan Daily Newspapers in Australia Today," *Journalism Quarterly,* XLV, No. 4 (Winter, 1968), 717.
3. *Ibid.,* p. 715.
4. All circulation figures courtesy of The Australian News and Information Bureau, December, 1968.
5. Holden, "Metropolitan . . . Today," *op. cit.,* p. 716.

Bibliography

Books, Pamphlets, and Papers

Albig, W. *Modern Public Opinion.* New York: McGraw-Hill Book Co. Inc., 1956.
Borrie, W. D., and Rodger, R. *Australian Population Projections 1960–1975.* Canberra: Australian National University, 1961.
——— (ed.). *A White Australia: Australia's Population Problem.* Sydney: Australasian Publishing Co., 1947.
———. *Immigration.* Sydney: Angus and Robertson, 1949.
———, and Dedman, R. *University Enrolments in Australia, 1955–1970.* Canberra: Australian National University, 1957.
Cairns, J. *Living With Asia.* Melbourne: Lansdowne Press, 1965.
Calwell, Arthur. *Australian Tradition In Immigration.* Canberra: Government Publications, 1949.
———. *Danger For Australia.* Canberra: Government Publications, 1949.
———. *How Many Australians Tomorrow?* Melbourne: 1945.
Casey, R. G. *Australia's Place In The World.* Melbourne: Robertson & Mullens, 1931.
Dennery, Etienne. *Asia's Teeming Millions: Its Problems for The West.* London: Jonathan Cape, 1931.

Dixon, R. *Immigration and The White Australia Policy.* Sydney: Communist Party, 1945.
Dougherty, T. N. P. *White Australia Policy Was Key To Our High National Standards.* Brisbane: Australian Workers Union, 1962.
Downer, A. *Commonwealth Club Luncheon.* Canberra: Government Publications, December 4, 1959.
——. *Influence of Migration on Australian Foreign Policy.* Roy Milne Lecture. Sydney: Australian Institute of International Affairs, 1960.
Fairchild, H. P. (ed.). *Dictionary of Sociology.* New York: Philosophical Library, 1944.
Forsyth, W. D. *Myth of Open Spaces.* Melbourne: Melbourne University Press, 1942.
Gilmore, R. J., and Warner, D. (eds.). *Near North.* Sydney: Angus and Robertson, 1948.
Gizen-No-Tek (pseudonym). *Colorphobia.* Sydney: R. T. Kelly, 1903.
Gordon, Milton. *Assimilation in American Life.* New York: Oxford University Press, 1964.
Greenwood, Gordon. *Australia: A Social and Political History.* Sydney: Angus and Robertson, 1955.
——, and Harper, N. *Australia in World Affairs 1950–1955.* Melbourne: Cheshire Publishers, 1957.
——. *Australian World Affairs, 1956–60.* Vancouver: University of British Columbia, 1963.
Hancock, W. K. *Australia.* London: Ernest Benn Ltd., 1930.
Hodgkin, Mary. *Australian Training and Asian Living.* Perth: University of Western Australia, 1966.
Holden, W. Sprague. *Australia Goes to Press.* Melbourne: Melbourne University Press, 1962.
Horne, Donald. *The Lucky Country.* Adelaide: Penguin Books, 1964.
Huck, Arthur. *Australian Attitudes to The Chinese* (mimeographed pamphlet). Melbourne: August, 1964.
Hughes, Alan. *Political Attitudes In A Sample of Melbourne Voters: A Survey During The Federal Elections of 1963.*

Canberra: Australian Political Science Association Conference Paper, August, 1964.

———. "Political Conversation In A Small Group" (seminar paper). Political Science, Australian National University, March 29, 1967.

Immigration Reform Group. *Control or Colour Bar?* Melbourne: 1960.

Jupp, James. *Australian Party Politics.* Melbourne: Melbourne University Press, 1964.

Kristianson, G. L. *Politics of Patriotism.* Canberra: Australian National University Press, 1966.

Latham, Sir John. *The Significance of The Peace Conference From An Australian Point of View.* Melbourne: 1930.

Levi, Werner. *Australia's Outlook On Asia.* Sydney: Angus and Robertson, 1958.

Lippman, Walter. *Public Opinion.* New York: Macmillan & Co., 1947.

Lyng, J. *NonBritishers in Australia.* Melbourne: Macmillan & Co., 1927.

Marshall, Eric, and Marshall, Elizabeth. *Asia, The White Australia Policy And You.* Melbourne: East-West Committee, 1949.

Oeser, O. A., and Hammond, S. B. *Social Structure and Personality In A City.* London: Routledge & Kegan Paul, 1954.

Opperman, Hubert. *Immigration Policy.* Canberra: Government Printers, 1966.

Palfreeman, A. C. *The Administration of The White Australia Policy.* Melbourne: Melbourne University Press, 1967.

Park, R. E., and Burgess, E. *Introduction To The Sciences of Sociology.* Chicago: University of Chicago Press, 1921.

Powell, N. J. *Anatomy of Public Opinion.* Englewood Cliffs, N.J., Prentice-Hall Inc., 1953.

Price, Sir A. Grenfell. *Australia Comes of Age.* Melbourne: Georgian House, 1945.

Rivett, Kenneth (ed.). *Immigration: Control or Colour Bar?* Melbourne: Melbourne University Press, 1962.

Seligman, E., and Johnson, A. (eds.). *Encyclopedia of The Social Sciences,* Vol. II. New York: Macmillan & Co., 1930.

Smith, M. G. *Stratification in Grenada.* California: University of California Press, 1965.
Trullinger, O. O. *Red Banners Over Asia.* Boston: Beacon Press, 1951.
Whyte, W. F. *William Morris Hughes.* Sydney: Angus and Robertson, 1957.
Wilkes, John (ed.). *Australia's Defence and Foreign Policy.* Sydney: Angus and Robertson, 1964.
———. *Forces In Australian Politics.* Sydney: Angus and Robertson, 1963.
Wilkinson, H. L. *The World's Population Problems and A White Australia.* London: P. S. King, 1930.
Willard, Myra. *History of The White Australia Policy.* Melbourne: Melbourne University Press, 1923.
Yarwood, A. *Asian Migration to Australia: The Background to Exclusion 1896–1913.* Melbourne: Melbourne University Press, 1964.

Articles

Adams, Roy, "Overseas Students in West Australia," *Hemisphere,* July, 1965.
Aitkin, Don, "Political Review," *Australian Quarterly,* June, 1966.
"Australia: Asians, Keep Out!" (editors), *Time Magazine,* December 13, 1963.
"Australia For The White Man?" (editorial), *The Bulletin,* January 25, 1961.
Ball, W. Macmahon, "Our Record of Double Think," *Nation,* May 7, 1960.

Bernard, William S., "The Integration of Immigrants," Unesco, 1956.
Bevan, E. H., "So Kind of The Professor," *The Poultry Farmer*, July 20, 1963.
Borrie, W. D., "Aspects of Australian Demography," *Foreign Affairs*, 1947.
C. G. H., "Time To Change 'White Australia,' " *The Catholic Worker*, December, 1962.
Chipman, L., "Student Action in Victoria," *Vestes*, Vol. V, No. 1 (March, 1962).
Clunies-Ross, Anthony, "Student Life: The Fifties," *Mum*, Spring, 1961.
"Color Blindness" (editors), *Nation*, July 2, 1960.
Cooksey, Robert, "Foreign Policy Review," *Australian Quarterly*, June, 1966.
Elkin, A. P., "A White Australia," in W. D. Borrie (ed.), *A White Australia: Australia's Population Problem*. Sydney: Australasian Publishing Co., 1947.
Gott, K., "White Ants in The A. L. P.," *Nation*, May 5, 1962.
Greenwood, Gordon, "The Australian Political Scene," *Pacific Affairs*, 1947.
Harper, Norman, "Asian Students and Asian Studies in Australia," *Pacific Affairs*, Vol. XXXI, No. 1 (March, 1958).
———, "Asian Students In Australia," *Vestes*, No. 6 (June, 1963).
Harris, H. L., "Australians From Overseas," in W. D. Borrie (ed.), *White Australia*. Sydney: Australasian Publishing Co. Pty. Ltd., 1947.
Hodgkin, Mary, "Asian Student In An Australian University," *Educand*, November, 1958.
———, "When Australians Marry Asians," *Quadrant*, August/September, 1964.
Holden, W. Sprague, "Metropolitan Daily Newspapers in Australia Today," *Journalism Quarterly*, Vol. XLV, No. 4 (Winter, 1968).
Johanson, David, "History of The White Australia Policy," in K. Rivett (ed.), *Immigration: Control or Colour Bar?* Melbourne: Melbourne University Press, 1962.

Jones, G., and Jones, M., "Australia's Immigration Policy: Some Malaysian Attitudes," *Australian Outlook,* Vol. XIX (December, 1965).

Lang, J. T., "The Defence of White Australia," *Century,* June 3, 1966.

Latham, Sir John, "Australian Immigration Policy," *Quadrant,* Vol. V, No. 2 (Autumn, 1961).

"A Less White Australia" (editors), *Roundtable,* June, 1963.

London, Herbert, "Liberalizing White Australia Policy: Integration, Assimilation or Cultural Pluralism," *Australian Outlook,* Vol. XXI, No. 3 (December, 1967).

Mackie, J., and Rivett, K., "A Reply to Sir John Latham," *Quadrant,* Vol. V, No. 4 (Spring, 1961).

McInnes, Neil, "To Indians: Distant, Insignificant," *The Bulletin,* December 28, 1960.

Meeking, Charles, "Little or Nothing," *The Bulletin,* January 25, 1961.

Nairn, N. B., "White Australia Justified," *The Catholic Worker,* April, 1962.

"Open Letter" (editors), *Crux,* Vol. LXVII, No. 3 (June/July, 1964).

Palfreeman, A., "Administration of White Australia Policy," *Rural Life,* June, 1959.

Park, R. E., "Assimilation Social," in E. Seligman, A. Johnson (eds.), *Encyclopedia of The Social Sciences,* Vol. II. New York: Macmillan & Co., 1930.

"The Parson Bows Out of Politics" (Perth correspondent), *The Bulletin,* December 2, 1961.

Price, Charles, "White Restrictions on Colored Immigration," *Race,* Vol. VII, No. 3 (1966).

Richards, J. M., "Off The Floor and Into The West," *The Listener,* August 9, 1962.

Samuel, Peter, "Racial Discrimination," *The Catholic Worker,* April, 1962.

Soon, Alice Tay Er, "What Malayans Think of Us—Young Brother To Tuan Besar," *The Bulletin,* January 4, 1961.

Stanley, Massey, "We Are a Compulsory Subject," *The Bulletin,* January 11, 1961.

Tregonning, K. G., "Australia's Imperialist Image In Asia," *Australian Quarterly*, September, 1961.
Turnbull, Clive, "White Australia," in R. J. Gilmore and D. Warner (eds.), *Near North*. Sydney: Angus and Robertson, 1948.
Westerway, Peter, "Pressure Groups," in J. Wilkes (ed.), *Forces In Australian Politics*. Sydney: Angus and Robertson, 1963.
"The White Australia Policy" (Australian correspondent), *West Indian Economist*, March, 1960.
"White Australia—Yes or No?" (editors), *Peacemaker*, February, 1963.
"White Policy—Anti Asia Policy" (Oriental observer), *East Wind*, May/June, 1962.
Williams, Robin, "The Reduction of Intergroup Tensions," Social Science Research Council, *Bulletin 57*, 1947.
Young, Edmund, "Asian Student Organizations in New South Wales," *Asiana*, Spring, 1956.

Selected Primary Materials

Australian Gallup Polls.
Australian International Aid. Canberra: Department of External Affairs, October, 1967.
Australia's Way Forward. Program of the Communist Party of Australia, 21st National Congress, June, 1967.
Commonwealth Official Yearbook 1966. 1967, Bureau of Census and Statistics. Canberra: Government Printers, 1966, 1967.
Commonwealth Parliamentary Debates.
Daly, F., *Recommendations: For A. L. P. Immigration Committee* [unpublished], August, 1965.

———, *Report of Immigration Review Committee of the A. L. P.* August, 1965.
Department of Immigration, "Brief Notes On Australia's Established Immigration Policy," December, 1963.
Department of Immigration, "Summary of Rules Generally Applying to Entry of Non-Europeans," August 25, 1966.
Methodist Church Statement of Policy on Social Issues.
New South Wales Association For Immigration Reform, "Statement of Aims," 1962.
New South Wales Association For Immigration Reform, *White Australia: Time For A Change.* Sydney, 1963.
Official Minutes. 1960–65 Returned Servicemen's League Congress.
Official Report of The Proceedings of the 26th Commonwealth Conference. August 2–6, 1965.
Overseas Trade 1967–68. Bulletin No. 65, Commonwealth Bureau of Census and Statistics, Canberra, 1968.
Report of Survey at Twelve Universities. National Union of Australian University Students, 28th Annual Council Meeting, 1964.
Report of The Australian Labor Party Conference. 1961.
Report on White Australia Debate at National Union Council of National Union of Australian University Students. 1959.
Returned Servicemen's League Constitution.
Returned Servicemen's League Standing Policy.
Secretary of Student Action, *Notes.*
United Nations General Assembly, *Official Records.* 1966, 1968.
United Nations Special Political Committee, *Official Records.* 227th Meeting, March 21, 1961.
Victorian Association For Immigration Reform, *Why Does White Australia Matter?* Melbourne, 1960.

Foreign Newspapers and Journals

Kuala Lumpur Daily
Manila Times
New York Post
The Fiji Times
The Hindu (India)
The Manchester Guardian
The New York Times
The Star (Hong Kong)
The Straits Times (Kuala Lumpur)
The Straits Times (Singapore)
The Times of India
The Times (London)
Time (magazine)
West Indian Economist

Theses

Dodd, C., *Changing Attitudes To The White Australia Policy 1945–56* (honors thesis). University of Queensland, 1964.
Palfreeman, A. C., *Australia's Policy on Non-European Immigrants* (Masters thesis). Australian National University, 1962.

Paul, Geoffrey, *The White Australia Policy and South East Asia* (unpublished Masters thesis). Harvard University, 1952.

Yong, C. F., *The Chinese in New South Wales and Victoria 1901–1921* (Ph.D. thesis). Australian National University, 1966.

Index

Aboriginal affairs, 119–20
Aborigines, 54, 57, 89, 119–20, 128, 157, 175, 187, 198, 238
Adelaide University, 175
Administration of the White Australia Policy, The, xiii, xiv
Advertiser (Adelaide), 41–42, 127, 247
Advocate, 84, 89
Africa, Africans, 197–98, 212, *passim*. *See also specific countries*
Afro-Asian bloc, 215, 260
Ajala, Olabisi, 197–98, 249–50
"All the way with L. B. J.," 219
America, *see* Americans; United States
Americans, 147 (*chart*), 174, 200–201; Negroes, 169, 200. *See also* United States
Anderson, R. W. C., 227
Anglican Church, 118; General Synod, 137
Anglicans (Chinese), 58
Anglo-Japanese Treaty of Commerce and Navigation (1894), 11

Anglo-Saxon, 164
Anthropologists, 4
Anti-Chinese Leagues, 9
Anti-Communism, 26–27, 62, 80, 81, 138, 190, 207. *See also* Communism
ANZUS, 218, 220
Apartheid, 127, 131, 188, 197, 201, 202, 210, 211, 212
Apex, 18, 66, 132, 135
Arabia, 208
Armstrong, Mr., 111
Arndt, Heinz, 163
Asabi, 190
Asia, Asians, *see specific countries*
Asian Migration to Australia: The Background to Exclusion, 1896–1924, xiv
Asian Relations Conference (1947), 157, 185
Asian Students' Council, 66
Asian Students' Federation, 66
ASPAC, 209
Associated Chamber of Manufacturers, 227

307

Association for the Defence of the Family, 242
Associations for Immigration Reform, xii, 18, 39, 86, 87, 103, 108, 117, 125, 133, 135–38, 142. *See also* New South Wales Association for Immigration Reform; Queensland Association for Immigration Reform
Athenian Society (U. of Melbourne), 124
Australasian Steam Navigation Company, 9
Australia House, 102
"Australia for the White Man," 153, 154
Australia-Japan Business Cooperation Committee, 227
Australian, The, 46, 136, 156, 237
Australian Act (1901), 13
Australian-American Educational Foundation, xv
Australian Broadcasting Commission, 169, 243
Australian Chinese Association, 60
Australian Citizenship Conventions, 91, 92, 93, 119, 254
Australian Council of Churches, xii, 39, 107, 120–21, 137
Australian Gallup Polls, 88, 150, 151 (*and charts*), 152 (*and chart*), 153, 177, 208, 261
Australian Junior Chamber of Commerce, 108
Australian Labor Party, xiii, 13, 33–35, 77, 80, 81–96, 103, 104, 105, 115, 123–24, 126, 128, 142, 187, 211, 223, 251, 252, 264
Australian National University, xv, 67, 152, 158, 160, 218; Research School of Pacific Studies, 163
Australian Natives' Association, 84, 89, 108, 113–15, 141
Australian Quarterly, 256
Australian Railwaymen's Union, 116, 163

Australian Sales Research Pty. Ltd., 153
Australian Student Christian Movement, 156
Australian Workers Union, 84, 115–16
Australia's Immigration Policy (brochure), 42

"Bags," 251
Ball, Macmahon, 132, 163
Balmain (Sydney), 250
Baltinos, Mr. (New Settlers' Federation), 237
Balts, 147 (*chart*)
Bangkok, 50 (*table*)
Bank of Tokyo, 191
Baptist Church, 119
Barnes, Mr., 216–17
Barton, Edmund, 11–12
Beazley, K. E., 31–32
Bendigo Fields, 8
Bill of 1855 (Victoria), 8
Black Muslims, 175
"blackbirders," 9, 82
Bolivia, 166
"booming Pacific," 225
Borrie, W. D., 160, 162
Bowditch, Jim, 126
Brass, Douglas, 164
Brisbane, 16, 129, 247
British, 5–6, 7, 10, 11, 14, 44, 48, 147 (*chart*), 148 (*chart*), 149 (*chart*), 161, 168, 196, 202, 204, 206, 208–209, 263; heritage, 111, 113. *See also* Anglo-Saxon; Great Britain; United Kingdom
British Columbia, 5
British Empire, 206
British Foreign Office, 253
Broome, 57, 167
Buddha, 22
Bulgaria, 187
Bulletin, The, 87, 153–55, 163, 241
Burma, 29, 221
Burns, Arthur, 218–19

Index 309

Caiger, George, 69
Cairns, J. F., xv, 87, 94, 129
California, 5
Calwell, Arthur, xv, 3, 16, 17, 59, 81–86, 89, 91, 93–94, 95, 103, 104, 113, 118–19, 126, 128, 182, 185, 187, 199, 244
Cambodia, 29, 221
Cameron, Mr., 94
Canada, 5, 265
Canberra, 42, 63, 67, 69, 140, 166, 186, 188
Canberra Theater, 254
Canberra Times, The, 41, 156, 241, 246
Cariappa, General, 193
"Case for Reform, A" (A.I.R.), 135
Casey, Lord, 206, 210
Catholic Church, *see* Roman Catholic Church
Catholic Worker, 156
Catholics, *see* Roman Catholics
Central Methodist Mission, 241
Ceylon, 29, 86, 161, 193
Chamber of Commerce, 36
Chamberlain, F. E., 33, 86–87, 89
Chamberlain, Joseph, 11
Chamberlain(s), 4
Chan, Harry, 57
Chang, Paschal, 62–63
Channing, L. J., 61
Chifley, Joseph B., 82
China, revolution of 1948, 260. *See also* Chinese; Red China
Chinatowns, 56–57, 58–61, 74
Chinese, 5, 6, 7–11, 14, 28, 54–64, 74, 75, 78, 89, 96, 103, 114, 146, 147 (*chart*), 148 (*and chart*)–49 (*and charts*), 150, 158, 180, 182, 183, 185, 196–97, 260–61
Chinese Chamber of Commerce, 60
Chinese Citizens' Society of Victoria, 58
Chinese Community Centre, 59

Chinese Immigration Act (1881), 5
Chinese Presbyterian Church, 55
Chinese Restriction Act, *see* Immigration Restriction Act
Chinese Students' Society (Sydney U.), 66
Chinese Women's Association, 60
Chinese Youth League (Melbourne), 58
Chong, Fred, 60
Christ, Jesus, 140
Churches and religious groups, xii, 18, 39, 55–56, 58, 78, 107, 108, 112, 116–23, 124, 132, 135, 137, 140, 142, 156, 187, 241
Cilento, Raphael, 159
Citizenship Conventions, 121, 136; Canberra, 37
Cleaver, Richard, xv
Cold War, 134
Collard, F., 33, 89
Collins, Justice, 236
Colombo, 50 (*table*)
Colombo Plan, 18, 30, 64, 123, 182, 185, 189, 209, 224, 261
Columbia, 166
Common Market, 171, 172, 224, 225, 261
Commonwealth, British, 210–11, *passim*
Commonwealth of Australia, 176; inauguration of, 12
Commonwealth Luncheon (1959), 98
Commonwealth Parliamentary Debates, see *Hansard*
Communism, 20, 78, 119, 150, 154, 183, 193, 194, 207, 218, 219, 224. *See also* Anti-Communism
Communist China, *see* Red China
Communist organizations, 112
Communist Party, 77, 78–80, 82, 103, 128
Communist states, 216
Confucius, 22
Congo, the, 114

Congregational Union of New South Wales, 120
Conscription, 105
Control or Colour Bar? (pamphlet), 133, 134, 136
Coombe, Reg, 161
Country Party, 31, 95, 102, 103, 104. See also Liberal-Country Party
Courier-Mail, The, 41, 46, 247–48
Creation legend (Filipino), 189
Crux, 156

Daily Mirror, The (Sydney), 154, 240–41, 246, 247, 250–51
Daly, Fred, xiii, 28–29, 33, 88–89, 90, 91, 92–93, 94, 231
Darling, Dr., 169
Darwin (Australia), 18, 57, 126, 206
Darwinism: "natural selection," 5; social, 4, 5
Das, Seth Govind, 194
Deakin, 11, 12–13, 14
Debating Society (U. of Melbourne), 124
Declaration of Human Rights, 118, 188
Delamothe, Dr., 64
Democratic Labor Party, 59, 77, 80–81, 103, 128, 138, 241, 242, 252
Department of External Affairs, 38, 40, 42, 99, 222–23, 224
Department of Immigration, xii, 3, 4, 16, 17, 30, 34, 36, 37, 38, 39, 40, 47, 63–64, 69, 70–71, 98, 99, 100, 102, 109, 111, 130, 132, 137, 164, 201, 220, 229, 230, 232, 233, 234, 235, 237, 238, 241, 242, 243, 244, 245, 247, 248, 249, 251, 252, 253, 255, 256, 257, 264
Department of Public Works, 229
Department of Supply, 226
Department of Territories, 214, 215
Department of Trade, 38, 40, 42, 225
Depression, the, 174
Detroit (U.S.), 170
Diallo, Seydon, 215
Dictation test, 11, 14, 16, 96
Dixon, R., 79
Dixon Street (Sydney), 60
Djakarta, 50 (*table*)
Doko, F., 227
Dougherty, T., 116
Dowding, Keith, 87
Downer, Alexander, xiii, 3, 18, 96, 98, 99–100, 110, 111, 126, 127, 129, 130, 131, 173, 176, 201, 208, 209, 213, 228, 231, 232
"Downer's exports," 18
"Downer's Wong Move," 18
Dunstan, Donald, 33, 89, 91, 92
Duhig, Archbishop, 121
Dutch East Indies, 185. See also Indonesia
Duthie, Mr., 211
Dyason lecture, 222
Dynon, John, 245

Eastern Economist (India), 194
Eastman, M., 215
Ebony magazine, 100
Economic Commission for Asia and Far East (ECAFE), 209, 225
Edinburgh, 131
Eggleston, Frederick, 160
England, *see* Great Britain; United Kingdom
Europe, Europeans, *see specific countries*
European Economic Community (EEC), 224, 225
Evatt, H. V., 83–84, 209–10
Evening Chronicle (Philippines), 186
External Affairs, Department of, *see* Department of External Affairs

Index 311

Fabian Society (U. of Melbourne), 124
Fancher, Wiley, 200
Federated Ironworkers Association, 116, 163
Federation, xiii, 13, 20, 113, *passim*
Federation of Employers' Association (Japan), 191
Fiji, 85, 86, 114, 161, 215, 230, 233, 234, 235, 236, 237, 238, 239, 240, 241, 242, 243, 244, 245, 246, 248, 251, 253, 254
Fijian Times, 246, 251, 252
Fijians, *see* Fiji; Prasad case
Filipinos, 149 (*chart*), 186–90, 196, 220–21. *See also* Philippines, the
Fitzgerald, Senator, 33, 89, 252
Fitzgibbon, C. H., 115–16
F-111's, 220
Formosa, 166, 226
Foundation for Aboriginal Affairs, 120
Fraser, Allan D., 252–53
French, 147 (*chart*)
Friendly Society, 115
Full Supreme Court, 236

Gallup Polls, *see* Australian Gallup Polls
Gamboa, Sergeant, *see* Gamboa case
Gamboa case, 17, 83, 84, 120, 186–87, 190, 204, 220, 252, 261
Gan, Richard, 47
Geelong, 241
Gela, Bachi, 223
Genoa, 125
Germans, 147 (*chart*), 148 (*and chart*), 149 (*chart*)
Glebe (Sydney), 119
Gobineau(s), 4
Gold Fields Commission, 8
Gollan, Ross, 159
Good Neighbour Council, 161
Gorton, John, 72, 101, 104, 216, 219, 220, 221, 222

Grayndler, 231
Great Britain, 11, 19, 23, 89, 95, 98, 102, 147, 161, 174, 201, 207, 218, 219, 224, 225, 226, 261, 263. *See also* United Kingdom
Greece, 263. *See also* Greeks
Greeks, 148 (*and chart*), 149 (*chart*), 183, 191. *See also* Greece
Greenwood, Gordon, 162, 193
Grenada, 199
Griffith, Samuel, 10
Guardian, 202

Hamilton, Mr., 253
Hammond, S. B., 22, 146, 147, 148, 149
Hancock, W. K., 21
Hansard, xiv
Harlem (U.S.), 174
Harold, A. M., 92, 136
Harper, Norman, 65
Harris, H. L., 161, 263–64
Hasluck, Paul, 96, 213–14
Hawaii, 171
Hayden, Mr., 93, 255–56
H-bomb, 154
Henshaw, J., 86, 87
Henty, Senator, 250
Heydon, Peter, xv, 35, 71, 99, 100, 102, 233, 240
High Court, 16–17, 235
Hindu, The, 42–43
Hindustani, 243–44
History of the White Australia Policy, xiv
Hitler, Adolf, 15, 186–87
Holden, W. Sprague, xiv *n*
Holland, G. W., 109
Holt, Harold, 17–18, 36, 37, 38, 41–42, 43, 51, 96, 97, 100, 101, 104, 113, 187, 216, 219, 221–22, 223, 256, 265
Holt, R. W., 88

Hong Kong, 19, 26, 42, 50 (*table*), 61, 70, 130, 149, 150, 196, 211, 245, 251
Honolulu Conference, 217
Horie, Shigeo, 191
Horne, Donald, 136
House of Representatives, 19, 27, 28, 30, 35, 36, 87, 93, 101, 140, 211
Huck, Arthur, 148, 149, 150
Hughes, Alan (poll), 152, 153
Hughes, Wilfrid Kent, 159–60
Hughes, William, 13, 14, 206, 213
Hungarians, 183. *See also* Hungary
Hungary, 187. *See also* Hungarians
Hunt (Secretary of Immigration), 23

Immigration: Control or Colour Bar? 133, 137
Immigration, Department of, *see* Department of Immigration
Immigration Act, 10, 41
Immigration Advisory Committee, 39, 108, 136, 161
Immigration Advisory Council, 36–37, 110, 111, 113
Immigration Committee (A.L.P.), 33, 34
"Immigration Quarterly" (W.A.A.I.R.), 135
"Immigration Reform: Where Do We Go From Here?" (A.I.R.), 135
Immigration Reform Groups, 39, 125, 131, 132–33, 136, 138, 155, 170
Immigration Restriction Bill, 12
Immigration Restriction Act, 10, 11, 14, 55, 84
Immigration Review Committee (A.L.P., 1965), 88–91
Immigration and the White Australia Party (pamphlet), 79

India, 29, 42, 168, 185, 193–96, 224, 250, 251. *See also* Indians (Asian)
Indians (Asian), 10, 12, 14, 147 (*chart*), 149 (*chart*), 166, 182, 185, 193–96, 215, 241, 244, 252. *See also* India
Indonesia, 86, 149, 168, 180, 185, 213, 221, 224, 251. *See also* Indonesians
Indonesians, 149 (*chart*), 185. *See also* Indonesia
"Influence of Immigration on Australia's National Character, The" (lecture), 98
Intercolonial conferences: 1881, 9; 1896, 10–11
Intermarriage, 6, 18, 59, 60, 62–64, 69–70, 71, 74, 82, 118, 165–66, 215
Inter-Parliamentary Conference, 188
Irish, 147 (*chart*), 148 (*chart*), 149 (*chart*)
Italy, 263. *See also* Italians
Italians, 147 (*chart*), 148 (*and chart*), 149 (*chart*), 183, 191. *See also* Italy

Jamaica, 199
Jamaicans, 199
Japan, 11, 14, 15, 29, 79, 99, 100, 141, 158, 163, 166, 190–92, 208, 212, 213, 221, 222, 225, 226, 228. *See also* Japanese
Japanese, 12, 14, 15, 21, 26, 40, 57, 99–100, 140, 149 (*chart*), 156, 163, 171, 190–92, 204, 205, 213, 216–17, 227–28; anti-, 190, 206. *See also* Japan
Jews, 147 (*chart*), 148 (*and chart*), 149 (*chart*)
Johanson, David, 9
"John Chinaman," 57
Johnson, John, 124

Johnson, L. R., 31
Johnson, Lyndon B., 219
Jones, C. K., 30, 93
Jones, Gavin, 184
Jones, Margaret, 184
Jupp, James, 80

Kanakas, 9–11, 82, 114
Karachi, 50 (*table*)
Karmel, P. H., 134
Kennedy, Robert, 176
Kenya, 100, 114, 161, 198, 204
Kew Civic Hall (Darwin), 126
Keys, Mr. (R.S.L.), 112
Kissinger, Henry, 219
Korea, 250. See also Koreans
Koreans, 158. See also Korea
Kuala Lumpur, 50 (*table*), 131
Kuala Lumpur Daily, 42
Ky, Marshal, 166

Labor, 113, 148, 267, *passim*. See also Australian Labor Party; Democratic Labor Party
Labor Party, *see* Australian Labor Party. See also Democratic Labor Party
Lambing Flat, 8
Lang, 179
Lang, J. T., 158–59
Latham, John, 97, 157–58, 205
League of Nations, 213; Covenant, 206
Leary, Mr. (Prasad case), 235
Lebanon, 250
Liberal Club (U. of Melbourne), 124
Liberal-Country Party, 17, 96, 99, 104, 105, 267. See also Country Party; Liberal Party
Liberal Party, 33, 95, 97–99, 101, 102, 103, 104–105, 113, 187, 252; Immigration Committee, 34; Victorian Council, 97. See also Liberal-Country Party

Liberia, 215, 216
Little Bourke Street (Melbourne), 58, 59
Locsin, Aurelio, see Locsin case
Locsin case, 37–38, 39–40, 42–43, 101, 187, 188, 190, 204, 220, 226, 256, 261
London, 202
London, Mrs., xiv
Lopez, Mr. (Philippines), 189
Luchetti, Mr., 181

Macapagal, Diosdado, 43, 190
McDonald, Charles, 12
McGoll, Mr. (A.N.A.), 113
Mackie, J. A. C., 132, 163–64
McManus, Senator, 59, 252
Macquarie, 181
Maher, E. B., 17
Malacanag Palace, 187
Malay Mail, 183
Malaya, see Malaysia
Malaya, University of, *see* University of Malaya
Malayan Seamen's Defence Committees, 16
Malaysia, 16, 29, 48, 84, 102, 149, 161, 176, 180, 181–85, 211, 217, 250, 251. See also Malaysians
Malaysians, 15–16, 31, 57, 73, 126–28, 130, 149 (*chart*), 173, 181–85, 218. See also Malaysia
Malaysian-Singapore Students' Association, 47
Malik, Mr. (U.S.S.R.), 187
Malta, 263
Maltese, 191
Manglapus, Raul, 222
Manila, 186, 188, 189, 251
Manila Conference (1966), 188, 217
Manila Times, 37, 44, 186
Mannix, Archbishop, 107, 121
Mantano, Justiniano, 188
Maori, 201

Marcos, President, 190
Marshall, Elizabeth, 163
Marshall, Eric, 163
Mascot Airport, 237
Mboya, Tom, 100, 198, 204
Melbourne, 16, 23, 55, 57, 58, 59, 67, 85, 103, 129, 132, 148, 152, 176, 262
Melbourne, University of, *see* University of Melbourne
Melbourne Buddhist Society, 58
Menzies, Robert, 17, 36, 77, 95–97, 104, 109, 126, 127, 131, 199, 210–11, 212, 216–17, 256
Mercury, The, 41, 247
Messina, 125
Methodist Church, 107, 116–18
Methodist Church Statement of Policy on Social Issues, 116–18
Methodists (Chinese), 58
"Metropolitan Daily Newspapers in Australia Today," xiv *n*
Migration Act (1958), 235
Migration to Australia, applications for (*table*), 50
Migration Review Committee (A.L.P.), 87–88
Mindszenty, Cardinal, 187
Monash University, 124
Mongolians, 5
Moyes, J. S., 118
Munich conference, 159
"My Experiences in Australia" (A.I.R.), 135
Myers, Justice, 235

Nairn, N. Bede, 158
Nairobi, 50 (*table*)
Nandi Airport, 254
Naples, 125
Natal, 114
Nation, 157, 241, 246
National Catholic Rural Movement, 108
National Civic Council, 18, 80, 81, 138, 139

National Union of Australian University Students, 72, 152 (*and chart*), 153
National Union of Students, 18, 123
Nationalist China, 26, 149–50
Nationalist Society (U. of Melbourne), 124
Naturalization of Non-Europeans (*table*), 48
Negroes, 147 (*chart*), 148 (*chart*), 149 (*chart*), 166, 169, 173–76, 200, *passim*
Nehru, Jawaharlal, 194–95
New Delhi, 185
New Guinea, 48, 96, 213, 214, 215, 216, 217. *See also* Papua-New Guinea
New Settlers' Federation of Australia, 237, 257
New South Wales, 6, 8, 92, 120, 122, 163; Equity Court, 235
New South Wales, University of, *see* University of New South Wales
New South Wales Association for Immigration Reform, 118, 133–35
New Zealand, 5, 201–202, 240
Newcastle, 93
Newman Society (U. of Melbourne), 124
News, The (Adelaide), 155, 247
News Weekly, 138
Nigeria, 197
North America, North Americans, *see specific countries*
Norton, Ezra, 154
Notting Hill (U.S.), 170

Oeser, O. A., 22, 146, 147, 148, 149
O'Keefe, Annie, *see* O'Keefe case
O'Keefe case, 16–17, 83, 185, 252
Oliver, C. T., 89, 92

Opperman, Hubert, xi–xii, xiii, xv, 27–28, 30, 31, 32–33, 34, 35, 36–37, 39, 41–42, 46, 47, 48, 50, 51, 77, 98–99, 100–101, 117, 127, 149, 179, 201, 229, 233, 234, 235, 239, 240, 241, 242, 243, 244, 245, 246, 247, 249, 251, 252, 253, 254, 256, 257, 258
Orsova (liner), 232
Overseas Students' Conference, 71
Oxley, 255

Pacific Islanders, 9–10
Pakistan, 193. See also Pakistanis
Pakistanis, 149 (chart). See also Pakistan
Palfreeman, A. C., xiii, xiv, 101
Palmer, Thomas, 87
Palmer Diggings, 9
Papua, 96, 214, 216. See also Papua-New Guinea
Papua-New Guinea, 213–17, 223, 224, 226
Parker, Robert, xv
Parkes, Henry, 6
Parliament (Federal), xv, 12, 101, 110, passim
Parliamentary Labor Party, see Australian Labor Party
Peacock, Andrew, 97
Pearce, George, 13
Perkins, Charles, 238, 239, 254, 255
Peters, E. W., 30
Philippines, the, 29, 38, 40, 42, 43–44, 84, 166, 185–90, 204, 220–21, 222, 226, 250, 251, 261. See also Filipinos
Plimsoll, James, 212
Political Science Society (U. of Melbourne), 124
Polynesian Labourers Act (1868), 10
"Populate or Perish," 206
Port Hedland Copper Mining Project, 227
Portugal, 129
Portuguese, 129
Powditch family, 234, 235, 236, 237, 238, 239, 240, 242, 243, 244, 245–46, 252, 253–55
Prasad case, xiv, 34, 37, 38, 46, 101, 154, 196, 229–58, 262
Prasad family, see Prasad case
Praser, Harbans Singh, 65
Pratt, Graham, 200
Presbyterian Church, 107, 118–19
Presbyterians (Chinese), 55, 58
Price, A. Grenfell, 214
Price, Charles, xv, 118
Prime Ministers' Conferences, 210, 211
Prince Alfred Hospital, 232
Public Questions Society (U. of Melbourne), 124

Qantas, 237
Queensland, 6, 8, 9, 10, 12, 64, 92, 113, 114, 165, 200, 248
Queensland Association for Immigration Reform, 248
Quota system, 34, 90, 107, 116, 117, 133, 155, 162

Rabaul, 216
Rahman, Tunku Abdul, 42, 84, 181–82, 183, 211–12
Railwaymen's Union, see Australian Railwaymen's Union
Ramos, Narcisco, 42, 188
Rationalist Society (U. of Melbourne), 124
Rawson, Donald, xv
Ray, Mrs. Jyotikana, 63
Red China, 19, 26–27, 61, 80, 130, 149–50, 218, 220
Reddaway, W. B., 134
Reform Movement, 87
Regional Banking Programs, 209
Religious organizations, see Churches and religious groups

Research School of Pacific Studies (A.N.U.), 163
Restriction Act, *see* Immigration Restriction Act
Returned Servicemen's League, 36, 108–12, 135, 141; Congress, 111; Constitution, 112
Returned Servicemen's Organizations, 85
Rhodesia, 102, 114, 161, 188, 200, 202
Ridley, John, 72
Rigg, Julie, 46–47
Rivett, Kenneth, xii, xv, 132, 137, 163–64
Roman Catholic Church, 80, 81, 107, 121–22
Roman Catholics, 138
Rome, 125
Roosevelt, Eleanor, 17
Ross, Lloyd, 163
Rotary Club, 66
Round Table, 156
Royal Melbourne Institute of Technology, 124
Royal Navy, 154
Rumble, Dr., 121
Russia, *see* Soviet Union
Russians, 147 (*chart*). See also Soviet Union
Russo-Japanese War, 11

Samabula (Suva), 242
Samuel, Peter, 163
San Francisco, 58, 209
Santamaria, B. A., 80, 138–39, 140
Schenk, John, 230
SEATO, 38, 189, 217, 218, 261
Selma (U.S.), 200
Sharpeville, 210
Shiba, Kempei, 190–91
Shogunate, 192
Short, Laurie, 163
Singapore, 26, 42, 50 (*chart*), 70, 85, 86, 149, 150, 176, 180, 206
Singhalese, 63

Slim, William, 158
Snedden, B. M., xv, 49–50, 100–101
Social Darwinism, *see* Darwinism, social
Soliven, Maximo, 37, 44, 188, 189, 251
South Africa, 23, 90, 114, 161, 169, 170, 188, 197, 198, 200, 202, 210–11, 212, 250
South America, 166. *See also specific countries*
South Australia, 8
South Korea, 166. *See also* Korea; Koreans
South Vietnam, 166. *See also* Vietnam; Vietnamese
South-China Morning Post, 42
Soviet Union, 187, 216
Spain, 125. *See also* Spaniards
Spaniards, 191. *See also* Spain
Special Political Committee, 212
Spencer, Herbert, 4
Spender, Percy, 95
Star, The (Hong Kong), 42
Steward, Mr., 33
Stewart, F. E., 89, 179
Stoddard(s), 4
Straits Times, The (Kuala Lumpur), 43, 73, 211
Strong, Archbishop, 118
Strong(s), 4
Student Action, 18, 39, 108, 123–32, 136, 140, 141, 202
Student Christian Movement (U. of Melbourne), 124
Students, 49, 55, 64–75, 85, 90, 94, 119, 123–32, 152–53, 156, 167, 184, 238, 255, *passim*
Students' Representative Councils, 18, 123
Suez, 219, 261
Sugarman, Justice, 236
Sumner(s), 4
Sun (Melbourne), 127
Sun, The (Sydney), 132 *n,* 241

Sunday Telegraph, 41
Sun-Herald, The, 242, 243
"Suriya," 66
Suva, 50 (*table*), 235, 240, 241, 242
Swedish, 147 (*chart*)
Swinburne Technical College, 69, 124
Sydney, 16, 23, 55, 57, 59–60, 119, 120, 165, 228, 230, 234, 240, 249, 250, 255
Sydney Airport, 237
Sydney Morning Herald, The, 40, 41, 159, 174
Sydney University, 67, 72, 170, 238, 249; Chinese Students' Society, 66
Syrians, 23

Tahiti, 214
Taiwan, 221
Tanzania, 215
Taxes, discriminatory, 9
Tet offensive, 219
Thai Students' Association, 66
Thais, 197
"thin edge of the wedge," 6, 166
Thomas, W. J. (Bill), 123, 124, 127, 129, 131
Thompson, Era Bell, 100, 200
"Time For A Change In Migration Policy" (handbill), 125
Time magazine, 201
Times, The (London), 129, 202
Times of India, The, 43
Togo, 215
Tokyo, 50 (*table*); Bank of, 191
Trade, Department of, *see* Department of Trade
Tranbie College, 119
Tregonning, K. G., 180, 208
Trieste, 125
Trullinger, O. O., 218
Trust Territories, the, 213–18
Truth, 153, 154
Tsiang, Dr., 61–62

Tylee (Swinburne Technical College), 69

Uggams, Leslie, 200
Unesco, 146
Unions, unionists, 9, 13, 79, 80, 84, 115–16, 126, 141, 158, 163, 191, 255
United Arab Republic, 215
United Kingdom, 90, 114, 161, 193, 199, 202, 209, 213, 218–19, 224, 263. *See also* British; Great Britain
United Nations, 17, 19, 95, 117, 186, 187, 189, 197, 210, 212, 214, 215, 216, 260; Charter, 17; Commission on Human Rights, 38, 42, 189; Declaration of Human Rights, 188
United States, 5, 10, 20, 23, 83, 90, 95, 114, 154, 160, 161, 169, 170, 171, 173, 174, 176, 200–201, 207, 209, 213, 218–20, 261
University of Malaya, 180, 184
University of Melbourne, 18, 72, 123, 124, 132
University of New South Wales, xiii, 69, 72, 195
University of Western Australia, 65

Vagholkar, M. K., 195–96
Vanderputt case, 102
Vanderputt family, *see* Vanderputt case
Versailles, Peace Conference (1919), 14, 157, 205, 213
Verwoerd, Dr., 211
Victoria, 8, 58, 80, 86, 123, 125, 242.
Victoria, Queen, 11
Victorian Association for Immigration Reform, 86, 88, 92, 129, 135–36
Victorian Australian Labor Party, 87; Conference, 86

Victorian Liberal Party Council, 97
Vietnam, 29, 105, 121, 188, 216, 217, 219, 225. *See also* Tet offensive; Vietnamese
Vietnamese, 164, 218. *See also* Vietnam

Walker, Alan, 117–18, 241
Walker, Patrick Gordon, 89
Walsh, Justice, 236
Wang, David, 59
Warner, Denis, 46
Waterside Workers Federation, 115–16
Watson, J. C., 12
Watt, Alan, 31, 109, 159–61
Watts (U.S.), 170
Wentworth, W. C., 97
West Australian, 41
West Australian Labor Party, 86
West Indian Economist, 199
West Indians, 199–200, 202
West Irian dispute, 213
West New Guinea, 149, 185
West Pacific High Commission (1875), 10
Western Australia, 86, 123, 135
Western Australia, University of, *see* University of Western Australia
Western Australian Association for Immigration Reform, 135
Westerway, Peter, 141

"White Australia: Time for a Change?" (A.I.R.), 135
White Man's Burden, 4
Whitlam, E. Gough, 37, 89, 92, 94, 103, 104, 223
"Why Does White Australia Matter?" (V.A.I.R.), 135–36
Wilkinson, J., 12
Willard, Myra, xiv, 6, 11
Wilson, Keith, 29
Wing, Ron, 58
Winks, Robin, xv, 173–77
Wong, Willie, *see* Wong case
Wong case, 18–19, 130–31
Woomera communications satellite project, 226
World War I, 205
World War II, xi, 15, 18, 19, 57, 79, 81, 83, 99, 104, 107, 109, 117, 145, 153, 162, 163, 181, 202, 206, 212, 213, 217, 218, 233, 259, 261; war babies, 140

Yale University, xv, 173
Yarra, 129
Yarwood, A., xiv, 13
"Yellow Hordes," 206
"Yellow Peril," 206, 207
Yong, C. F., 56
Young Chinese Relief Movement, 60
Youth and Student Seminar on International Affairs, 98